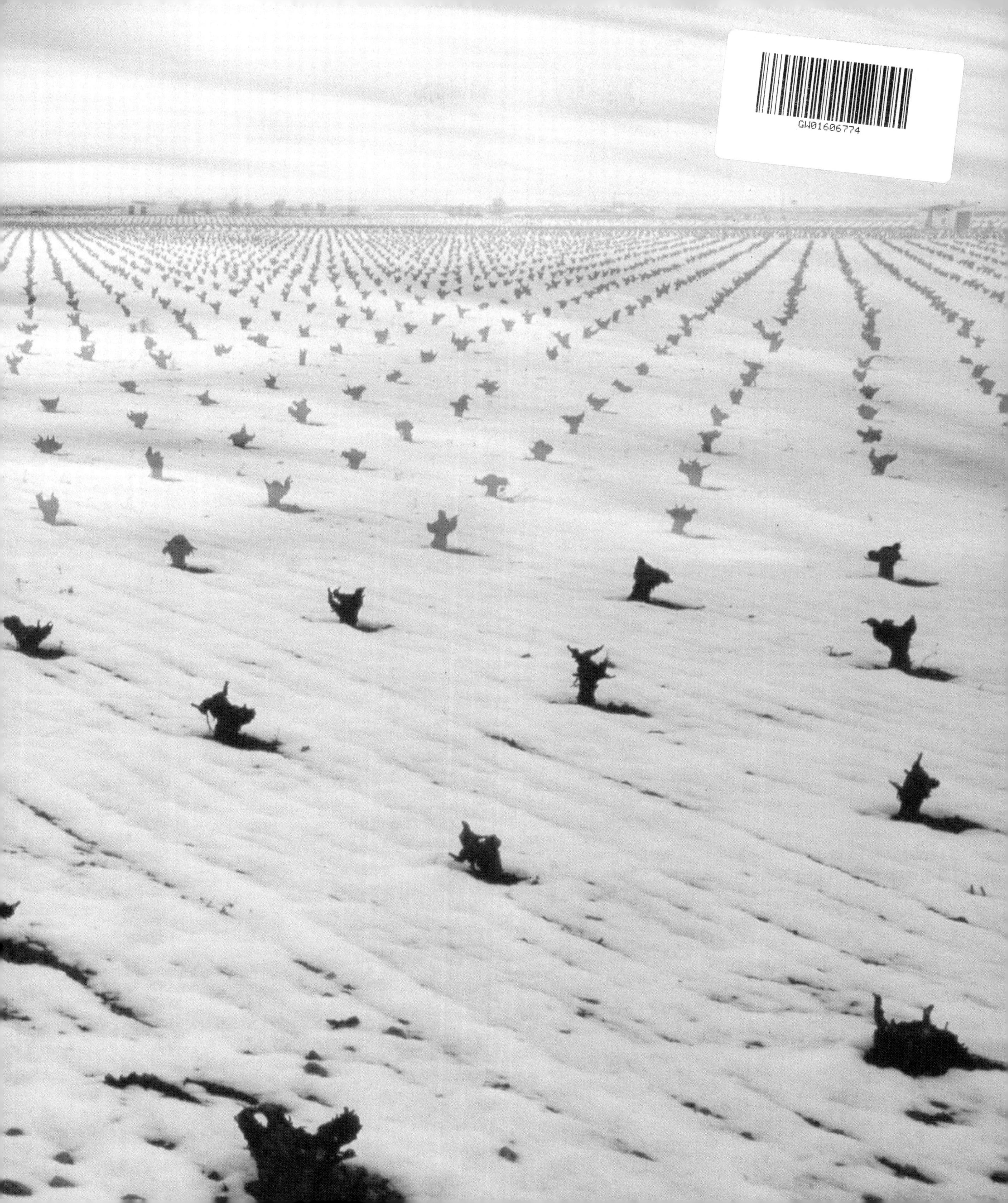

GW01606774

SPAIN

IN LIGHT AND SHADOW

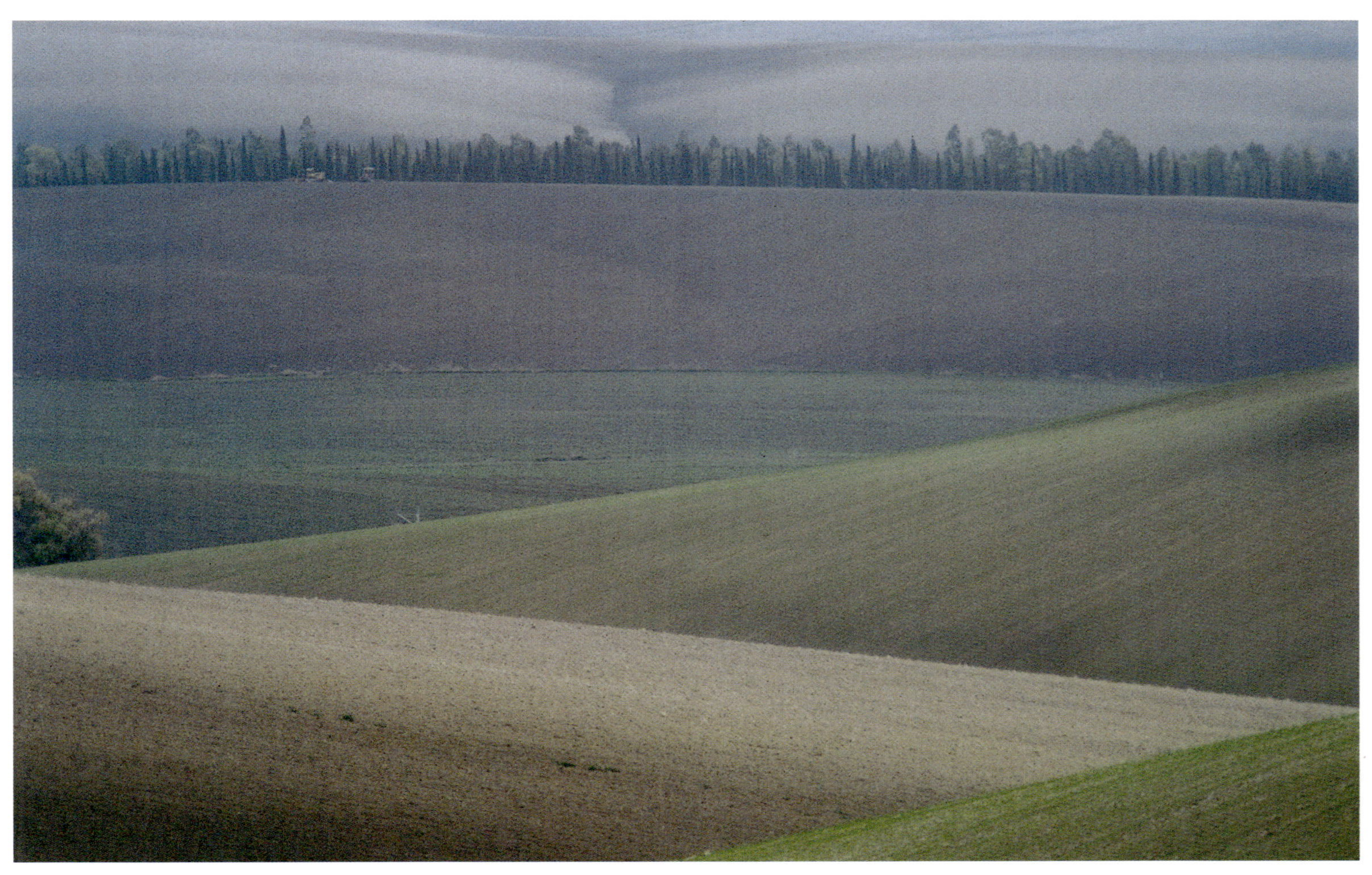

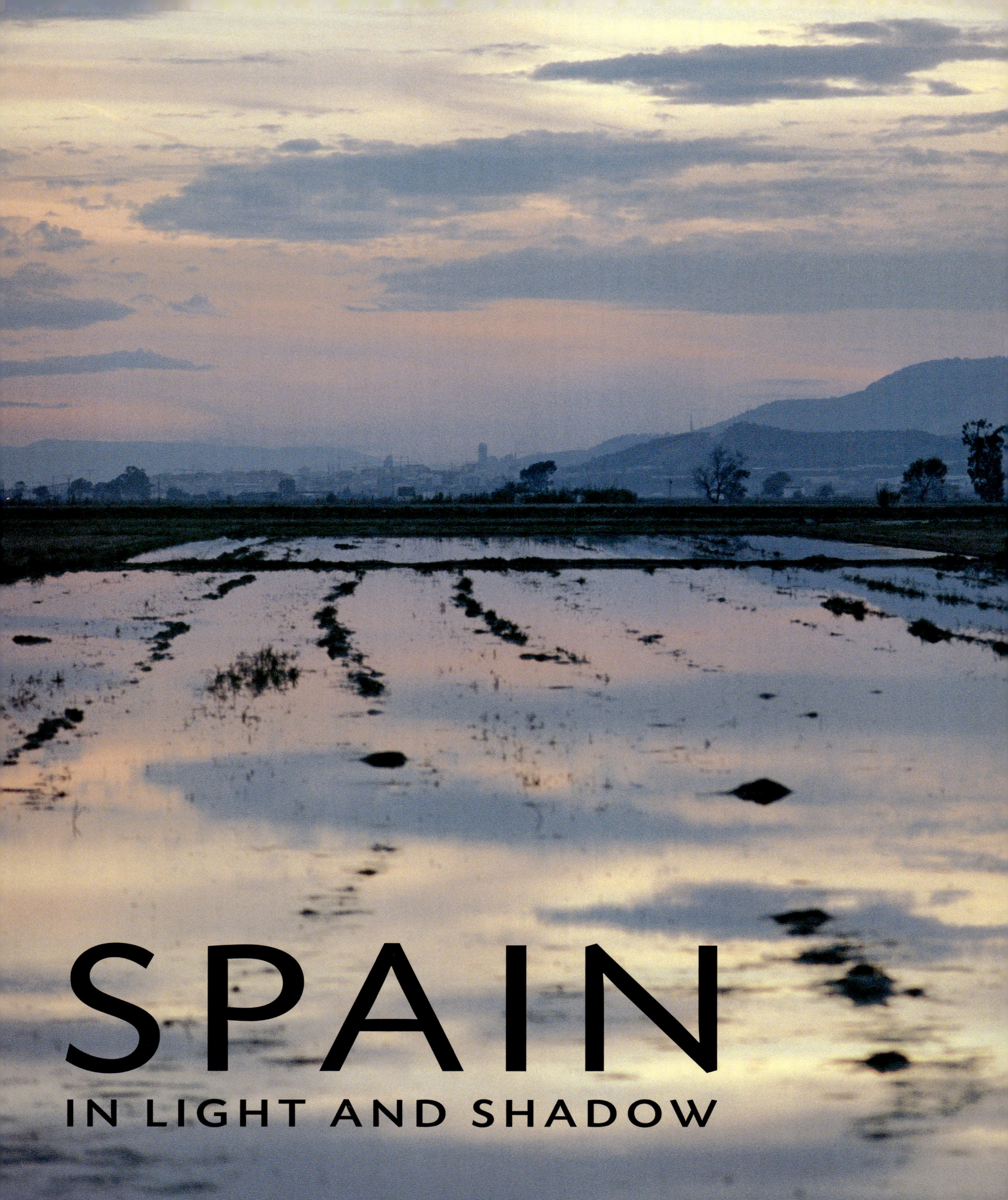

SPAIN
IN LIGHT AND SHADOW

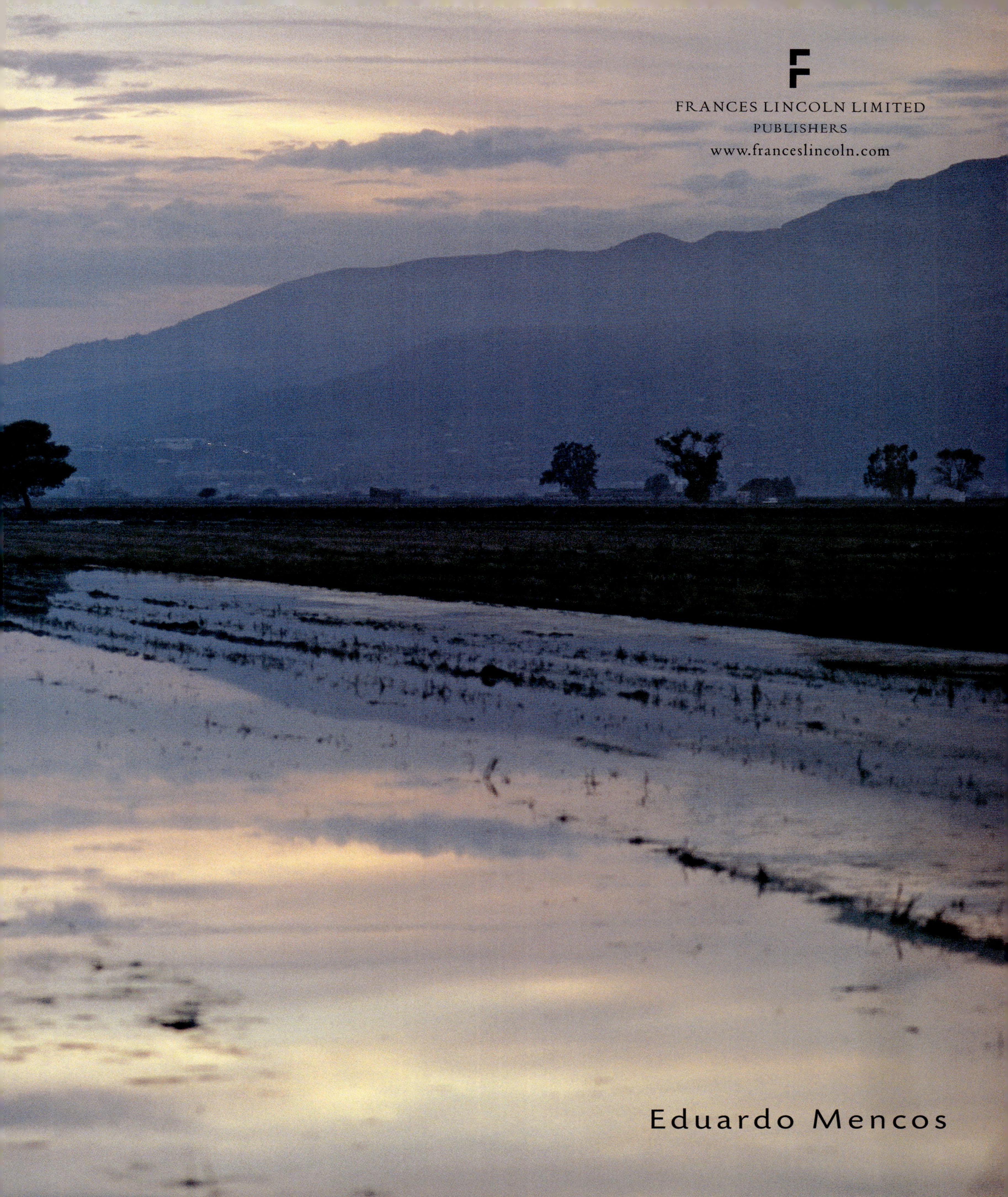
FRANCES LINCOLN LIMITED
PUBLISHERS
www.franceslincoln.com
Eduardo Mencos

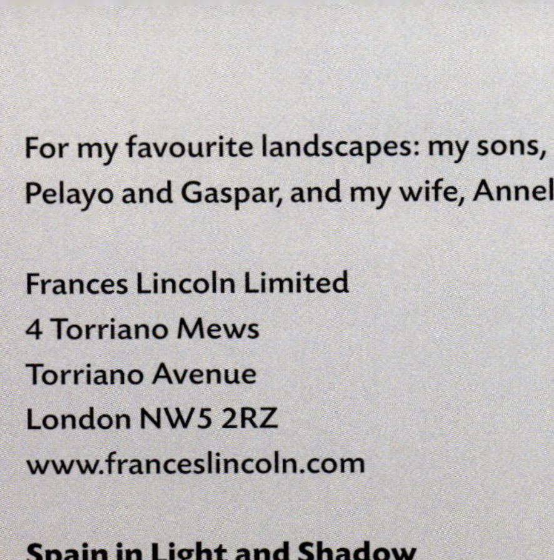

For my favourite landscapes: my sons, Pelayo and Gaspar, and my wife, Anneli

Frances Lincoln Limited
4 Torriano Mews
Torriano Avenue
London NW5 2RZ
www.franceslincoln.com

Spain in Light and Shadow

British Library Cataloguing in Publication Data
A catalogue record for this book is available from the British Library

ISBN 978-0-7112-2661-6

Printed in Singapore

9 8 7 6 5 4 3 2 1

Half-title page Cádiz, Andalucía, in December
Title page Tarragona, Catalonia, in November
pages 4-5 Albacete, Castilla-La Mancha, in June
pages 22-23 The Basque Country in June
pages 46-47 Ávila, Castilla y León, in March
pages 86-87 Cádiz, Andalucía, in October
pages 118-119 Minorca in May
pages 130-131 Gran Canaria in May

CONTENTS

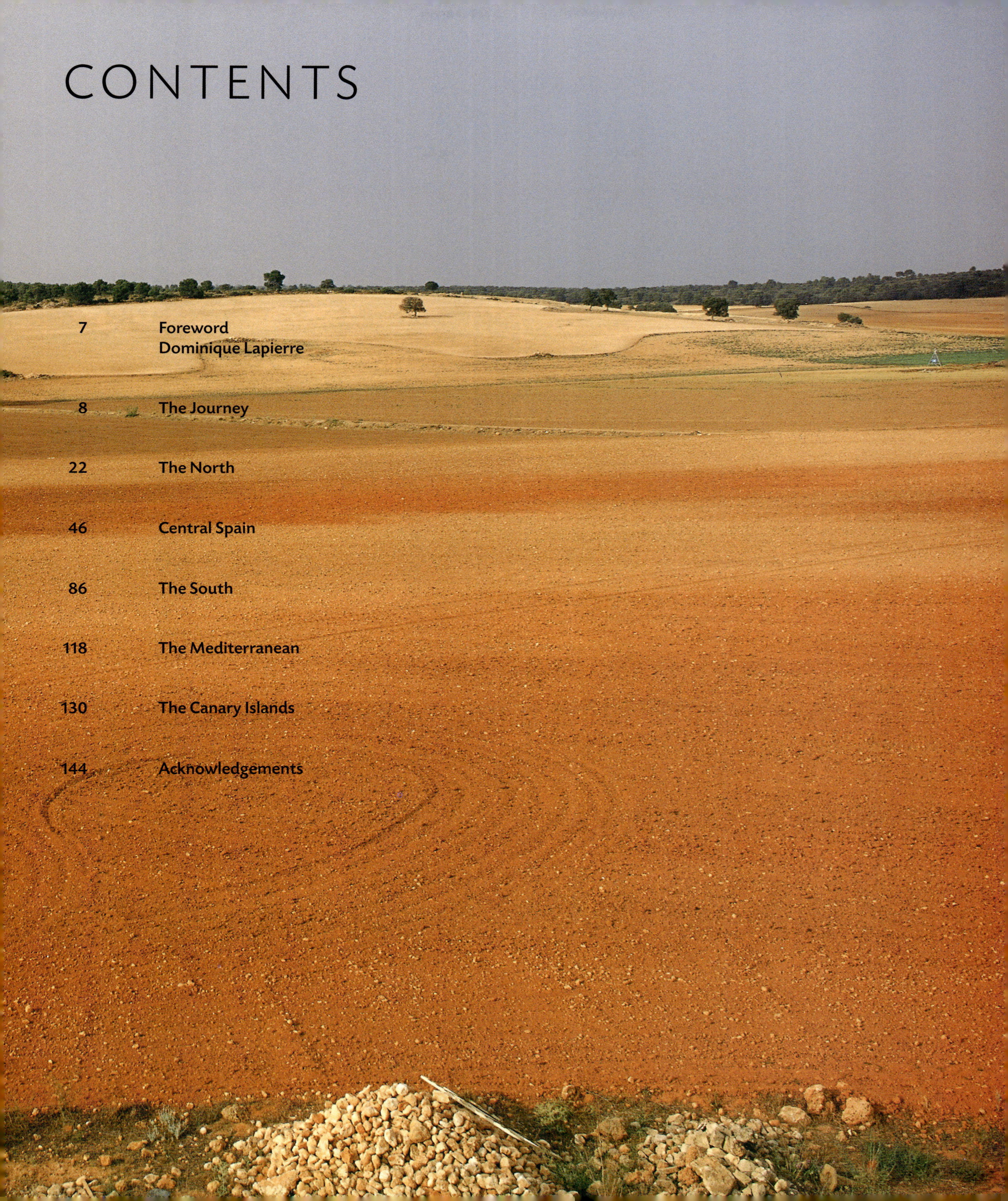

7 Foreword
Dominique Lapierre

8 The Journey

22 The North

46 Central Spain

86 The South

118 The Mediterranean

130 The Canary Islands

144 Acknowledgements

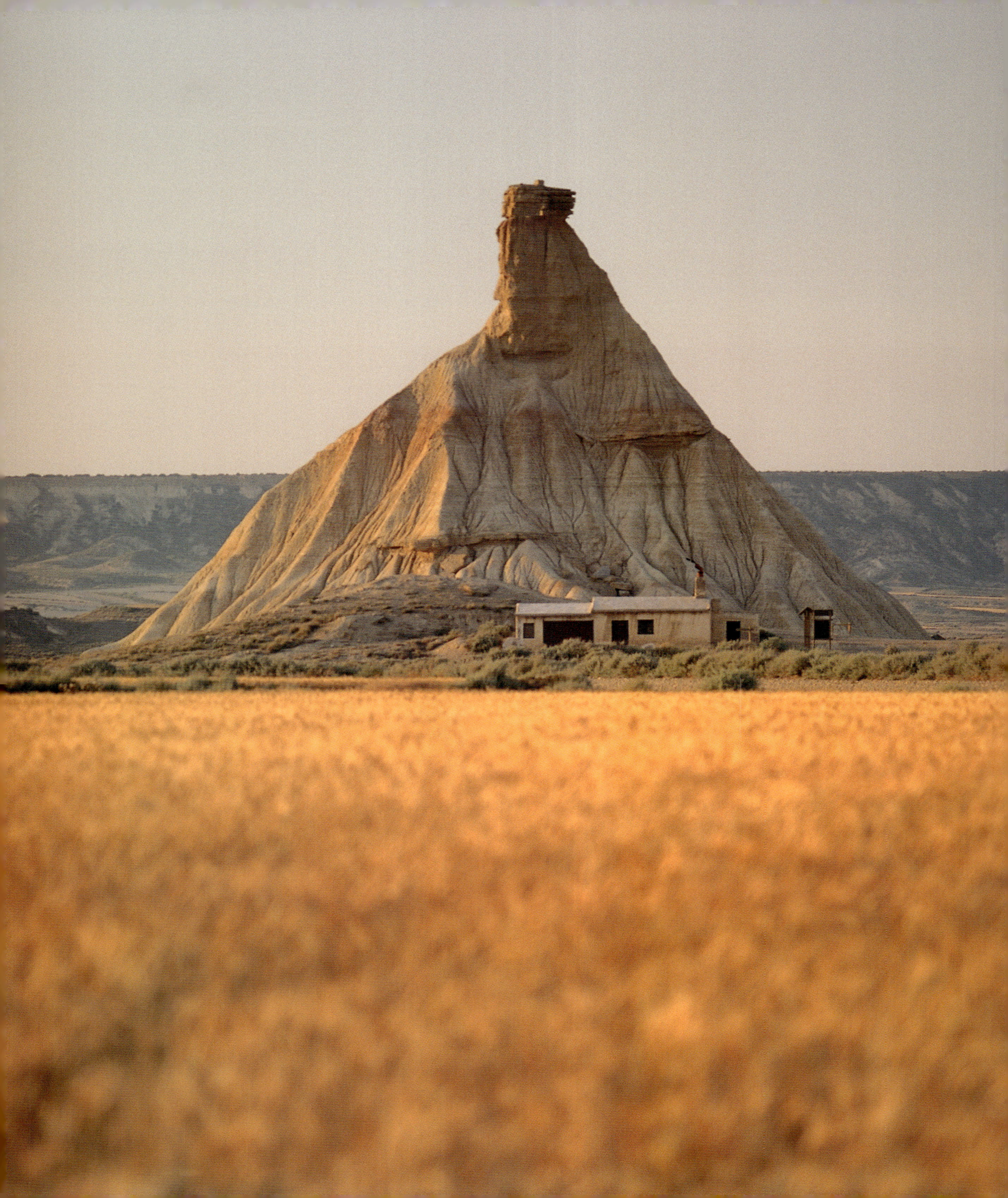

FOREWORD

In a lifetime of travel I have been privileged enough to have seen many different landscapes, but I have always had a particular fondness for Spain. My love of riding has given me the opportunity to see some of the most beautiful natural surroundings this planet has to offer – including Sierra de Gredos in early springtime. Its undulating plains lie just a few miles outside Ávila and there is no trace of humankind as far as the eye can see. That is real Nature, in all her wild, essential richness. Then there are the Andalusian paths I used to take each year with my friends from the Hermandad de los Palacios on our Pentecost pilgrimage to the mythical little church in El Rocío. How can I describe the utter beauty of a sea of yellow mustard and sunflowers parting before hundreds of riders in the wonderful spring light? And how, when there is so much ugliness in our world, can I express the sheer exhilaration of Guadalquivir horses and riders alike when, having crossed that sea of flowers to the opposite hillside, we galloped freely under the green canopy of the lovely Doñana forest?

I spent three years in the 1960s researching my book *Or I'll Dress You in Mourning*, which gave me the chance to travel all over Spain in the footsteps of Manuel Benítez el Cordobés. I was often filled with wonder by all kinds of Spanish landscapes. I will never forget my walks with troupes of aspiring bullfighters across the lunar landscapes of Castile and La Mancha. Nor will I forget the groups of wild bulls in the untouched wilderness of the Andalusian meadows. And I will always remember those lazy days between seasons on the as-yet-unspoilt beaches from Marbella to Gibraltar. It is hard to imagine that back in the 1950s the charming little port of Estepona just had a single motel. It was owned by a German man and boasted only nine small one-room bungalows built straight on the sand. They were so covered in bougainvillaea that they could hardly be seen from the road or the beach.

Since then, as we all know, Spain's coastline has been well and truly defiled. I passed through Estepona again recently as I was returning from Ceuta, where I had been honoured with the town's Grand Cross of Solidarity in recognition of my humanitarian work in India. I almost wept at the muddle of multicoloured apartment blocks threatening to engulf the seafront at the little beach I had so loved. It made me think of the peninsula I call home – St Tropez – which has miraculously escaped the developers' madness. In fact it is probably the only point in the Mediterranean from Naples to Gibraltar that remains intact.

Every time I return to my beloved Spain it strikes me that it is not just Estepona's fate nor the fate of all those poor disfigured Andalusian and Gallician villages which gives me reason to feel both sorry and angry for Spain. So much of the Spanish countryside is now suffering from a less visible and subtler form of leprosy – the leprosy of the pylons and power cables which are disfiguring the countryside with their hideous metallic web.

The other day I took the high-speed train to Seville to record the programme *Loco de la Colina*, and for five hundred miles I watched in horror as the power cables and pylons jostled and criss-crossed each other. There are so many lines running parallel to one another, each with its own set of pylons. It is as though the engineers simply ignored the first sets – not wanting to acknowledge that they could have used the existing infrastructure and preferring instead to erect their own. A recent car journey from Salamanca to Madrid provided the same horrific sight. Of course we can't deny a country's right to the electricity it needs for development, but neither do we have to condone such offences against the beauty and purity of creation. To do so is a crime against humanity.

DOMINIQUE LAPIERRE

Navarra in June

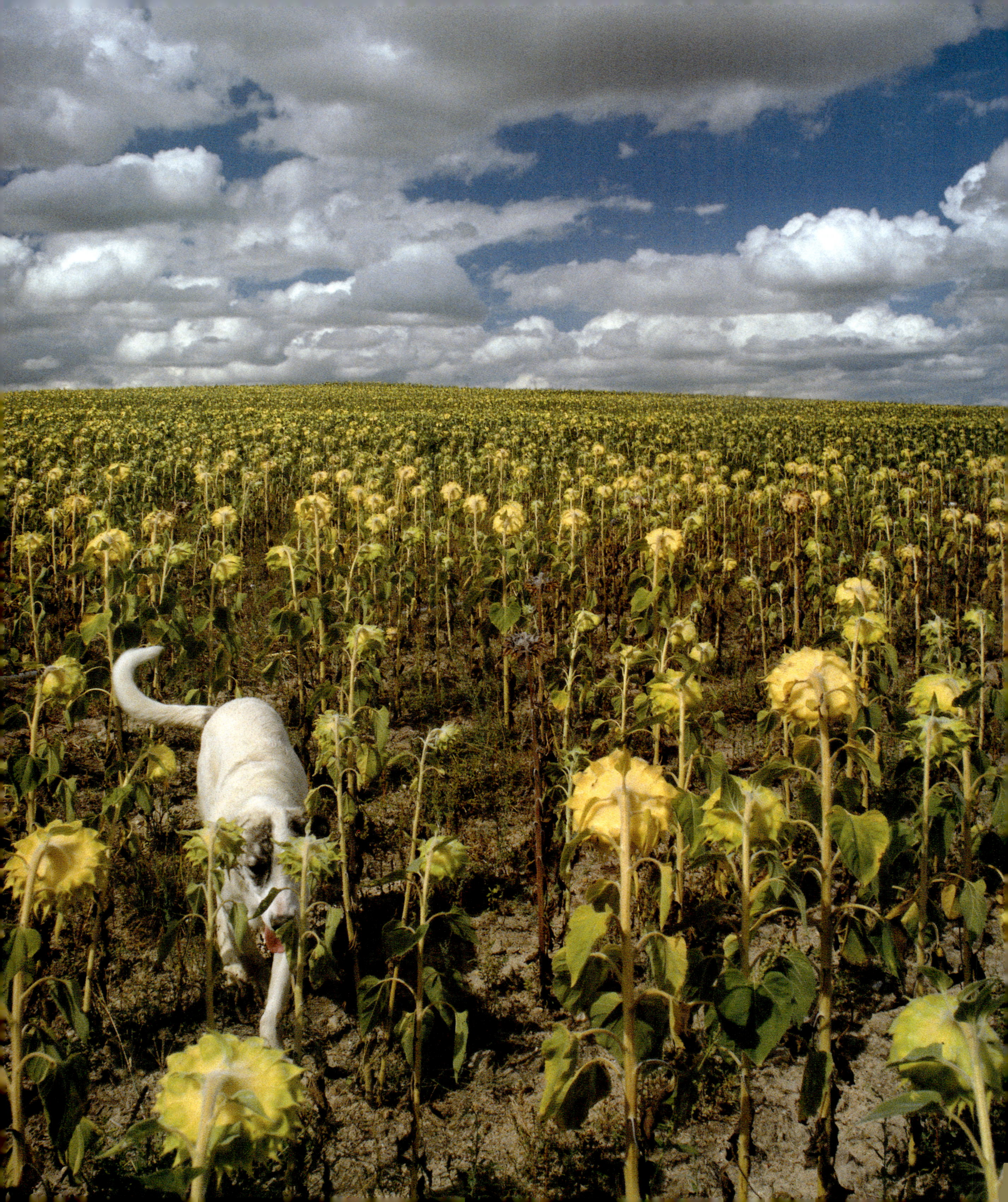

THE JOURNEY

It has come to an end. I've been on a journey round Spain for twenty-five years – with occasional stops, of course – and now I've finished my journey, I've started to explore what twenty-five centuries of historians, poets, painters and travellers have felt and written about these landscapes.

In offering up this collection of images, I propose that the thrill of a landscape, and of its contemplation, is one of life's great pleasures. I want to show what the land has shown me, seeing it as a kind of living canvas, redolent of the past and of the people who have lived there. Landscapes, like the human face, can record the effects of time.

Everyone needs a haven, an interior space, 'another country' where life's troubles can be shrugged off. Some find this in mountaineering, some on the golf course or tending a garden. Others prefer to hunt. I am one of those: since I was a teenager I have been hunting landscapes, looking for the most picturesque light so that the silent, naked Earth will show me its most beautiful face. Or in Keats's words, 'beauty is truth, truth beauty'.

This was a solitary affliction: there are few – and twenty-five years ago there were even fewer – who would accept an invitation to set off with no other aim than to see landscapes and capture them in photos. Of course this outlook on the world works as a kind of crucible for my relationships. If a girl didn't like the sound of these hunting trips, then she and I didn't have much future together. If I could persuade a girl to come with me, my plan was always roughly the same (though with the usual ulterior motives – I'm not that stupid). I took Sophie, a mademoiselle with eyes like blue moons, to see the dawn over Alcarria where the moon hangs red over the dark earth of Guadalajara. With Zhou Ling, Mandarin Chinese, beautiful as silence, I travelled the roads of Spain, worldlessly absorbed in the land and in each others' eyes. And my first decent proposal to my wife, Anneli, was an invitation to come and see the white moon rising in the pale hills of Cuenca. She agreed, of course, or we wouldn't be married now.

Like a Caravaggio, the Spanish landscape with its stark lighting and dramatic contrasts is a work of chiaroscuro, expressing the turbulent history and character of its people. These powerful forces seem to ignite a mysticism that rises from the land itself. How tiny the human figure seems, lost in the immensity of the Castilian plain beneath an infinite sky!

In a place so often harsh and hostile, where harvests are uncertain, men look to the skies for a redeeming God and the rain they are longing for. It is surely no coincidence that the mystics Saint Teresa and Saint John of the Cross lived in these dry desert lands where the rigours of the climate encourage thoughts to turn to the spiritual.

Taking a quick turn through time back to the earliest visitors. . . Ancient travellers were drawn here by stories of the wonders and natural riches of the remote, mythical lands to the west. Different peoples spread over the peninsula. The first inhabitants, originally from North Africa, were the people we know as Iberos. They were followed by Celts, and in 1100 BC by the Phoenicians, who founded Cádiz. Greeks, who had long known the peninsula as Iberia, derived from the word *Iber* which may have meant 'river', were present

Valladolid, Castilla y León, in June

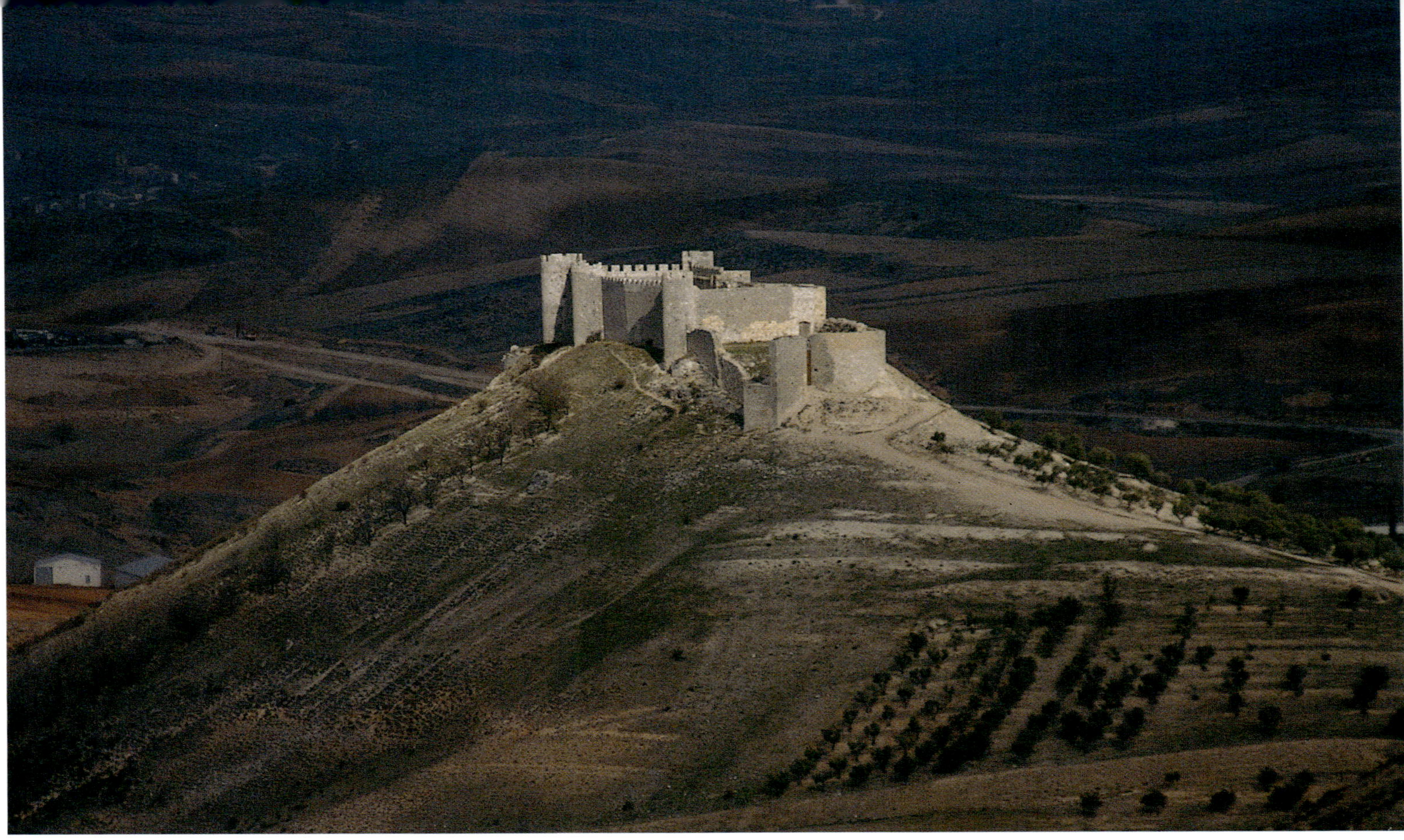

from the seventh century BC. The Romans knew it as Hispania, which is thought to derive from the Phoenician *Hi-shphanim* or 'The Island of Rabbits', as those animals were plentiful. There are not so many now (disease has taken its toll), but I remember in Madrid in the early 1990s I gave four rabbit snares to a group of destitute Nigerian refugees, and they were able to feed themselves through a long and bitter Castilian winter with what they caught.

But to return to our roots... From the third century BC, the Romans occupied the peninsula for nearly seven hundred years and left deep traces, above all in our language, culture and civil engineering. Under Roman rule, Spain became a rich source of food and men – including the emperors Trajan, Adrian and Theodosius – and one of the most important imperial possessions. Many roads were built: it was easier to travel round Roman Hispania than nineteenth-century España.

The Greek historian Strabo (*c.* 63 BC – *c.* AD 23), author of the compendious *Geography*, describes the landscape in the Roman era: 'For the most part barely inhabited, as it is covered in mountains, forest and plains of poor unevenly watered soil.' He also makes some rather modern-sounding observations about the influence of the environment on its inhabitants: 'The Northern region is very cold and cut off from the rest, and thus inhospitable.' His preference for the South is clear in his description of the region around the river Guadalquivir: 'From the riverbanks to the islets, all is carefully cultivated. To relieve the eye there are copses and plantations of all varieties, admirably cared for. Riches and fertility abound in these regions: they are nature's eternal store.' Strabo was the first to link Spain with the image of a bull, making resonant comparison between the map of Iberia and a stretched ox-hide. The bull is still a national symbol, whose imposing silhouette looms over the nation's roads in the shape of billboards for the distillers Osborne. (These were protected by law in 1994 after public outcry over their threatened removal: thus their position as an authentic part of the Spanish landscape was formalized.)

After the Barbarian invasions that brought an end to the Roman Empire, a Visigoth dynasty was established in Spain in the fifth century. An idyllic description of the country and its riches survives from this period in the words of Saint Isidore of Seville (550–636) in his *Historia Gothorum*: 'Hispania, rich in fruits, abundant in cereals, planted with olives, bordered with vines, with flowers in the fields, leaves in the mountains, fish at the shore. Under the most agreeable climate in the world, neither scorched by the summer heat, nor bitten by the rigours of winter, superior to Alfeo in horses, to Clitum in livestock... Of all the lands between India and the Western shore, you, Hispania, are the most beautiful.'

From 711 most of the peninsula was occupied by the Moors. Over eight centuries they turned Hispania into Al-Andalus, where Arab culture reached an artistic, scientific and architectural peak. This desert people used the water they found here to transform arid zones into places of abundance. Their long presence left a heritage in our history and landscape of palaces, mosques and gardens unique in Europe. The German traveller Edmundsen, who visited Al-Andalus at the

Guadalajara, Castilla-La Mancha, in January

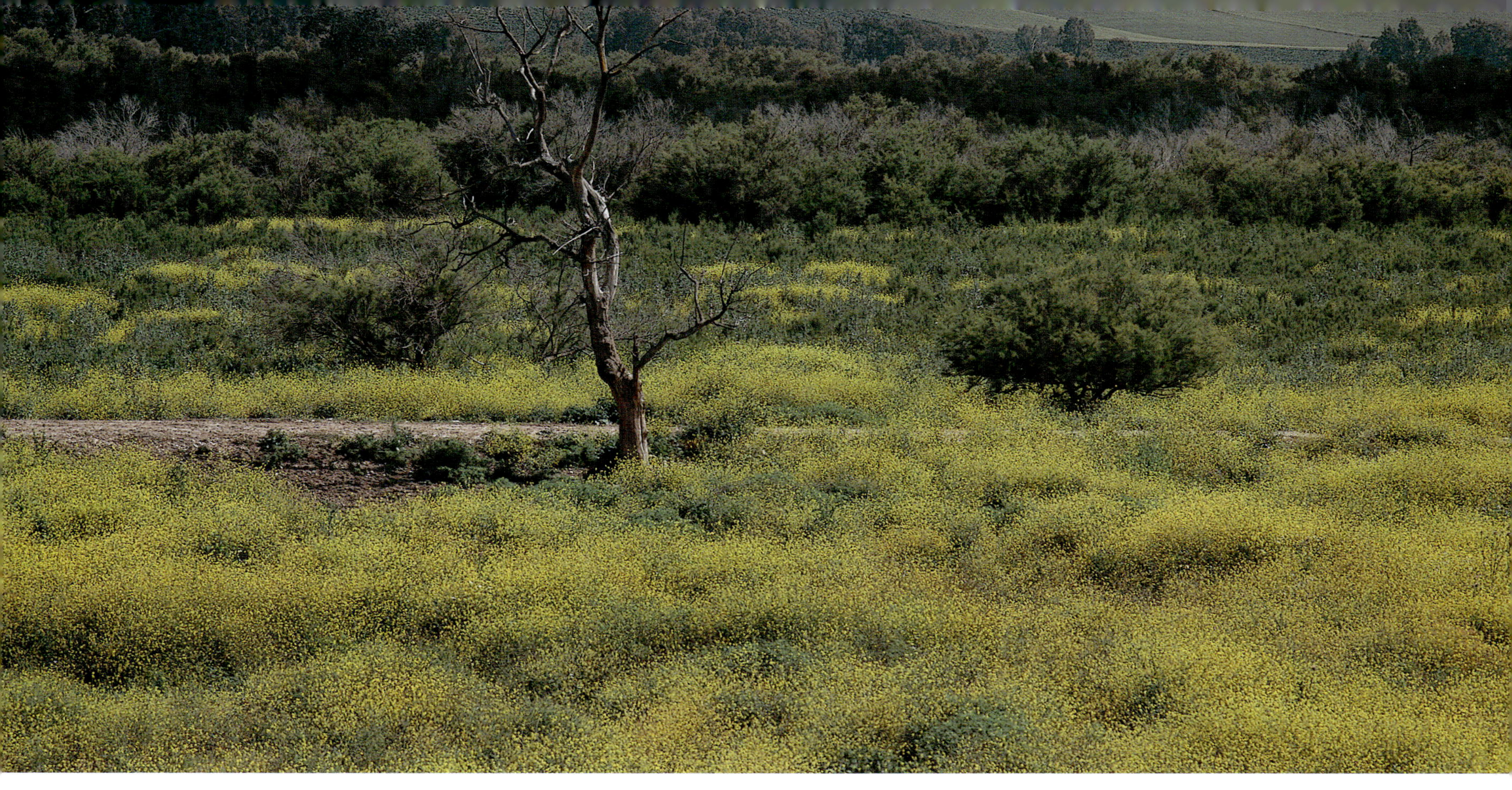

end of the fifteenth century, described it as a fertile land, with carefully tended fields. He wrote of Tabernas in Almería with its palms, fruit and olive trees, watered by irrigation channels and tanks, 'Like a paradise, cultivated in the Arab manner, which is the best'. Today, the Moors, with their talent for irrigation, long gone, Almería is the driest, least fertile place in Europe, used in the 1960s as a backdrop for innumerable spaghetti westerns because of its resemblance to the harsh desert landscapes of the Wild West. A powerful demonstration of how landscapes change through time and through the uses man makes of them. Perhaps tomorrow Tabernas will be a golf course. . .

The poets of Al-Andalus also used to praise the beauty of their land. In the eleventh century Ibi Alzaya wrote, 'Oh, people of Al-Andalus! How fortunate you are – water and shade, rivers and trees! Eternal paradise in your own lands. If I could live anywhere in the world I would live here. You need not fear Hell because it is impossible for you to go there, having once been in Heaven.' Two hundred years later the great traveller Ibn Battuta expressed his admiration for the country in his *Rihla*: 'I went to Granada, capital of Al-Andalus, foremost among its cities. Its surroundings are without equal in all the world, extending over forty miles, crossed by the famous river Genil and other streams. Orchards, gardens, pastures, farms and vines embrace the city from all sides.'

Granada, the last city of Al-Andalus, fell in 1492 to the forces of 'The Catholic Monarchs', Ferdinand and Isabella, who declared an end to the struggle for 'reconquest' that had lasted more than eight centuries. At the same time as the New World was discovered to the west, Ferdinand and Isabella created a unified kingdom, one of the most enduring in the world. Where only a handful of years earlier a harmonious mix of cultures and religions had prevailed, now Jews or Muslims who refused to adopt Christianity were expelled from the peninsula. In this land of extremes we switch from tolerance to bigotry, from modernity to ultra-conservatism, from impulsive creativity to indolence, from idolatry to iconoclasm, while the land, the setting for these rhythms of history, goes from drought to flood, from light to shadow, in starkest chiaroscuro.

Our 'Golden Age' ran from the sixteenth to seventeenth centuries, as the Renaissance became the Baroque. Despite underlying problems this was the richest and most glorious period in the art and culture of Spain. The great Córdoba poet Luis de Góngora writes in a sonnet of this period, 'Oh fertile plain! Oh lofty peaks that grace the sky and adorn the day! Oh my eternally glorious country, gained as much by the pen as by the sword!' The first paintings of the Spanish landscape date from this period. One of these, exceptional for its lack of any subject other than the landscape itself, is El Greco's dramatic, intensely subjective, *View of Toledo* (1597–1607), now in the Metropolitan Museum in New York. Although not specifically landscape paintings – a category more properly of the nineteenth century – the views of the Sierra de Guadarrama in the background of Velázquez' equestrian portraits are imbued with that cold wintry light so typical of Madrid. Centuries later, the American film producer Samuel Bronston was

Cádiz, Andalucía, in April

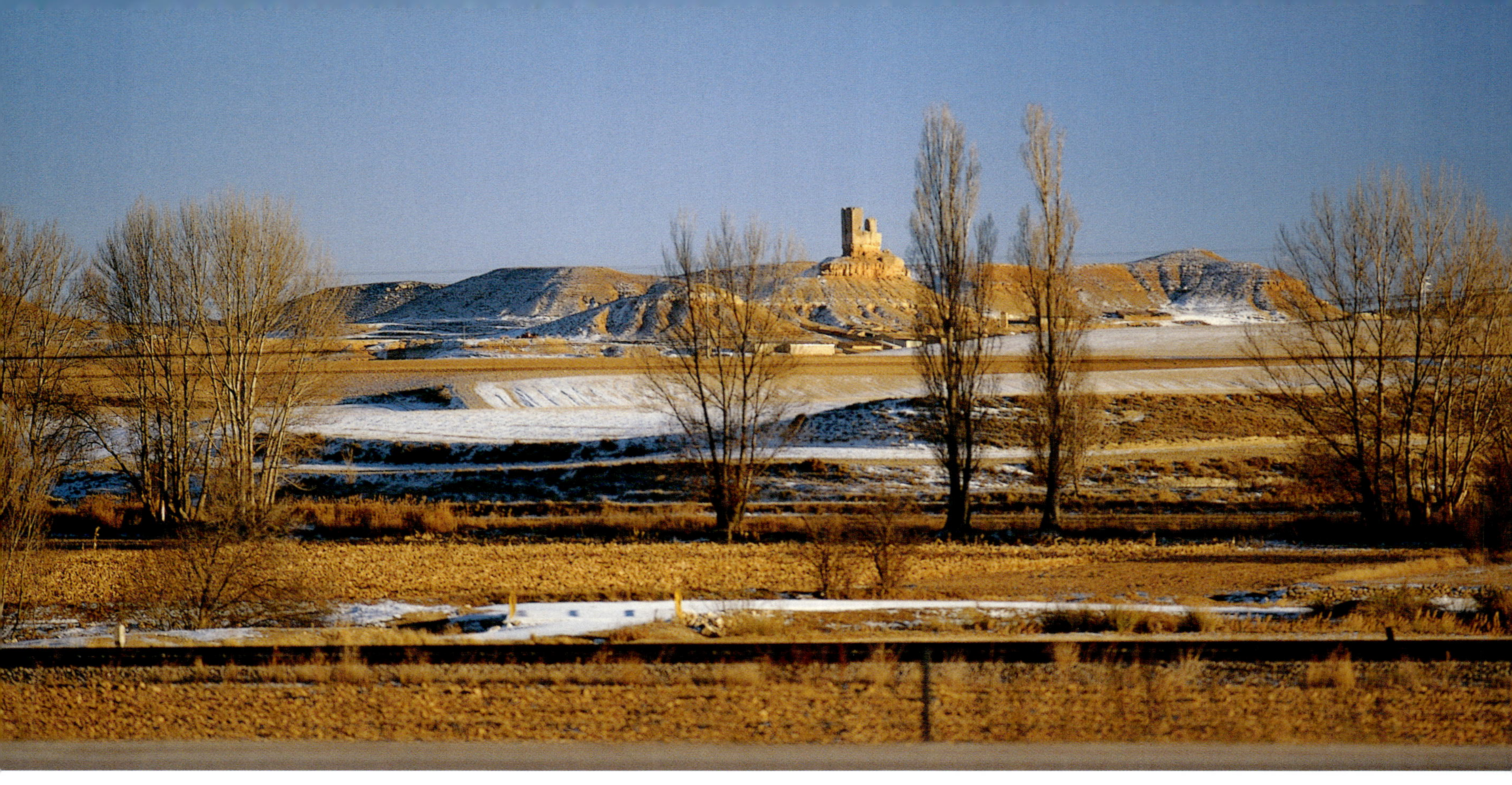

seduced by the same clear light and the variety of landscapes, and used the same settings for films like *Fifty-Five Days in Peking* or *The Fall of the Roman Empire* in the 1950s and 1960s.

Until well into the nineteenth century Spain was largely unknown to outsiders and rarely included in the Grand Tour. The few travellers who did visit tended not to comment on the landscape. However, there were exceptions, among them the French poet Vincent Voiture, who wrote in 1633, 'Andalucía has reconciled me to the rest of Spain. Here you see in one cast of the eyes snow-capped mountains and fruit-laden fields; there are snows in August and grapes in January. Winter and summer are mixed here and even when all is white in the year's dotage there are always green laurels, orange trees and myrtle.'

It is still very common to fall in love with Spain by way of Andalucía. Even today there are few who appreciate the infinite plains of Castile, the emaciated land, a bare and abstract canvas. La Mancha was described in 1775 by the English traveller Henry Swinburne as 'a bare corn-country, ugly and tedious beyond expression... scarce a fresh leaf was to be seen... and the weather cold and raw'.

Alexander Jardine, travelling in the North of Spain, wrote on his arrival in Asturias in 1777, 'The landscape now changed; here the mountains appeared more steep and magnificent' and after that, as he reached Galicia, 'again a different kind of country from the last ... and inhabited by a distinct race of people. Other nations are divided into provinces arbitrarily, but Spain is so by nature.'

As he followed the river Orduña to Bilbao in 1789 Joseph Baretti, another Briton, wrote, 'every step offered a new landscape of inexpressible beauty, and the frequent tumblings of that water delighted the sight.'

In 1782, the statesman Gaspar Melchor de Jovellanos praised the green meadows of his native Asturias in these terms: 'Oh Nature! How wretched are those who cannot adore you in these sublime scenes, when you offer up your beauty so magnificently and display all your majesty!'

The English traveller Sir John Talbot Dillon commented in *Travels Through Spain* in 1778, 'Nothing can be more bleak and dismal than the general aspect of the country round the seat of its Monarch, with a great want of trees, to which the Castilians have such a dislike, from a false notion that they increase the number of birds to eat up their corn.' I am often reminded of this comment travelling in Castile when I see the towns and fields so bereft of trees. If it were up to me, I would line our roads, motorways, towns and cities with trees, to give shade and fresh dashes of colour, providing relief for the eye as well as the body.

Adolphe Blanqui, travelling to Madrid in 1825, wrote, 'The same desolate dryness reigns in the country. If the Spanish do not take great care, old Castille will be a desert in 100 years. Already in many places the sand has taken over from the soil, the streams have run dry, and the few trees to have survived the war have a parched look.' This may sound apocalyptic, but as I write I hear on the radio that 80 per cent of European land destroyed by forest fire is in Spain.

Visiting Madrid in 1822–3, the English journalist Michael Joseph Quin described how, 'standing almost, like Palmyra, in the midst of a desert. . . no shady groves, no

Zaragoza, Aragón, in December

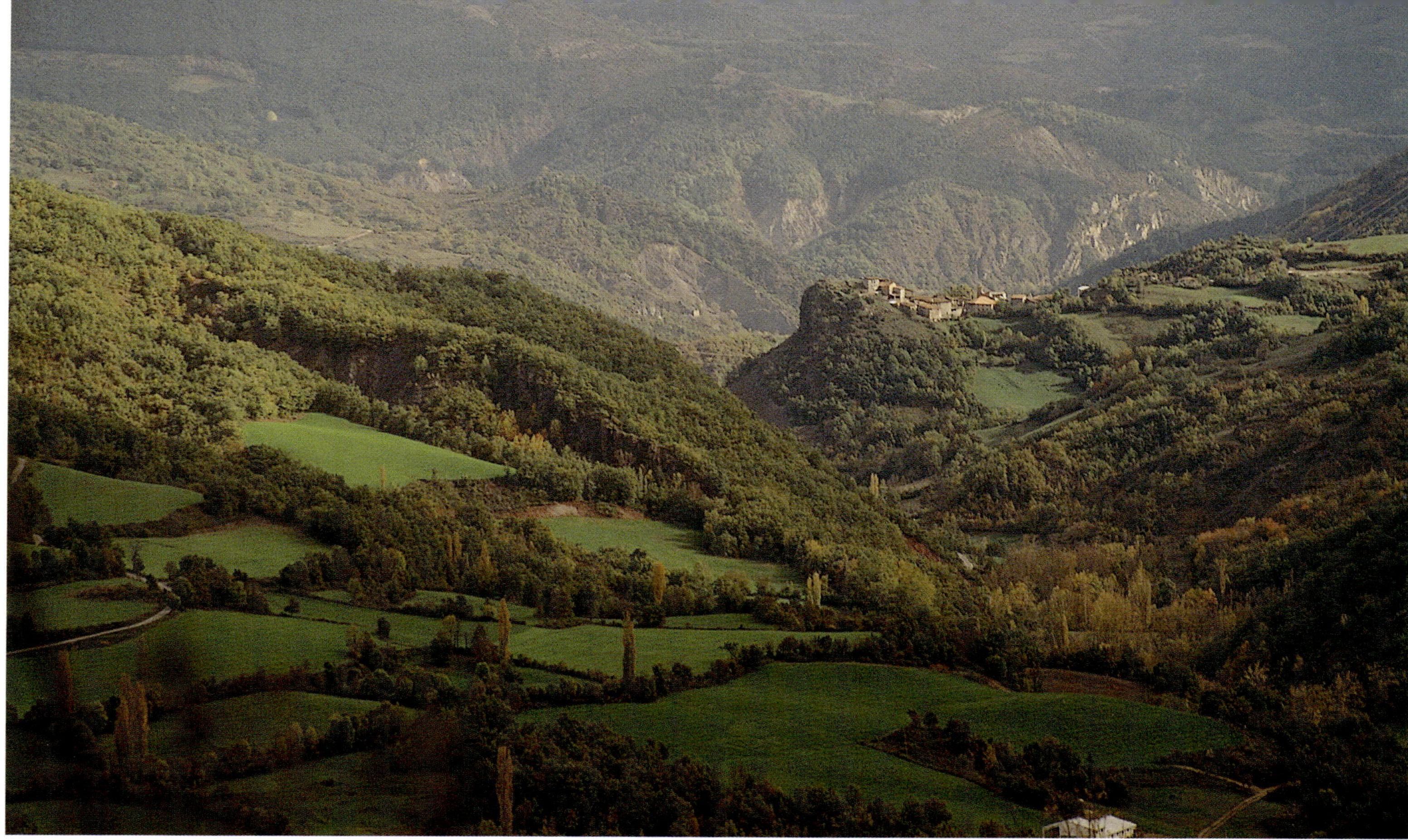

avenues, no country seats, bespoke the approach of a great capital.' Even today after the construction boom of recent years, there are still many cities in Spain that are like islands or oases in the middle of countryside.

In the Romantic period the land gained a character independent of the uses it was put to by man: it became a literary and artistic construction with a value of its own. Mountains, crags and isolated hill towns became objects of fascination. Nature became a protagonist in charged scenes like those painted by Carlos de Haes. Landscape painting in the hands of this artist, and others throughout Europe, became the dominant genre of nineteenth-century art.

My images draw on this idealizing spirit of the Romantics: abstracts, like an endless mosaic filling the Castilian plain, barren for man but fertile for the camera.

The Marquis Astolphe de Custine in *Spain in the Reign of Ferdinand VII* (1838) had this to say about the landscape: 'The look of the land, of the skies where spring clouds, full of hail and snow, stand out against the dark blue, the physiognomy and character of the people, and even the air one breathes, all is harsh in Spain... Spain is a forceful land: those skies insist on independence, on originality.' I too have been impressed by that tormented sky Custine describes: days when the clouds seem to be painted, days of sun and shadow, bringing the power and drama of chiaroscuro to the landscape. At dawn and dusk I am most richly rewarded, when with my camera I capture a fleeting moment of that light. The English writer Richard Ford in his *Handbook for Travellers in Spain*, written between 1830 and 1833, also recommended that travellers take advantage of the light at the two ends of the day, as 'In these almost tropical countries, when the sun is high, the effect of shadow is lost, and everything looks flat and unpicturesque.'

Andalucía held a particular attraction for the Romantics, who saw it as decadent, abandoned and mysterious, with sublime sunsets and totemic mountains. According to the French poet Theophile Gautier, the enchantment began at the Pass of Despeñaperros, the doorway to Andalucía, where 'the scene changes instantly, as though one had suddenly passed into Africa. All is bathed in a splendid refulgent light, as though illuminating an earthly paradis. . .' His compatriot the Marquis Astolphe de Custine wrote from Toledo in 1831, 'I look out on the flowering and perfumed desert of La Mancha, where the Spain of song begins. The winds it sends me are harmonious, and from here I will press on to Sierra Morena, beyond which paradise awaits. I know of it by the music of the air and the perfume of the land. My soul is ruled by one sole desire, the desire to fly across this space and rest in the valleys of Andalucía.'

Alexandre Dumas, who visited Spain in 1846, described Andalucía in his *Impressions of a Journey from Paris to Cadiz*: 'There, beyond the mountain, you can hear the approach of beautiful, joyful Andalucía, with castanets in her hand and a crown of flowers.'

'This country is exhausting to cross, with bad roads, worse inns, no good maps, and bandits and a feeling of adventure at every turn,' wrote Theophile Gautier in 1840. In this period it was indeed hazardous to travel in Spain, full of the unexpected, and Gautier regarded the gradual improvement in this situation as one of the great calamities of

Huesca, Aragón, in November

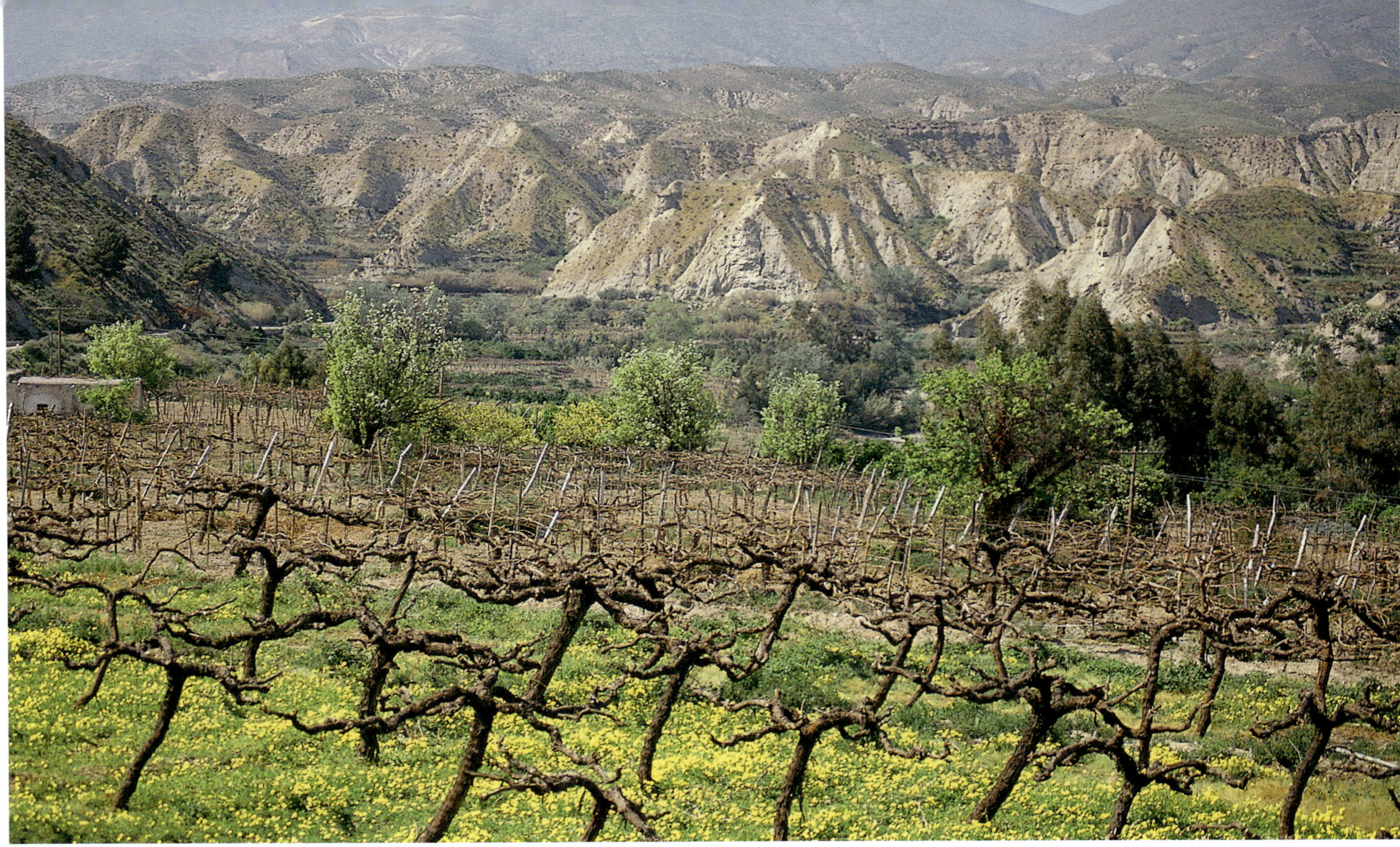

modern life. The Romantics yearned for places far from the rationality of the industrialized North. For them, Spain was a country of the strongest character, of startling customs and fascinatingly exotic landscapes. Uniquely in Europe, there was also the legacy of the Arabs, which carried all the connotations of the Orient: luxury, fantasy and sensuality. They relished the sumptuous architecture and the luminous colours of unfamiliar landscapes. Or in Victor Hugo's words, 'mythical, oriental Spain'.

One of the begetters of this Romantic image, who still informs the Anglo-Saxon attitude to Spain, is the New York writer Washington Irving. Settling in Spain between 1826 and 1832, Irving made numerous records of his responses to the landscape, insisting on the enormous difference between Spain and 'voluptuous Italy'. 'For the greater part, it is a stern, melancholy country, with rugged mountains, and long sweeping plains, destitute of trees, and indescribably silent and lonesome, partaking of the savage and solitary character of Africa. What adds to this silence and loneliness, is the absence of singing birds, a natural consequence of the want of groves and hedges... But though a great part of Spain is deficient in the garniture of groves and forests, and the softer charms of ornamental cultivation, yet its scenery is noble in its severity, and in unison with the attributes of its people; and I think that I better understand the proud, hardy, frugal and abstemious Spaniard, his manly defiance of hardships, and contempt of effeminate indulgences, since I have seen the country he inhabits... There is something too, in the sternly simple features of the Spanish landscape, that impresses on the soul a feeling of sublimity. The immense plains of the Castiles and of La Mancha, extending as far as the eye can reach, derive an interest from their very nakedness and immensity, and possess, in some degree, the solemn grandeur of the ocean.'

His British near-contemporary George Barrow, or 'Don Jorgito el Inglés', spent the years from 1836 to 1840 in Spain. Author of *The Bible in Spain,* he wrote in an English newspaper article, 'Spain is indeed a weary land; how cheerless are her elevated central plains, storm-blown and frost-bitten in winter, and calcined in summer! No trees break the blasts, no shade refreshes the eye, no singing bird the ear, in this disputed heritage of the wild bee, the locust, and the vulture...'

Richard Ford's *Handbook for Travellers* offers a series of observations, some of which are still very relevant, including: 'The natives themselves attach little or no importance to views, ruins, geology, inscriptions, and so forth, which they see every day, and which they conclude cannot be of any more, or ought not to be of more, interest to the stranger.'

The Romantic travellers – whose routes are promoted as tourist trails – played an important role in teaching us to appreciate the treasures so close at hand.

For these nineteenth-century travellers, the romance of the South was embodied above all in Granada and the Alhambra. In Washington Irving's words, 'the ancient kingdom of Granada, into which we were about to penetrate, is one of the most mountainous regions of Spain. Vast sierras, or chains of mountains, destitute of shrub or tree, and mottled with variegated marbles

Almería, Andalucía, in February

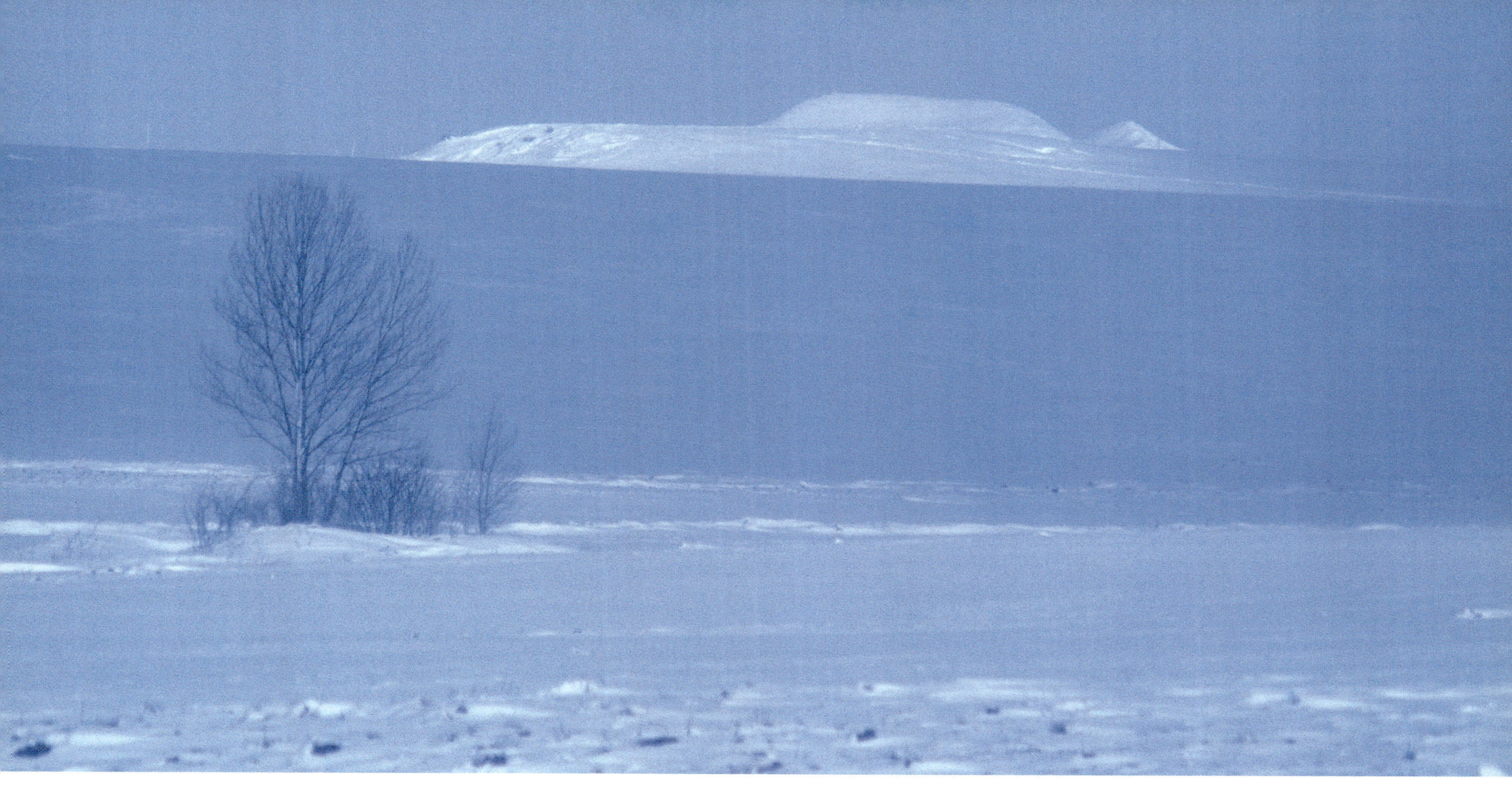

and granites, elevate their sunburnt summits against a deep-blue sky; yet in their rugged bosoms lie engulfed verdant and fertile valleys, where the desert and the garden strive for mastery, and the very rock is, as it were, compelled to yield the fig, the orange, and the citron, and to blossom with the myrtle and the rose.'

In 1831 Richard Ford visited Granada. 'The line of irrigation, like a Rubicon, divides the desert from a paradise, while all within its influence is green and fruitful, all beyond it is barren and tawny – a feature frequent in this Land of Contrasts. In objects of interest Granada, and there is attraction in the very name, contains the Alhambra. The alpine range of the *Alpujarras*, grand beyond conception, is the Switzerland of Spain; nor can anything be more sunny and Mediterranean than the littoral districts.'

The Mediterranean coastline was another favoured destination of the nineteenth-century traveller. In Spain, Mallorca was particularly attractive to artists and visitors. In 1838 the French writer George Sand arrived with her lover Chopin, and wrote *A Winter in Mallorca* in which she praised the beauty of the island's landscapes: 'This is one of those discouraging places that leaves nothing to the imagination. Anything the poet or painter can dream of has already been created by nature here. Vast range, inexpressible variety, bewildering shapes, thrilling heights and hazy depths, all are here and there is nothing that art can add.'

Another who left a mark on our perception of the island was the Archduke Luis Salvador of Habsburg, who was so beguiled by his first visit in 1867 that he rarely left it thereafter. The author of *The Balearics*, an extensive work covering the entire archipelago, he placed great importance on the preservation of the Mallorcan landscape and acquired estates on the dramatic Tramuntana coast, where he created a series of lookouts to enjoy the impressive views of the Mediterranean. At the same time he built roads to allow access to the public, so that they might come to appreciate the landscape as a thing to be shared and treasured, setting a precedent for today's national parks.

The nineteenth century ended in calamity for Spain with the loss in 1898 of the remnants of Empire: Cuba, the Philippines and Puerto Rico. This disastrous turn of events left the country slumped in an attitude of decadence and despair. Writers known as the Generation of '98 set out to capture and understand the soul of Spain through its landscapes. Miguel de Unamuno, Valle-Inclán, Pío Baroja, Azorín and Antonio Machado were the core of this group who left the cities in search of the cultural identity of their country and its regions through the character of the land itself.

They found what they were looking for in the austere Castilian plain, describing in detail the poverty of the towns, the simplicity of the people and the extremes of the climate. This flat, dry landscape became a metaphor for a country that had been neglected and abandoned. In 1908, Antonio Machado wrote about the region of Soria, 'Can you call this our native land, these bare limestone mountains, that once were thickly covered in trees, surrounding this noble and ancient city? This is a corner of the earth where men have

Burgos, Castilla y León, in January

passed, not to make a nation, but to unmake one. You are not patriots, who think that you would die to defend these barren rocks. Think instead of bearing trees and seeds, the plough and the miner's pick, to these dour, desolate places where the nation is still to be built.'

Or, in the words of Azorín, 'Lonely, melancholy Castile has no view of the sea. The sea is far from this flat, open, uninhabited, dusty country, from these stony ravines, from these red steppes where the torrential rains have carved deep notches, from these low hills where tracks zigzag down to a stream. The sea airs do not reach these drab towns of crumbling shacks, with a copse of poplars at the common.'

The idea of Castile as an austere and severe place is a persistent one. In his first published work, *Impressions and Landscapes* (1918), Federico García Lorca conjures up a desolate land: 'These plains, an immense symphony of dried blood, treeless, without cool shade or any rest for the mind, full of superstition, broken iron, enigmatic towns, sombre men, painful products of the race of Titans and the proud, cruel shadow. . .

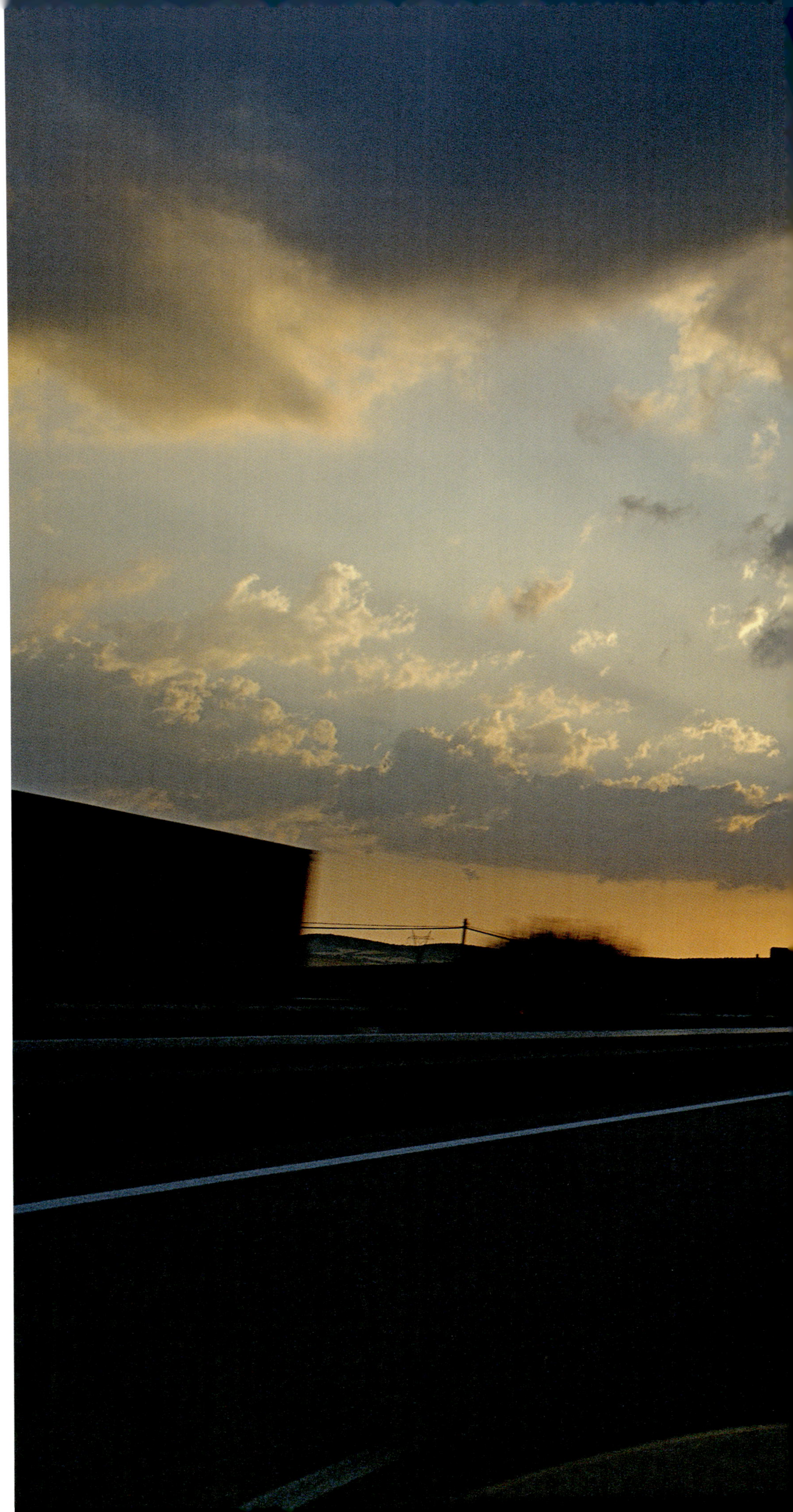

Silhouette of an Osborne bull in the Castilla La-Mancha countryside in December

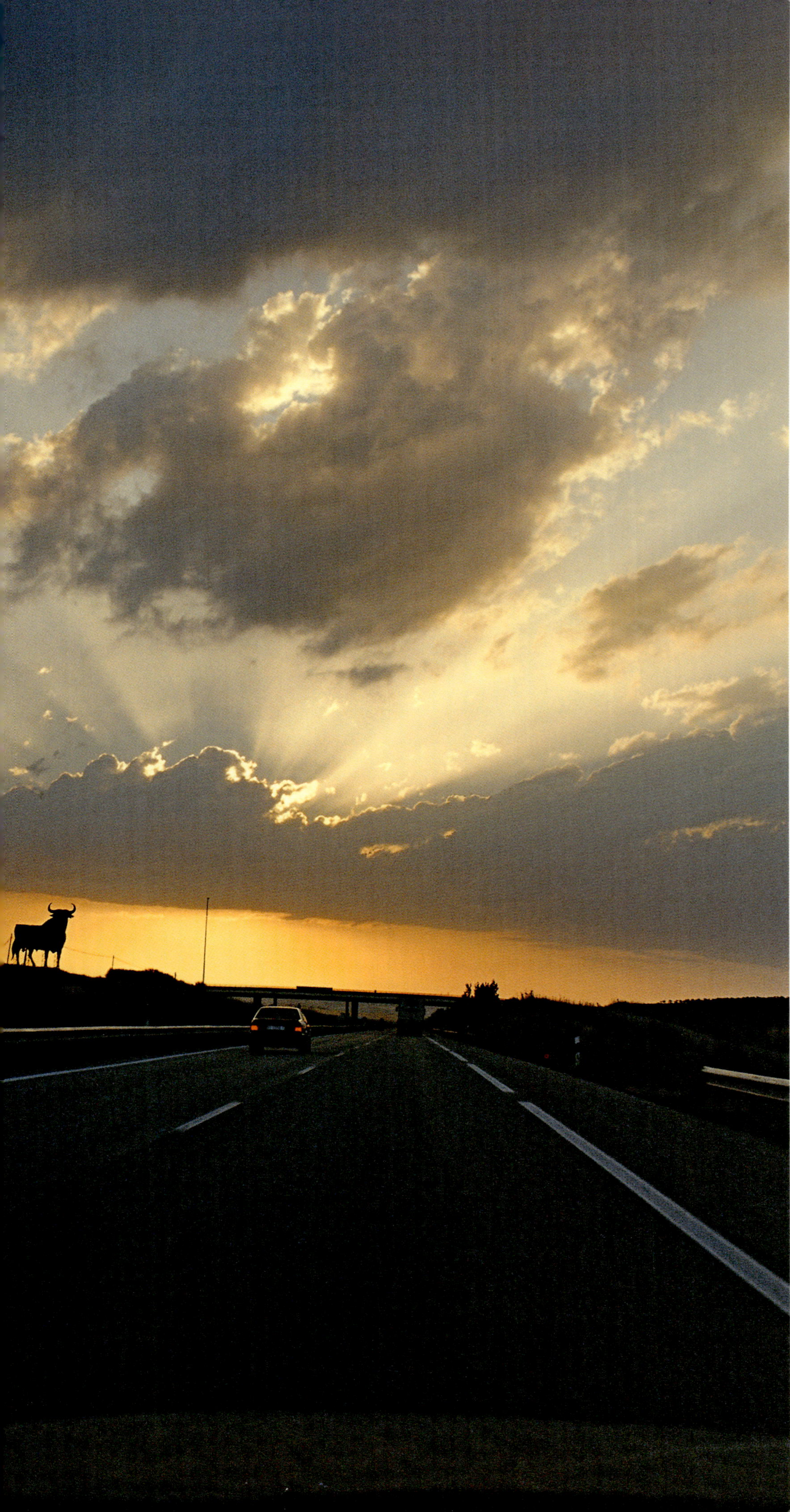

The red fields, the sun like a clod of earth... the labourers pass by hunched on their steeds. . . a few specks of gold glint in a sweet stream.'

Nature imitates Art, says Oscar Wilde, and there is no doubt that without these works of art we would see the Castilian landscape rather differently. 'The Castilian landscape is a new sensation, created by contemporary artists, largely writers. This is to say that art has created a direct connection between the spectator and the landscape, who sees it as though for the first time, with senses cleansed and memories banished of other landscapes which conform to ideas of "good taste" and which could be labelled "academic"', wrote Ramón Pérez de Ayala (1880–1962).

The British writer Gerald Brennan, who lived in Andalucía from 1919 until his death in 1987, published *The Face of Spain* in 1950. This took up where Brannan's Romantic compatriots had left off a century earlier. His description of the journey from Castile to Andalucía recalls these earlier writers: 'All at once, as we crawled up a little pass, the train

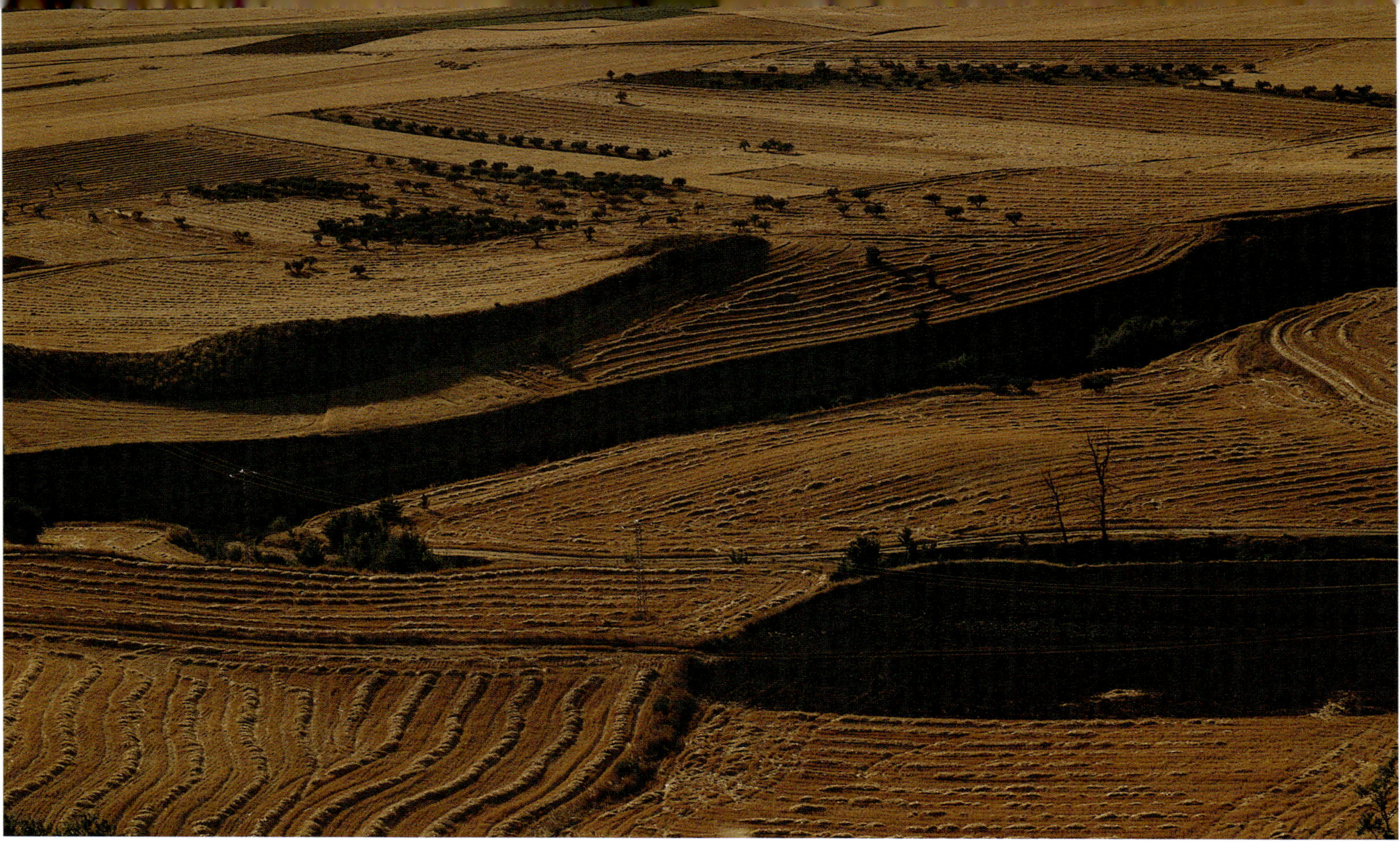

began to move faster and looking out we saw that we were racing down a steep grassy valley; jagged cliffs and rock pinnacles sprouting ilex and umbrella pine stood up on either side, rising above one another in distant recession. In an instant the whole scene had changed from the motionless and classical to the picturesque and romantic. We were in the Pass of Despeñaperros, the only breach in the three hundred mile wall of the Sierra Morena.'

Brennan was also moved by the sight of Spain from the air: 'Instantly we are over uninhabited country. The earth below us is magenta red, for the corn that covers it is too thin to hide the colour of the soil. Then come mountains and rivers, and after them more mountains, till we reach the sea and so leave the great spread ox-hide, as Strabo described this peninsula, behind us.'

It is impossible to mention the literature of the skies without referring to the French writer and pilot Antoine de Saint-Exupéry, who flew over the peninsula many times during the Civil War of 1936 to 1939. 'Every time I fly I find myself hypnotised at the window, and never fail to be impressed by the sophisticated tapestry formed by the Spanish landscape: a harmonious chaos, spun in the mysterious pattern of the centuries, a child of time and the history of the land.'

What is left of this romantic, poetic vision of Spain? This is now a country that has leapt headlong into modernity, and is different from the rest of Europe for better and for worse. It has undergone the most dramatic sociological and economic transformation of any European country in recent decades. Fifty years ago, fully half of the population worked the land. Today, that figure is 4 per cent.

In making that leap, the human form has changed abruptly: Spaniards have lost their earthy colours, and bodies once sculpted by the sun, wind and hunger are now toned in air-conditioned gyms and tanned at leisure. The cities and landscapes have also changed, sometimes in defiance of their past, as a result of the flight from the country to the city. Chaotic, speculative developments reflect the frenetic glamour of a society striving to bury its poverty, determined to prosper and become unrecognizable, even to itself.

Seas of plastic have turned some of the poorest land in Europe into some of the most abundant. The abstract beauty of these plastic greenhouses stretching to the horizon creates cosmic, unreal landscapes. Powerful cars ride the old mule tracks. From a high-speed train or a motorway the landscape flies past in air-conditioned comfort and with help only a mobile phone call away.

Critical voices have begun to be raised against this 'speeding', and steps have been taken with the creation of protected landscapes such as Menorca, Lanzarote, the Sierras of Cazorla and Segura, and Urdubai Reserve in the Basque Country. Apart from protecting these natural spaces like Indian Reservations, we have to learn to see the landscape as a work of art, and to appreciate the great variety among the regions of Spain, preventing the landscape from being spoiled by industry or buildings whose disproportionate scale or inappropriate materials offend the eye. A great inspiration in this area is the work of César Manrique in turning his native Lanzarote into a treasure and a symbol, protecting it and proving that

Guadalajara, Castilla-La Mancha, in July

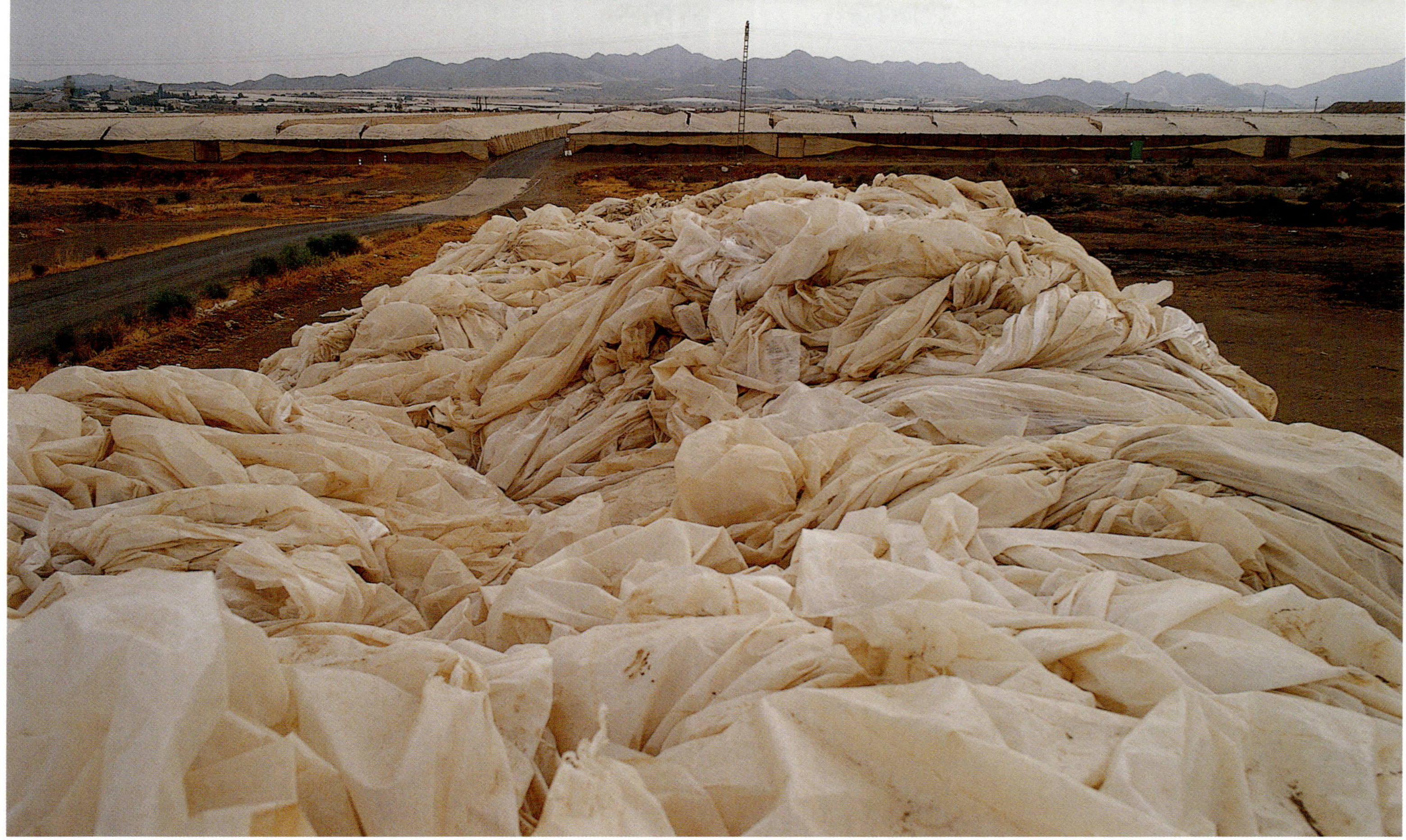

a well looked-after landscape is a cultural heritage as well as good business. I am drawn to Lanzarote by the fine balance between man and Nature and to be free from visual pollution, as well as by its magnetic beauty.

The Spanish landscape – so exotic to outsiders – is undoubtedly a draw for the sixty million visitors to Spain each year. Many come in search of sun, sand, sangria and all the other clichés, but there are more and more who come in search of something different. English, German, Scandinavian, they come to walk the old roads, drawn by their love of Nature to retrace the old Romantic dream of the South.

Hemingway said that Spain was 'the colour of a copper coin' and responded profoundly to the colours of the raw, bare earth, its wildness and intensity. Knowing a landscape helps one to understand a people, its history and culture. What would the work of Picasso, Dalí or Buñuel look like if they hadn't carried those landscapes in their souls? Spending time away from Spain made them see it with redoubled clarity and passion, like those foreign travellers whose rapt curiosity uncovered so many of our characteristics.

It is our duty to teach our children to read the landscape so that they can describe what inspires them, and how it makes them feel, and explore themselves through it. They must understand that our landscapes are the home of our past and the mother of our emotions. We should teach them to look at a landscape as though it were a movie screen where things happen because the observer's gaze fills them with meaning. We should teach them to travel for its own sake, to take minor roads and forget about the motorways, fast food for the eyes.

Spain is not a smooth country. Everything here is compulsive, intense: the geography; the views; the climate; the people. Here is Finisterre the westernmost point of Europe, Madrid the highest capital city, Tarifa the closest point to the equator, Grazalema the wettest, Almería the driest, Écija the hottest. This is a passionate land, always in chiaroscuro, like the bullrings where the seats in the sun and the seats in the shade are worlds apart.

Well, I sound very Spanish, don't I? A bit melodramatic. I can't help myself. . . It's been a long time since it rained. I'm descended from an Irishman who came to Spain at the end of the eighteenth century looking for merino sheep: Patrick Garvey, my ancestor, was shipwrecked in the Bay of Cádiz by a great storm and almost lost his life. He was rescued by the captain of the ship, and invited to stay at the captain's house while he recovered. There, he was left in the care of the captain's daughter, who was such a tender nurse that he fell in love with her, and with Spain. . . and this may be why I look at my country today with something like the fascination of an outsider.

If you decide to follow the blessed paths through this ancient but youthful land because I have given you a taste for it here, then you will find the road is endless. If this book prompts someone in a position of authority to act on the realization that the landscape is a 'garden for all', I will consider myself well rewarded. If you have read this far, my humble thanks.

¡*Gracias y Buen viaje*!

Murcia in June

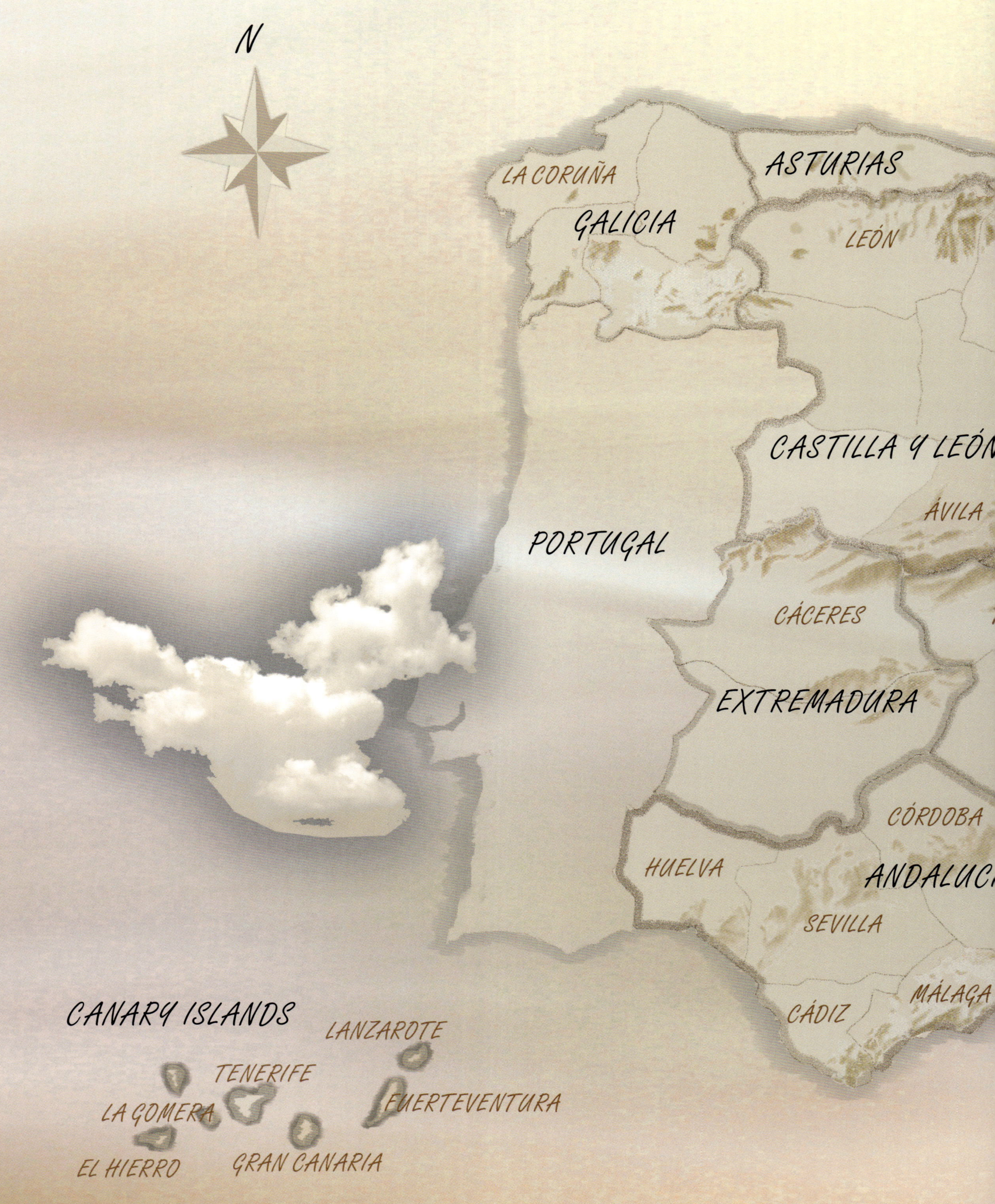
N
LA CORUÑA
ASTURIAS
GALICIA
LEÓN
CASTILLA Y LEÓN
ÁVILA
PORTUGAL
CÁCERES
EXTREMADURA
CÓRDOBA
HUELVA
SEVILLA
CÁDIZ
MÁLAGA
CANARY ISLANDS
LANZAROTE
TENERIFE
LA GOMERA
FUERTEVENTURA
EL HIERRO
GRAN CANARIA

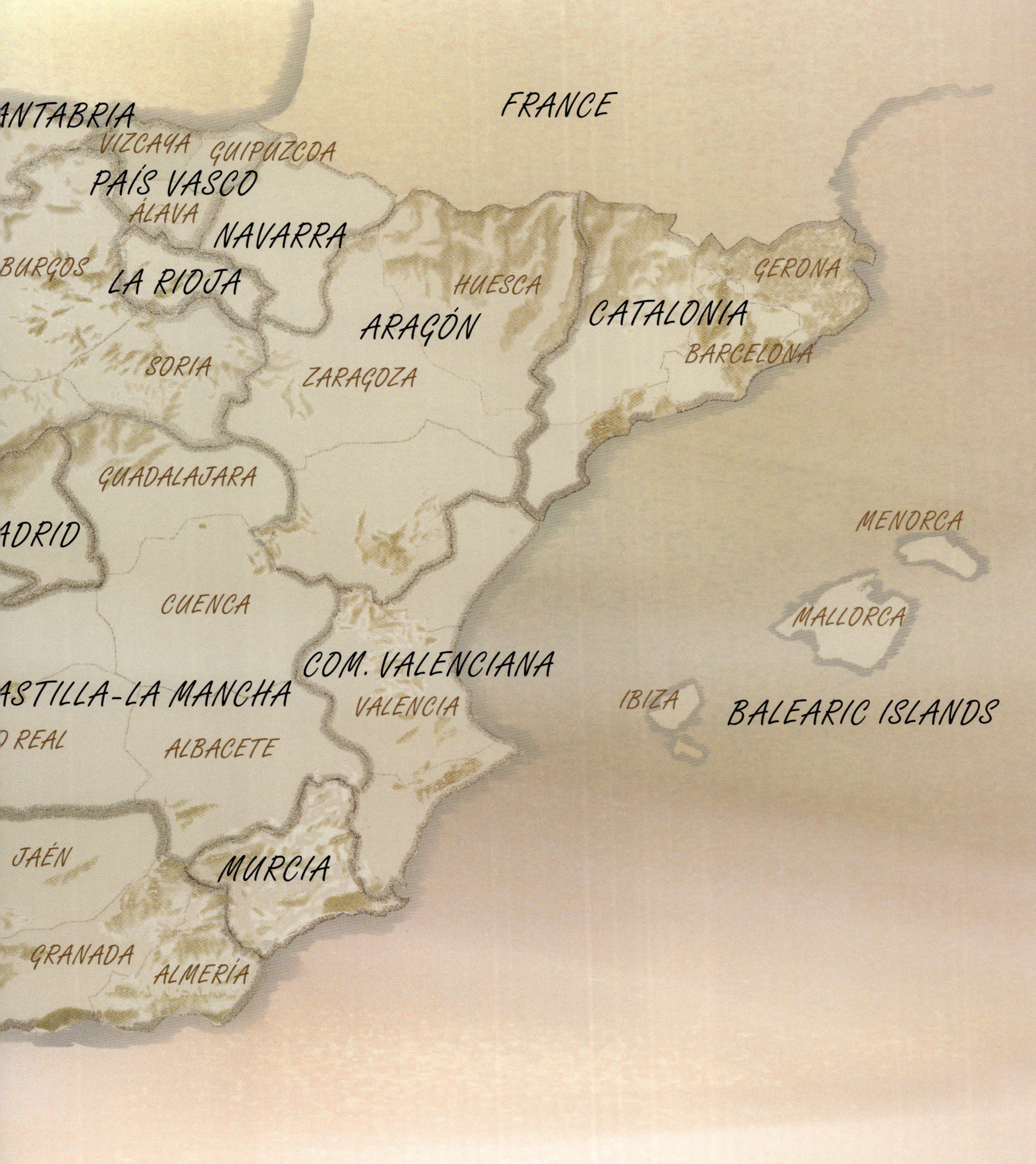
ANTABRIA
VIZCAYA
GUIPÚZCOA
PAÍS VASCO
ÁLAVA
NAVARRA
BURGOS
LA RIOJA
FRANCE
HUESCA
ARAGÓN
CATALONIA
GERONA
BARCELONA
SORIA
ZARAGOZA
GUADALAJARA
ADRID
CUENCA
COM. VALENCIANA
ASTILLA-LA MANCHA
VALENCIA
REAL
ALBACETE
MENORCA
MALLORCA
IBIZA
BALEARIC ISLANDS
JAÉN
MURCIA
GRANADA
ALMERÍA

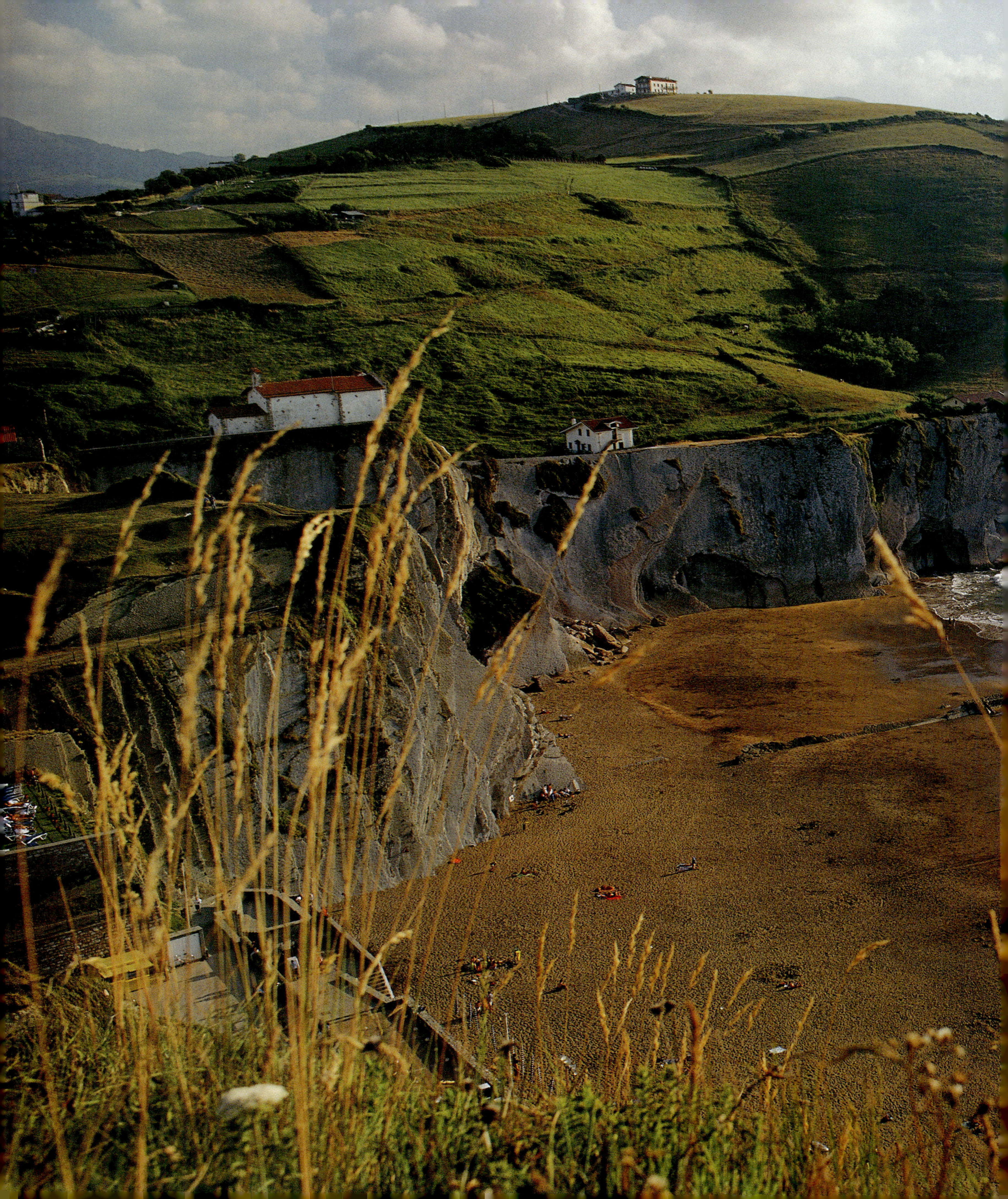

THE NORTH

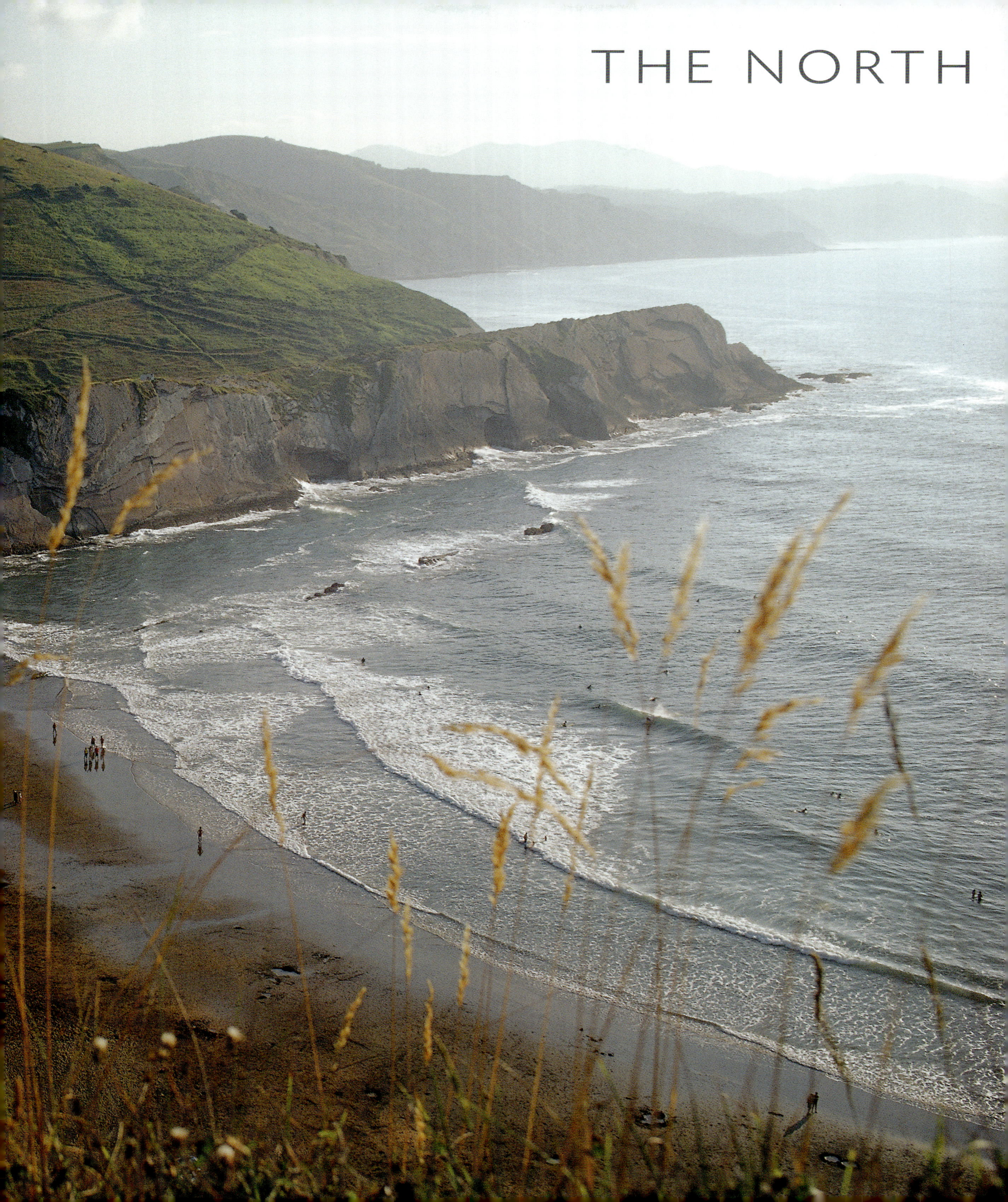

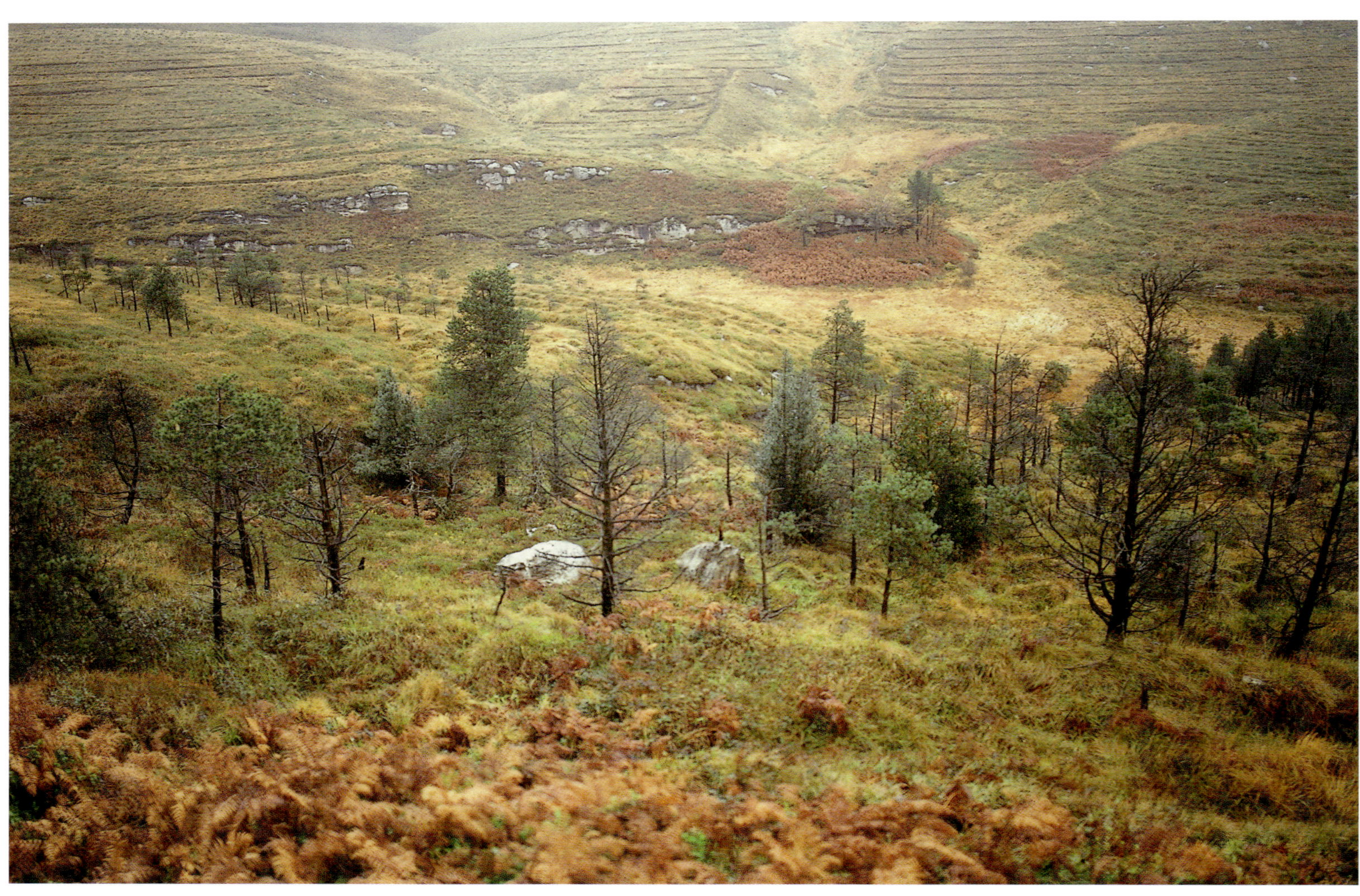

ABOVE
Cantabria in February

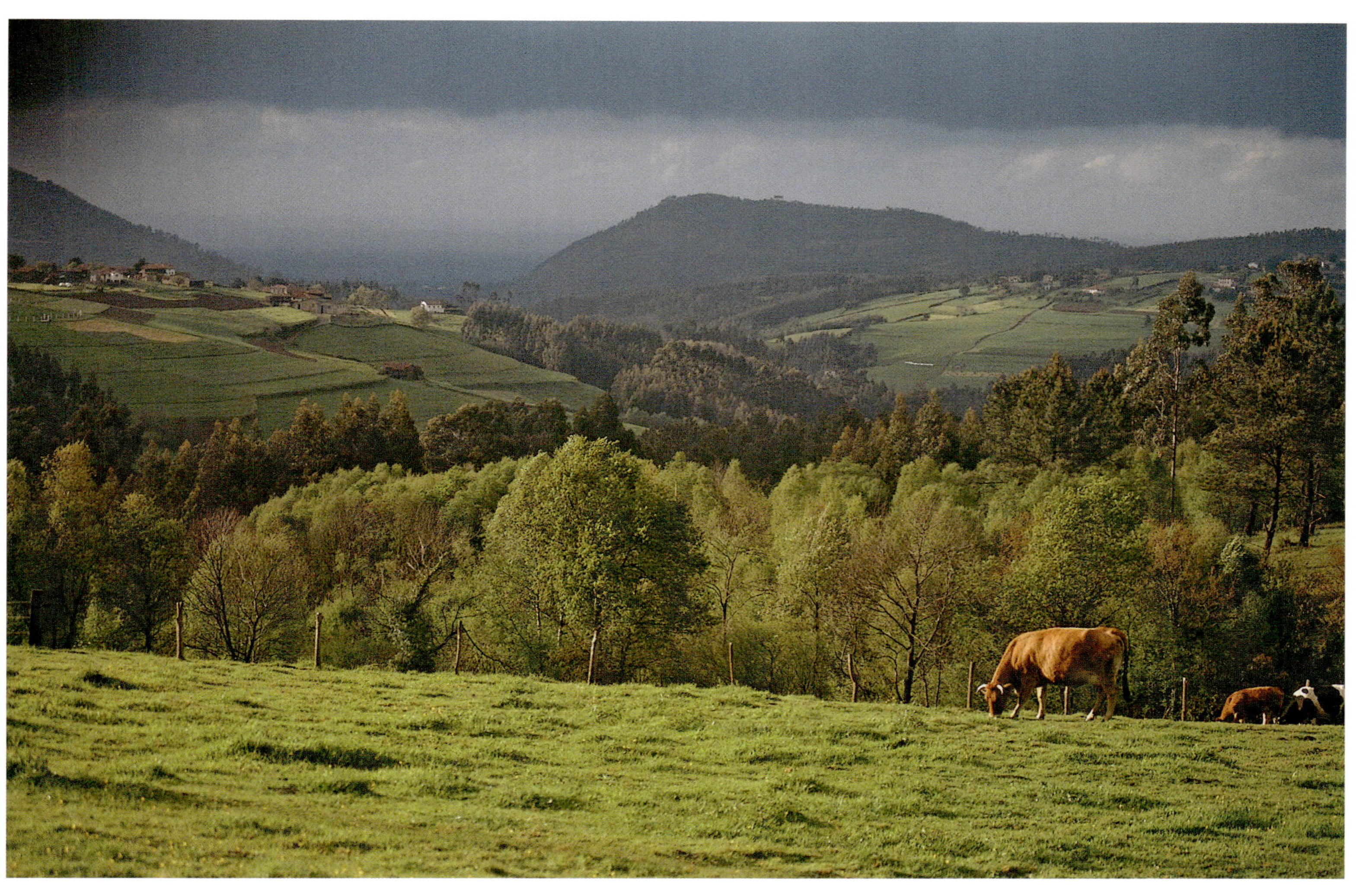

ABOVE
Asturias in July

FOLLOWING PAGES
Navarra in June

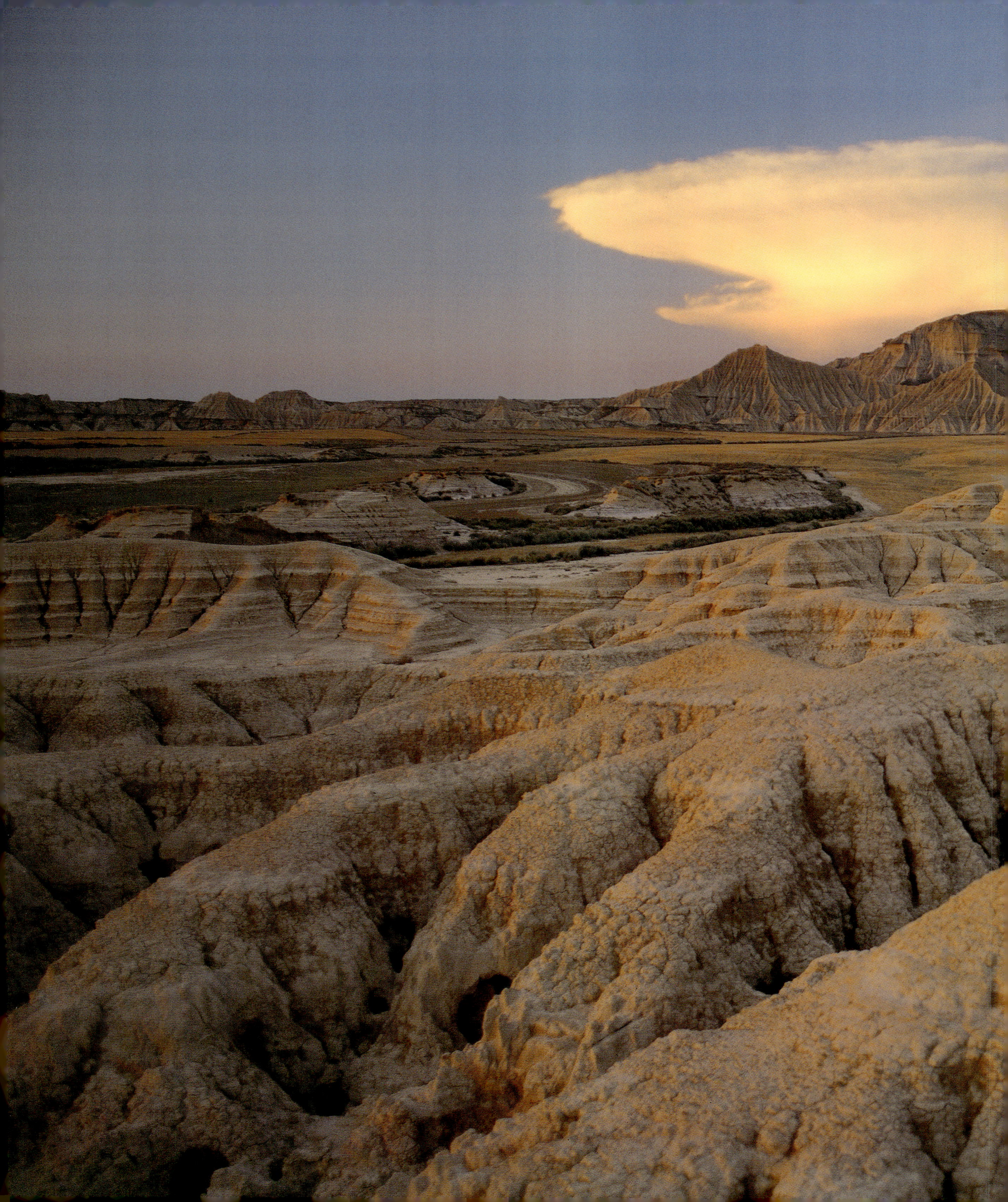

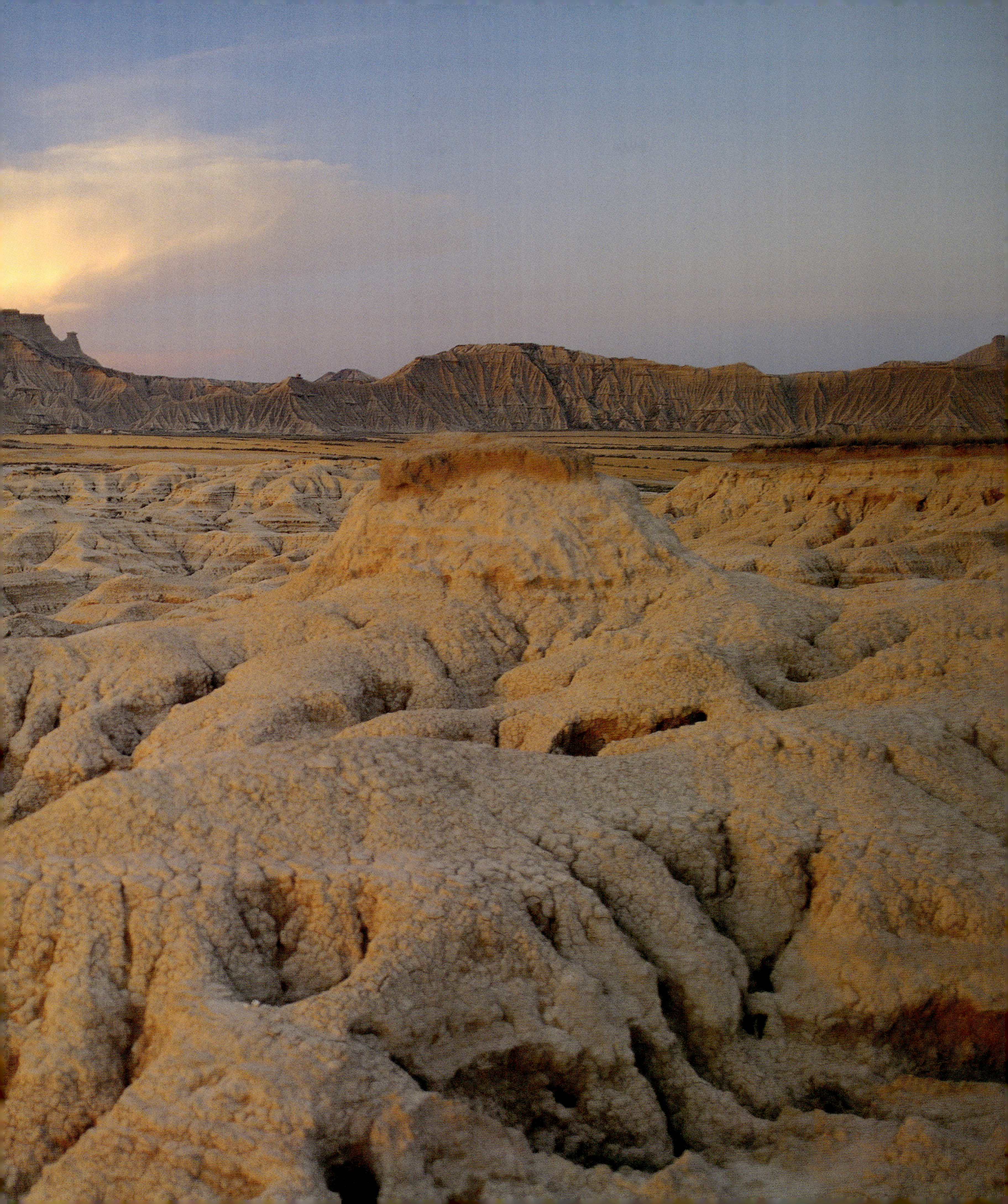

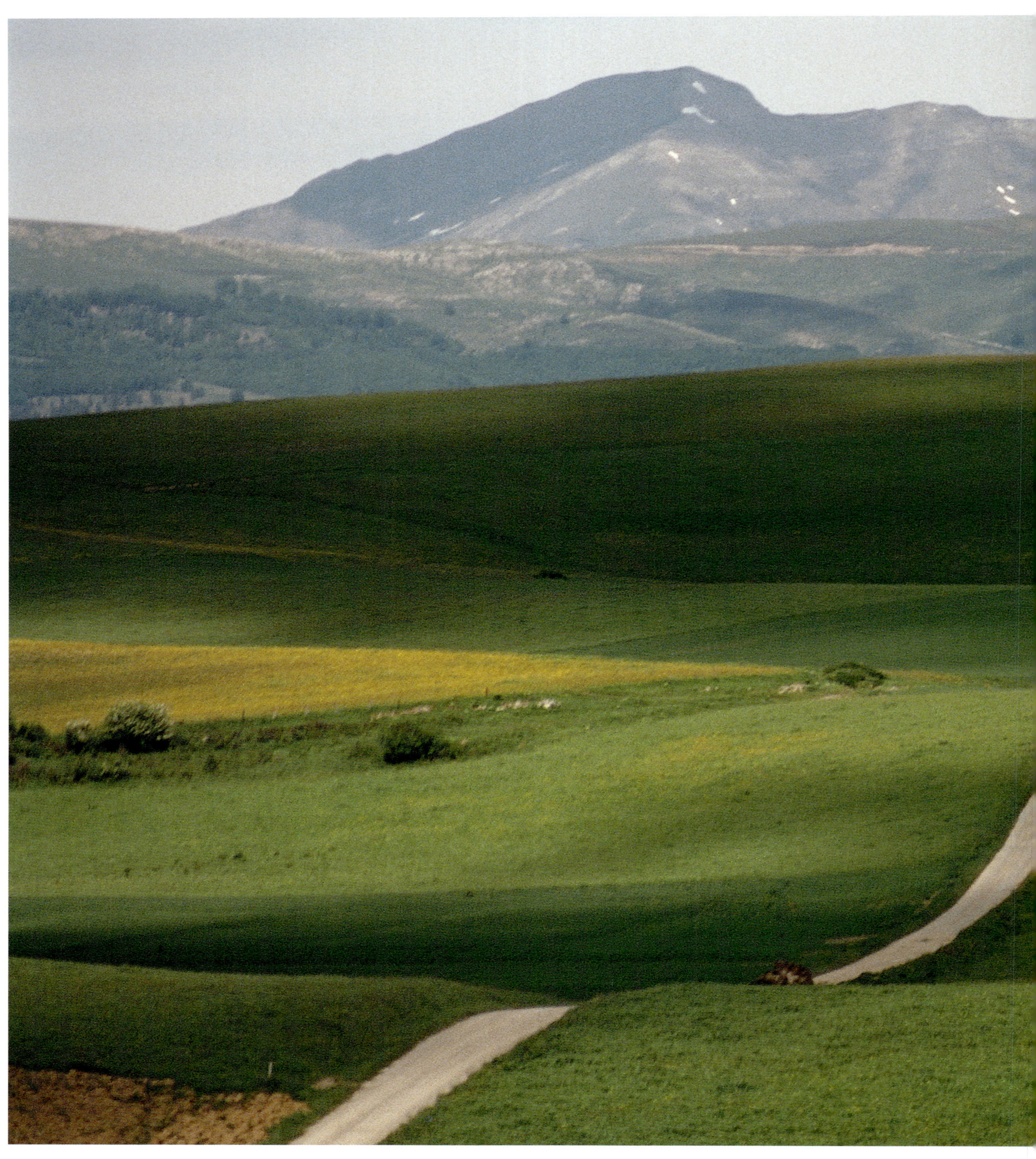

ABOVE
Navarra in June

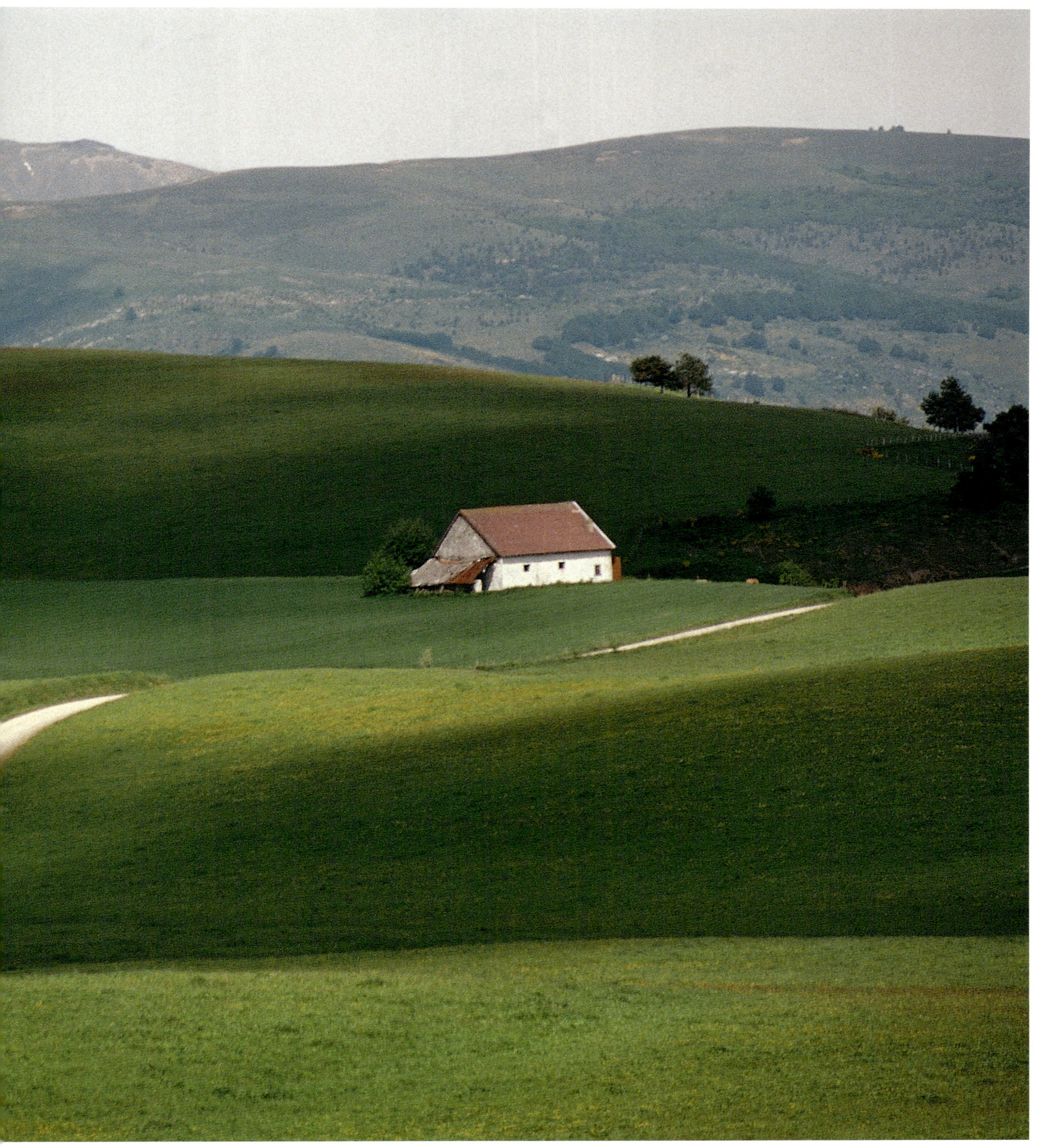

FOLLOWING PAGES
Vizcaya, Basque Country, in July

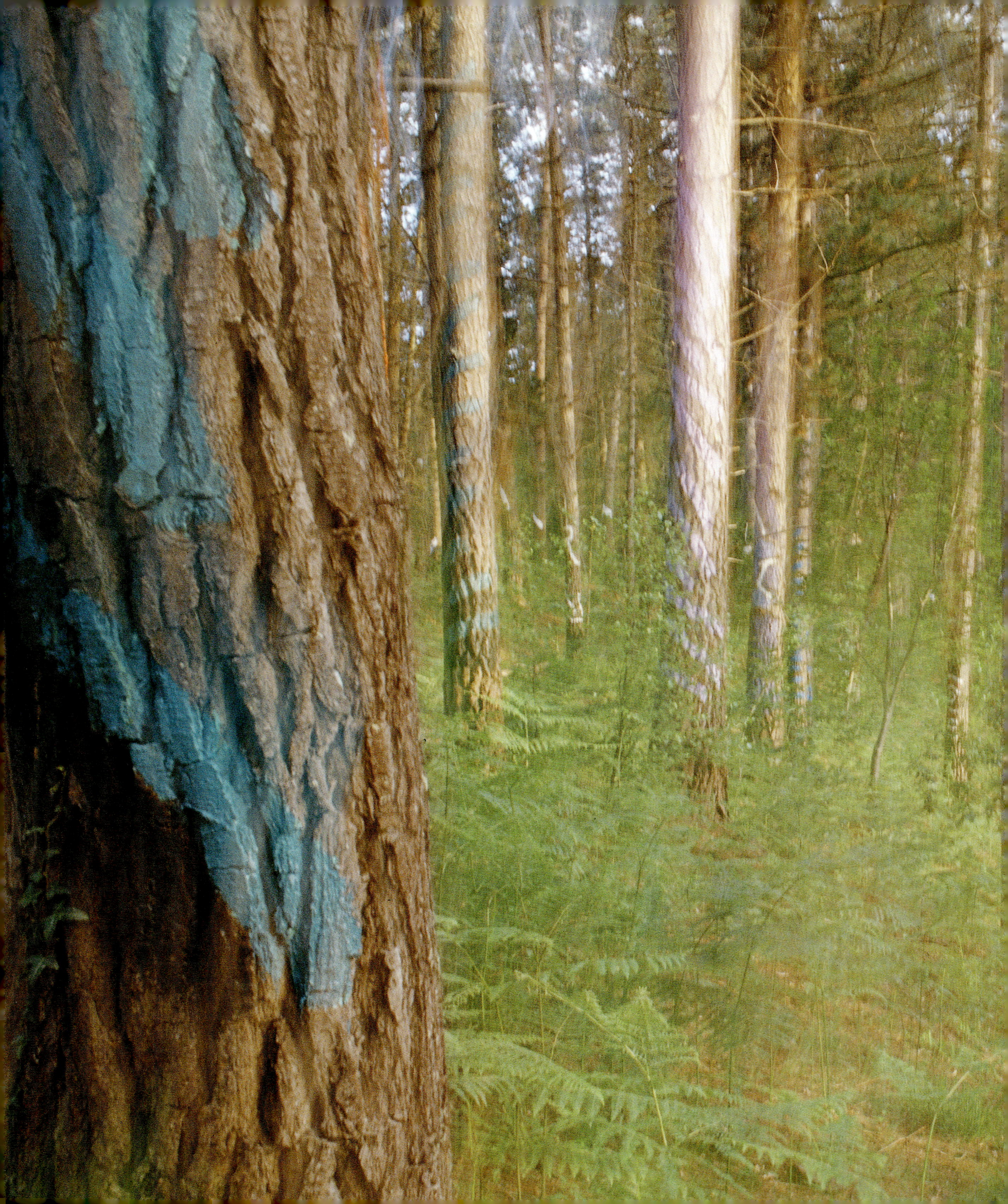

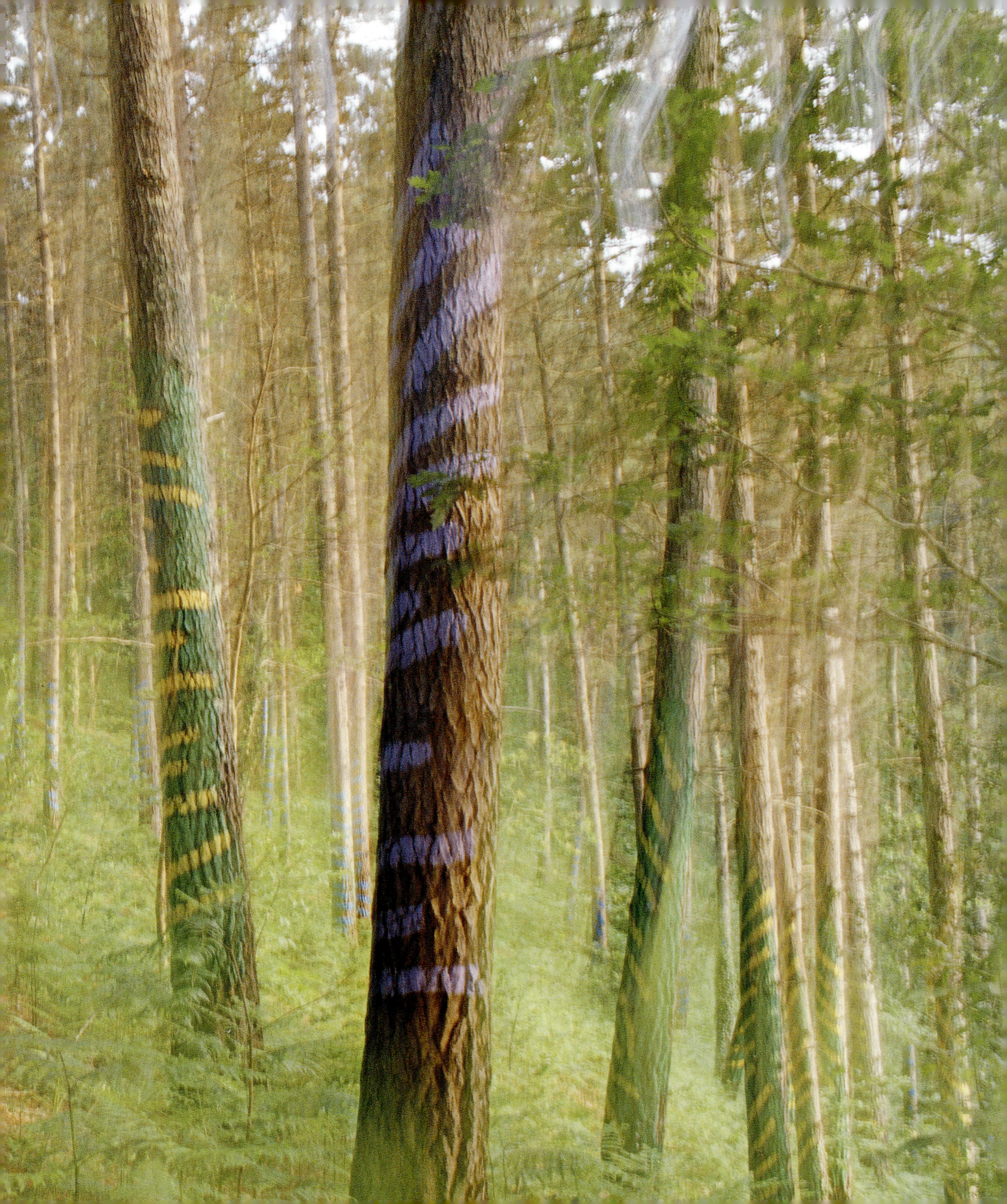

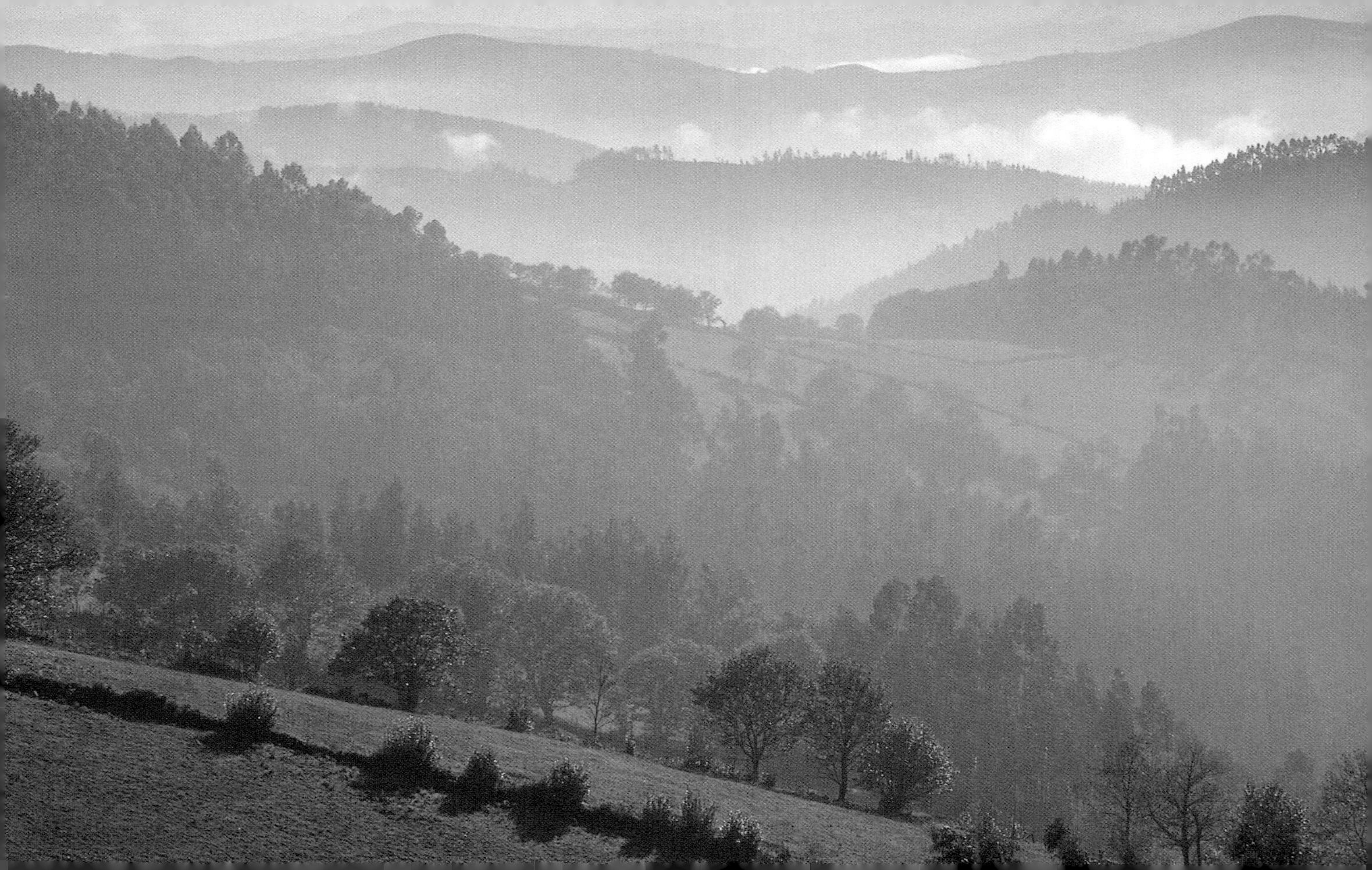

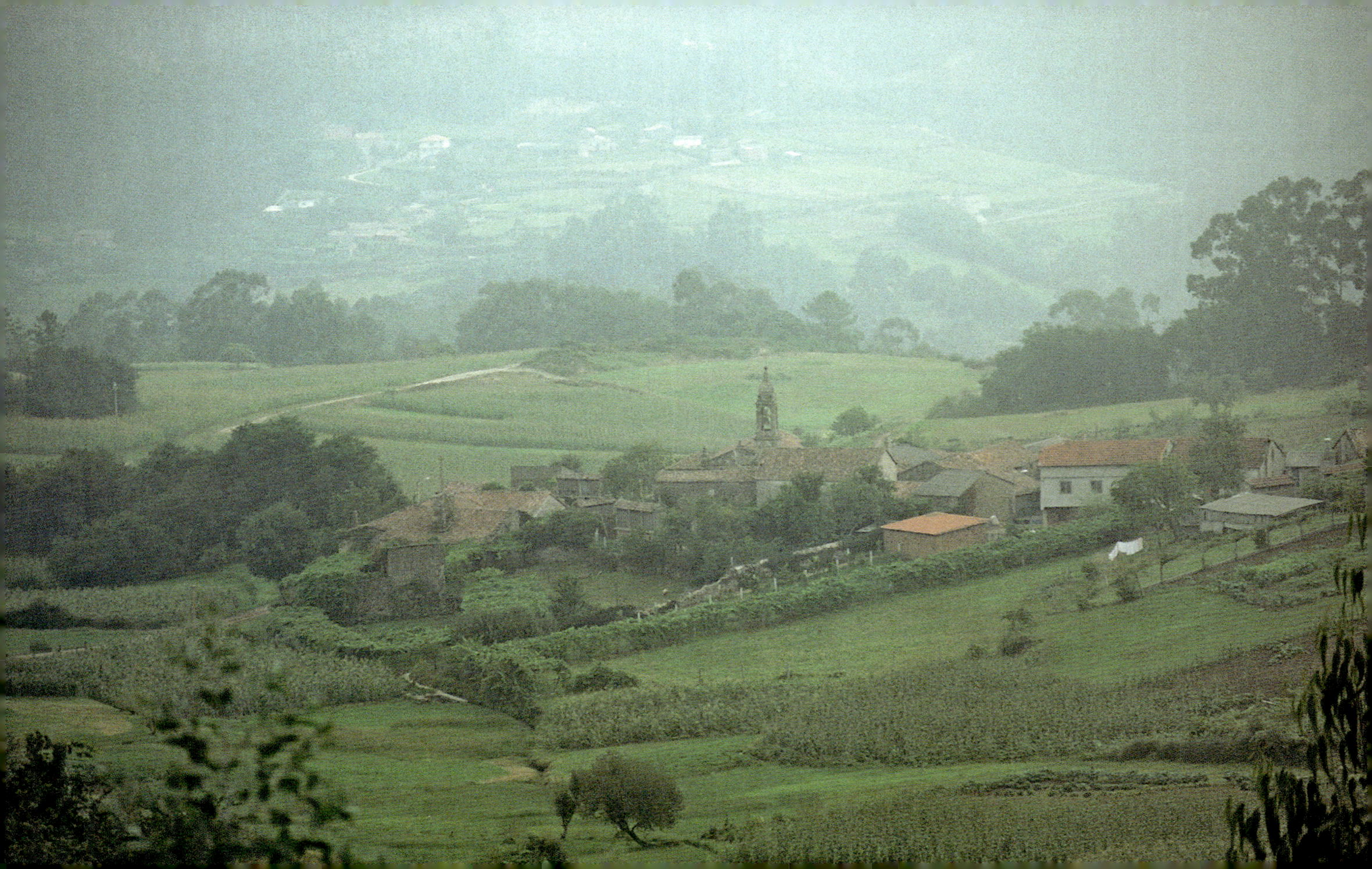

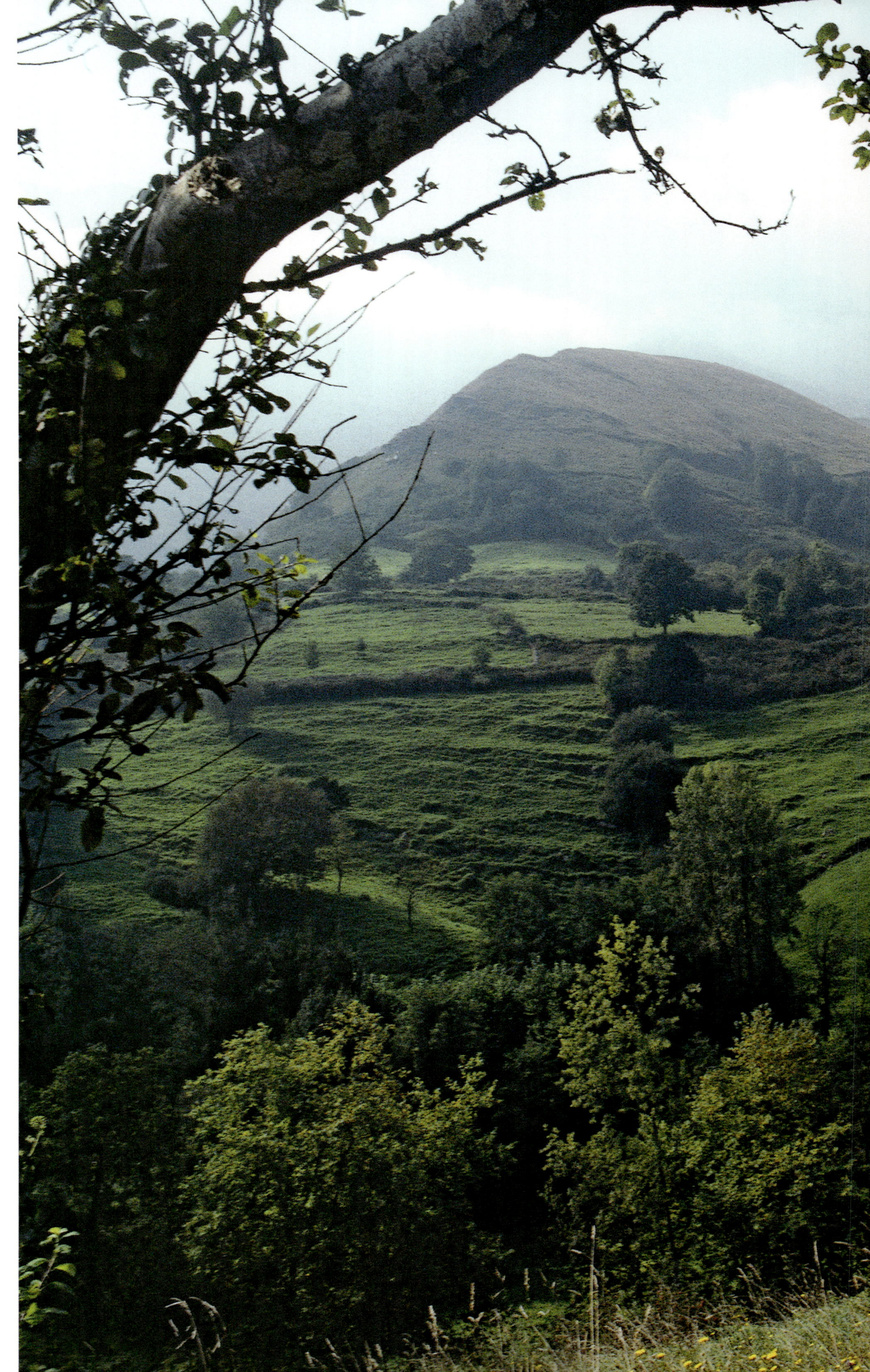

PREVIOUS PAGES
LEFT Asturias in August
RIGHT La Coruña, Galicia, in August

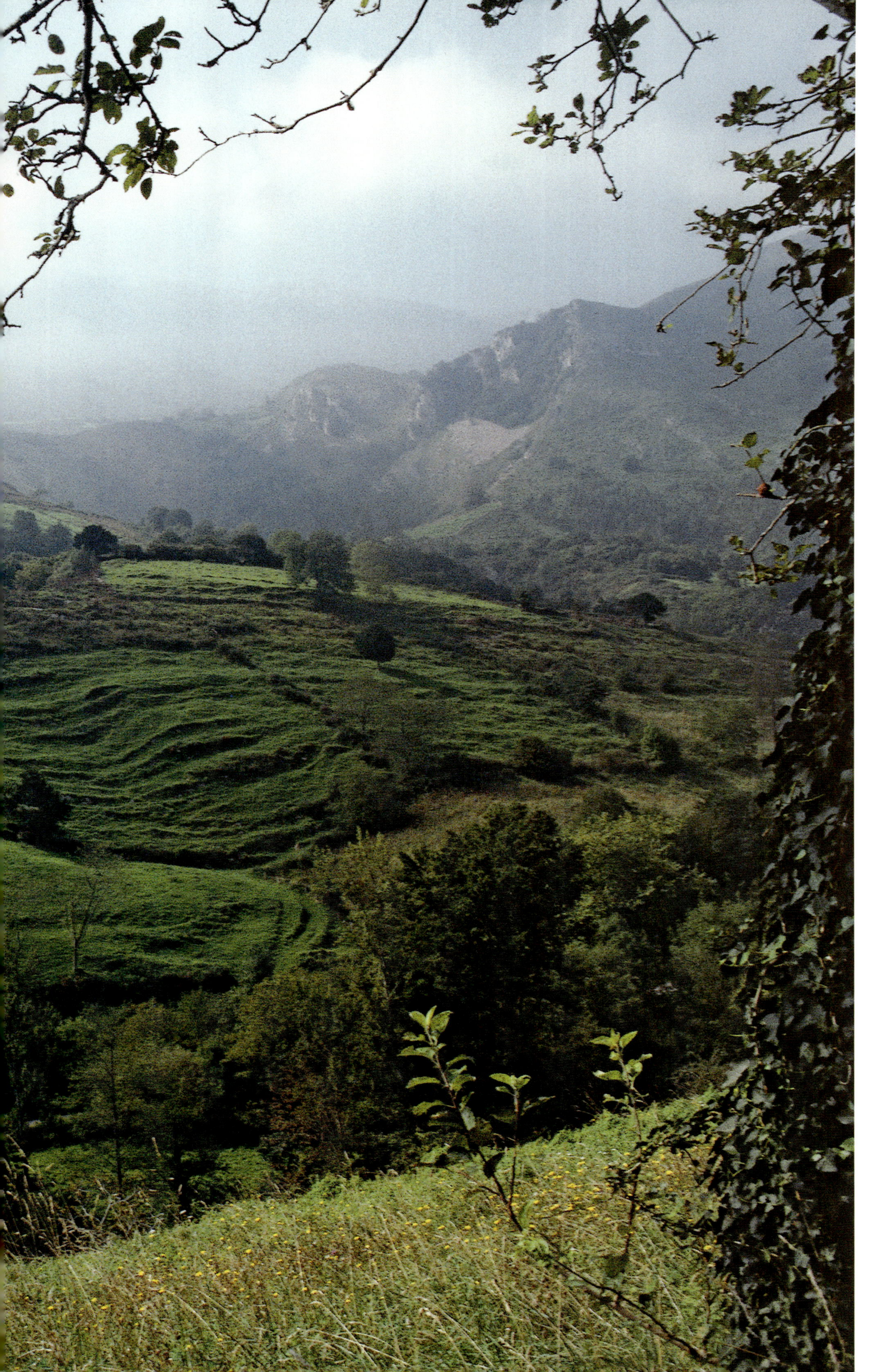

LEFT
Asturias in September

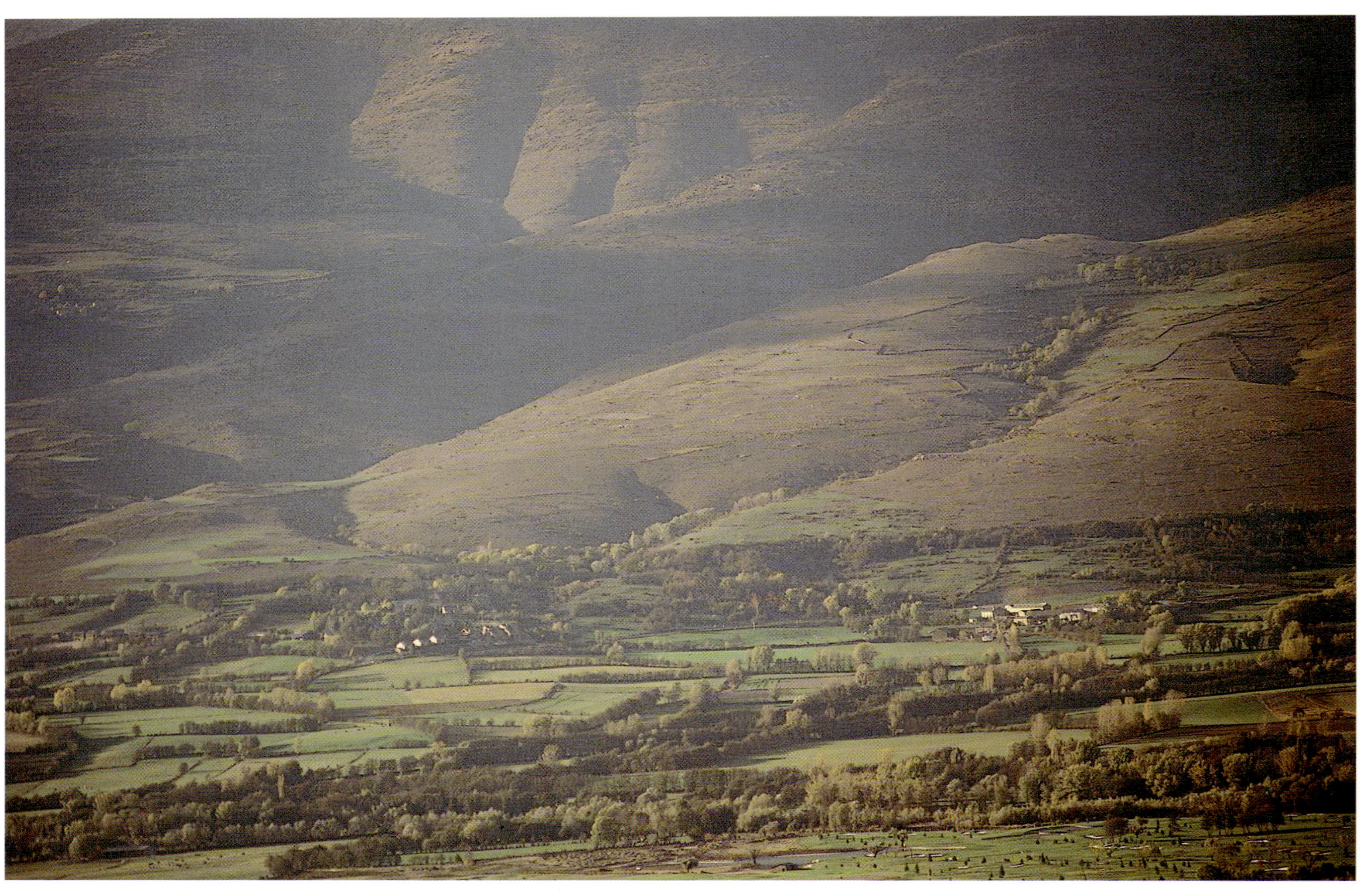

ABOVE
Barcelona, Catalonia, in October

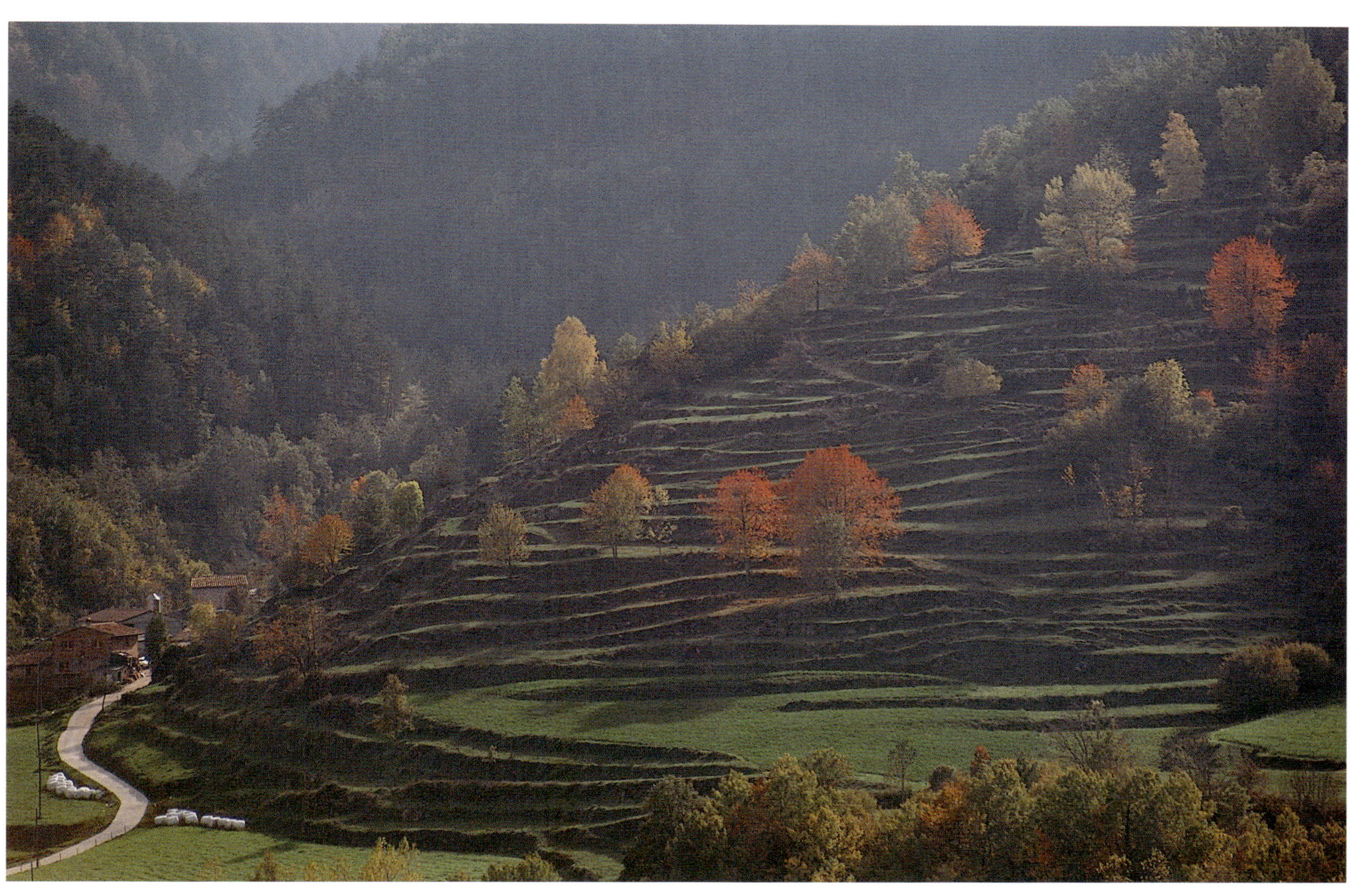

ABOVE
Huesca, Aragón, in October

FOLLOWING PAGES
LEFT Asturias in November
RIGHT Cantabria in November

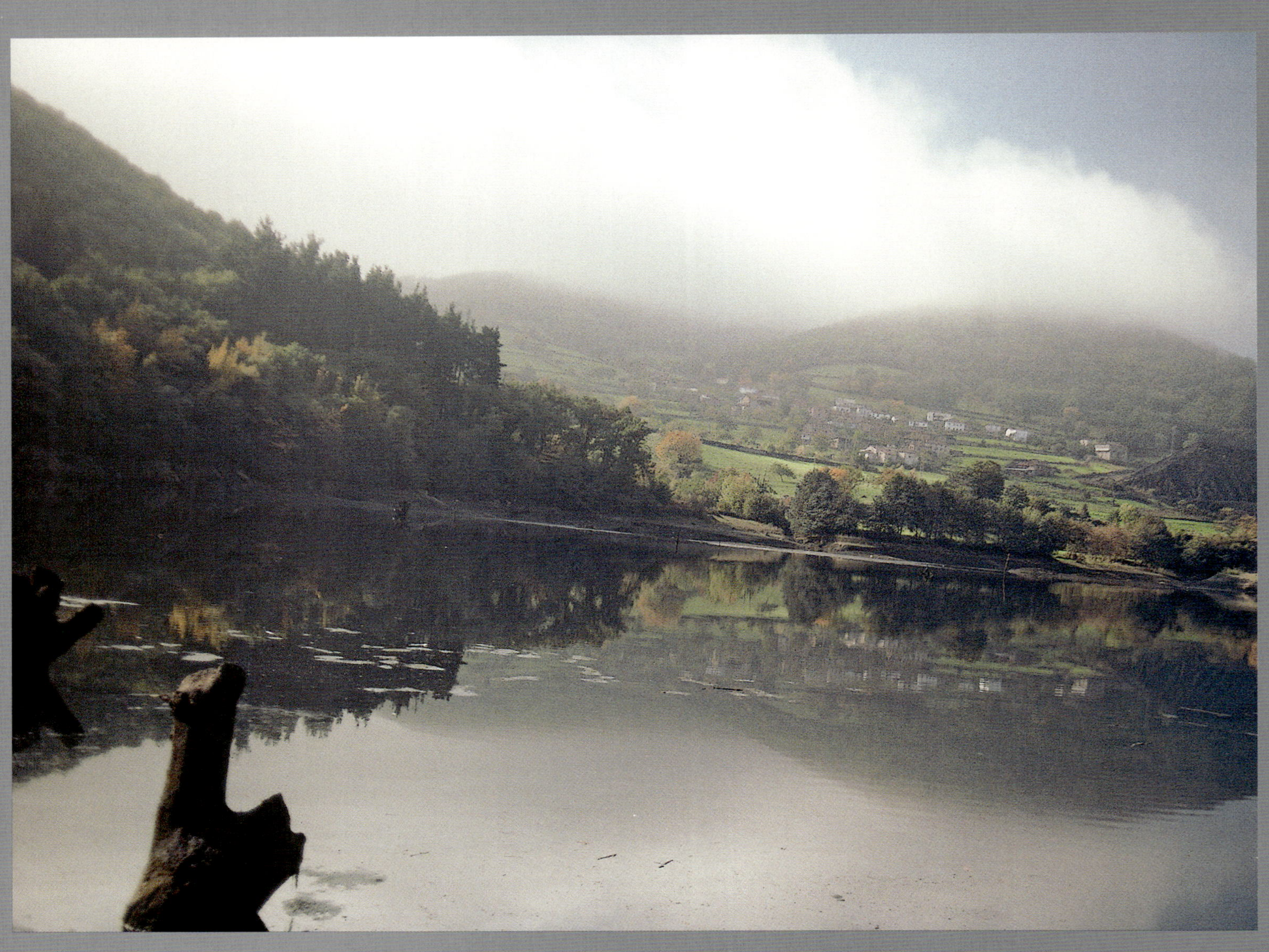

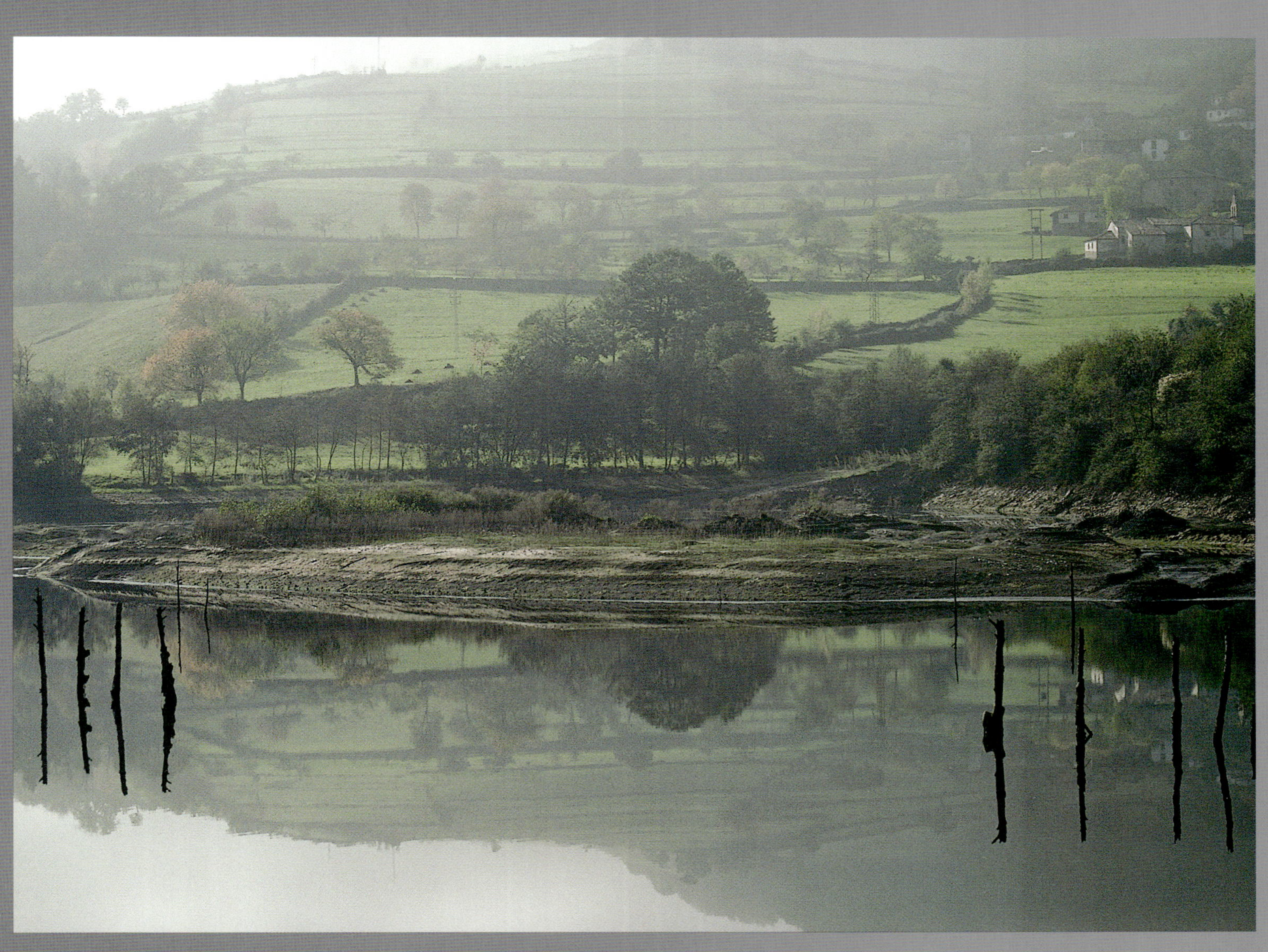

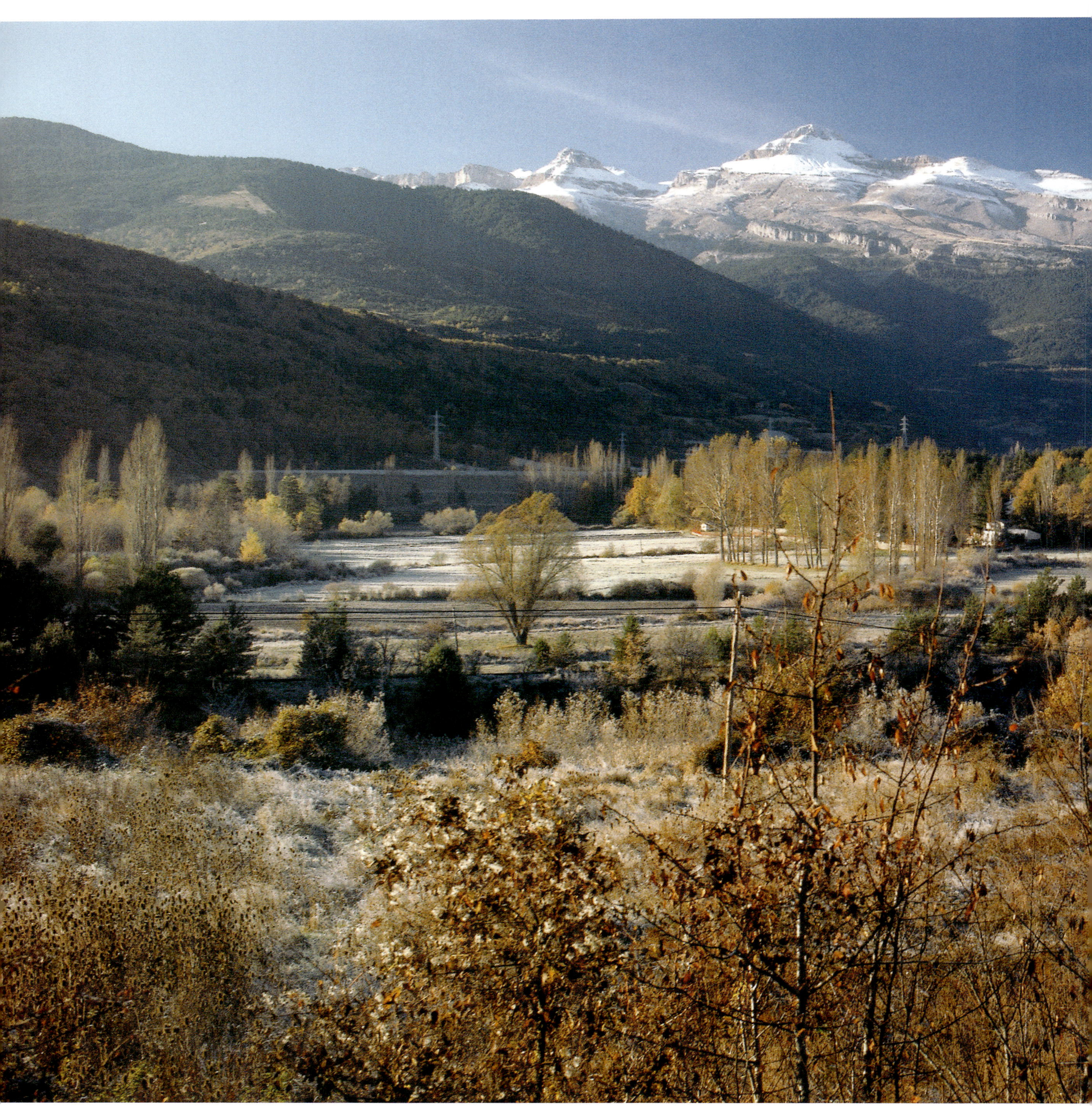

ABOVE
Huesca, Aragón, in November

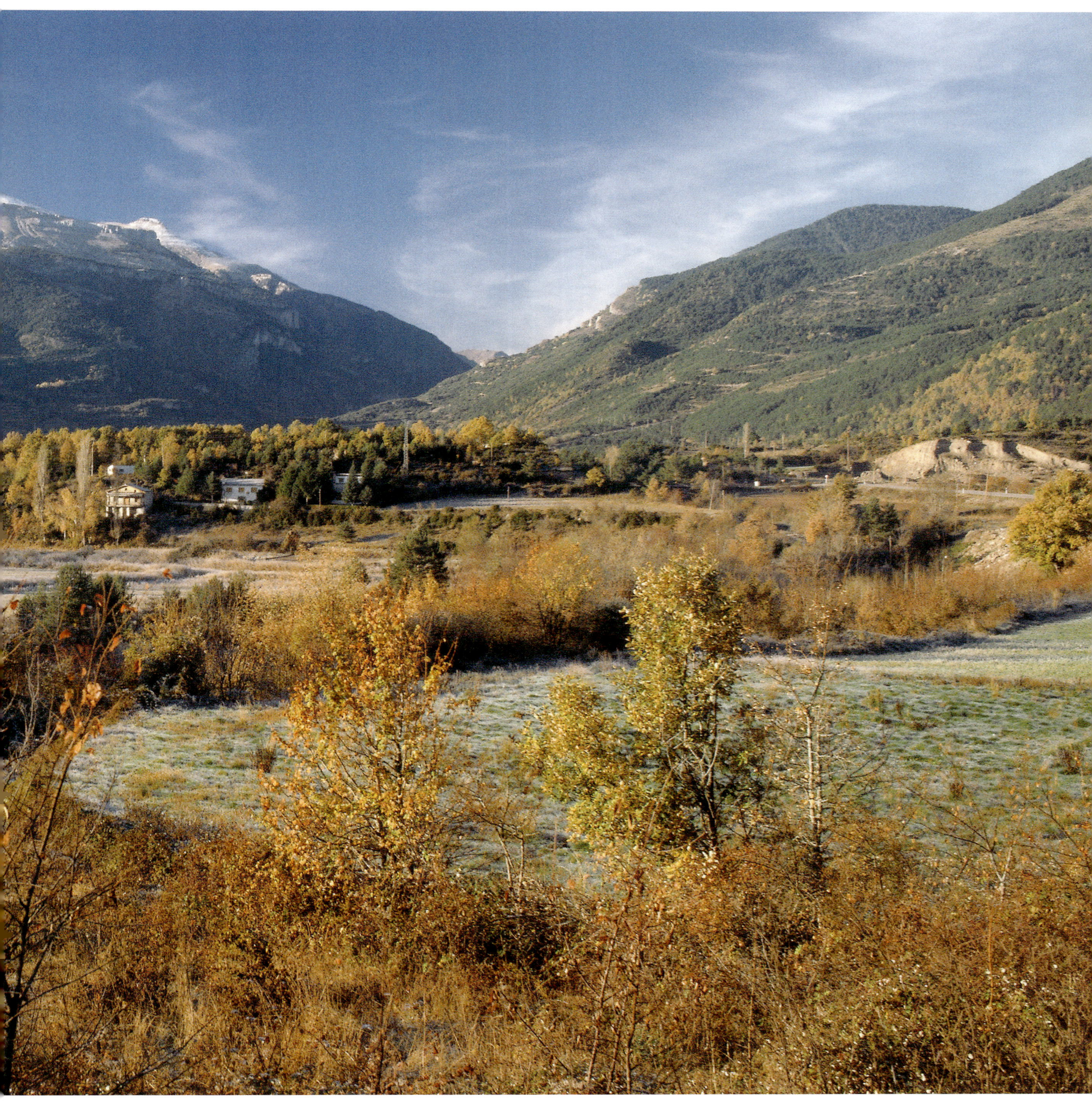

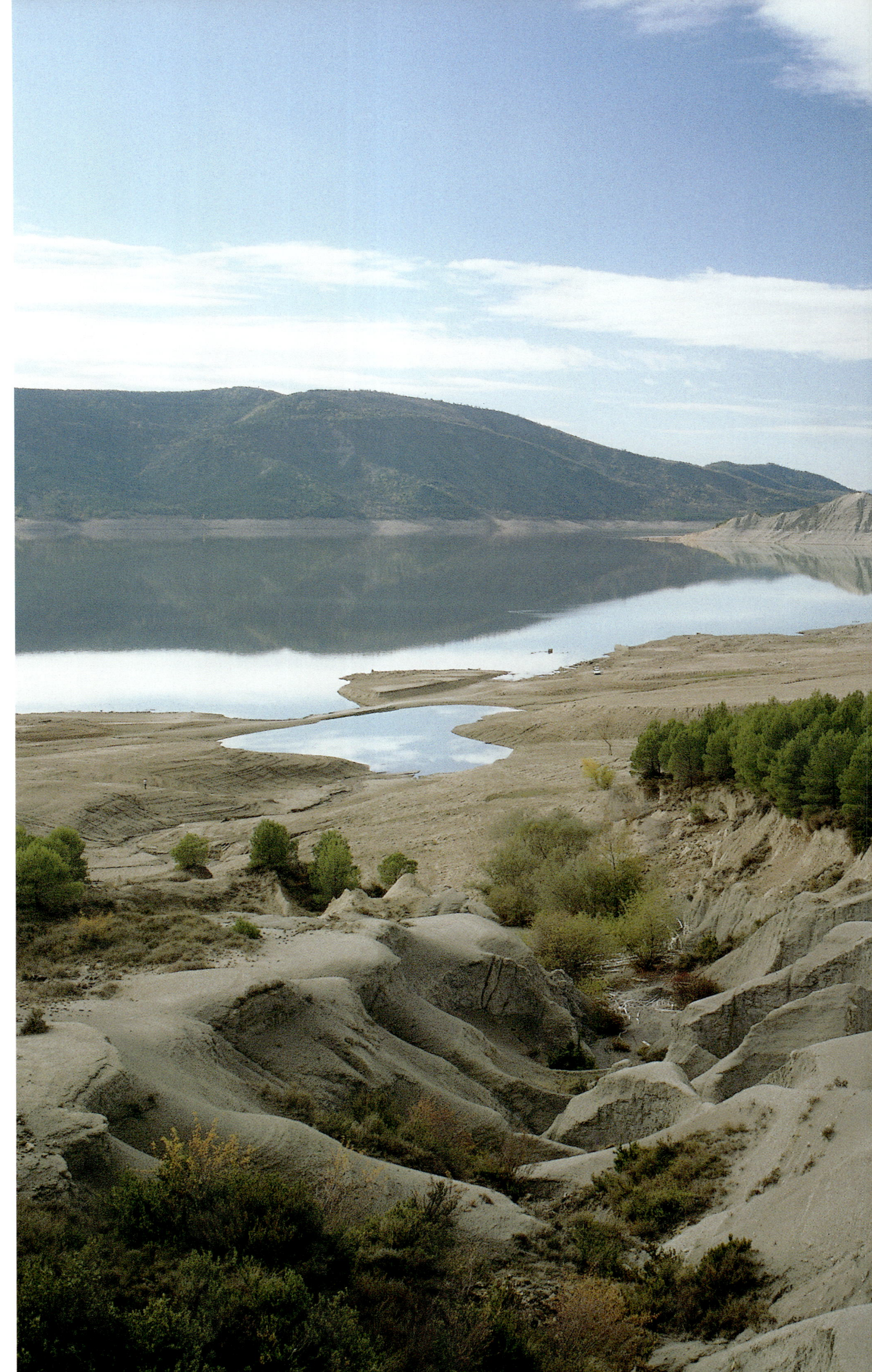

RIGHT
Navarra in November

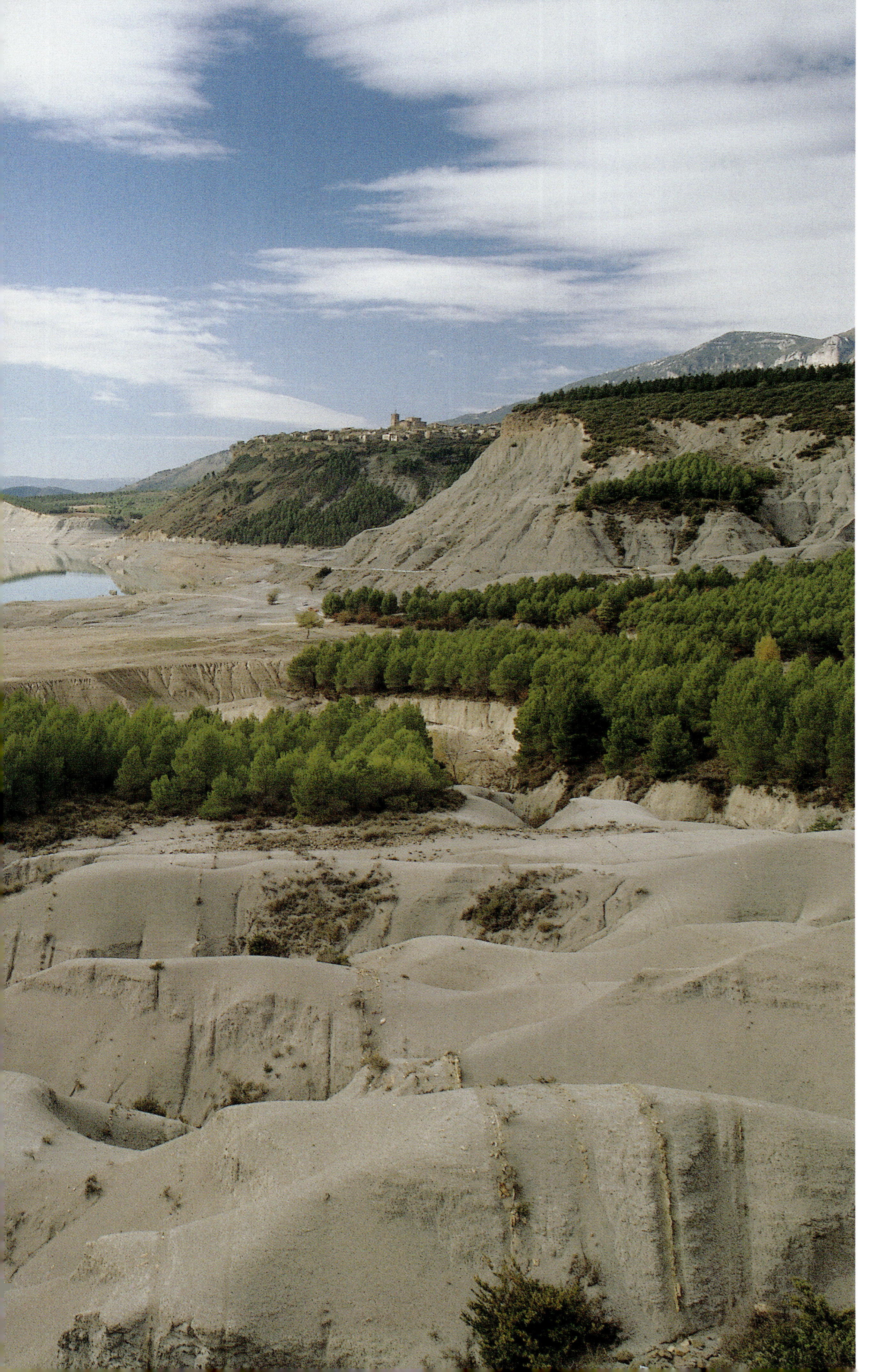

FOLLOWING PAGES
Álava, Basque Country, in July

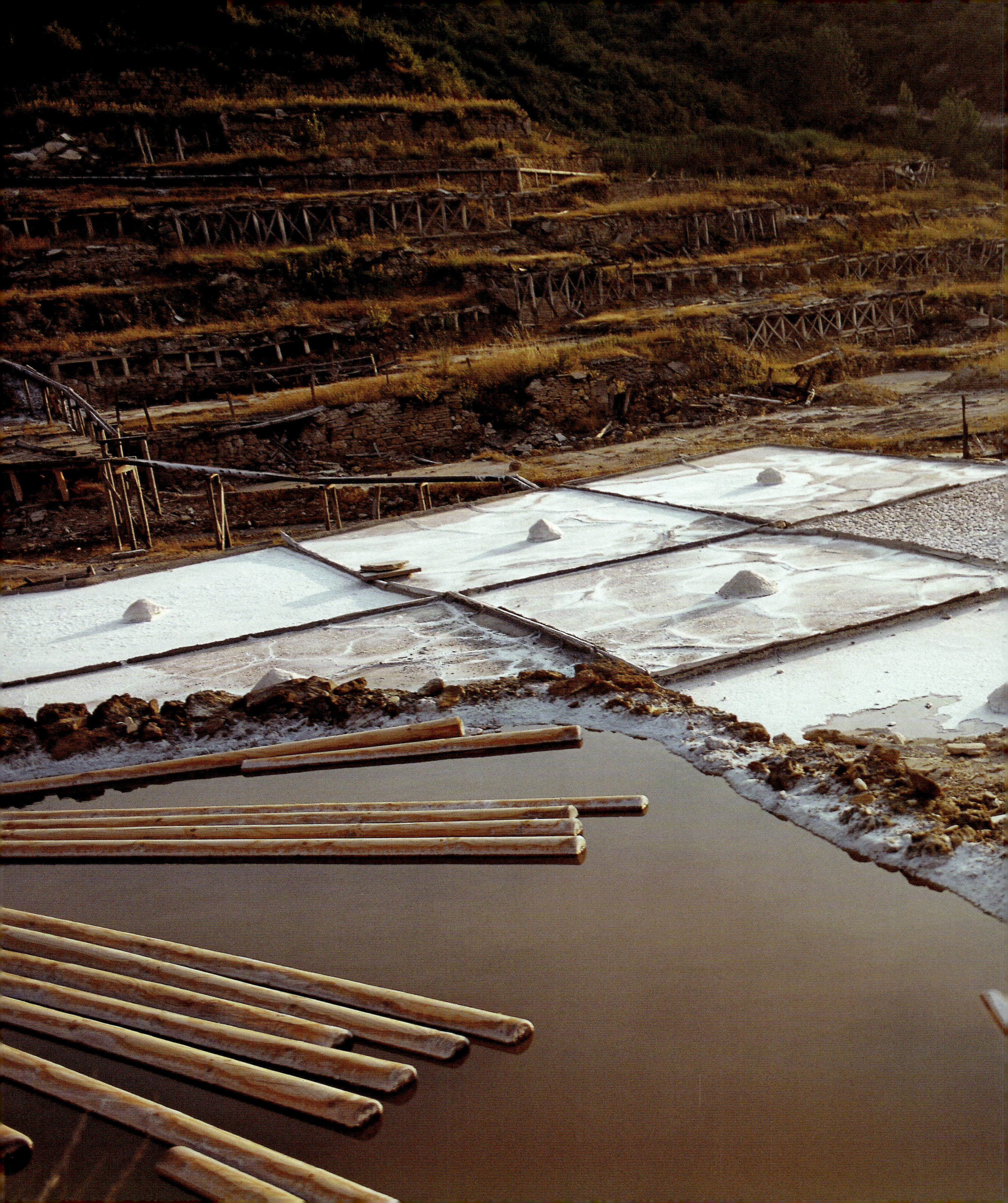

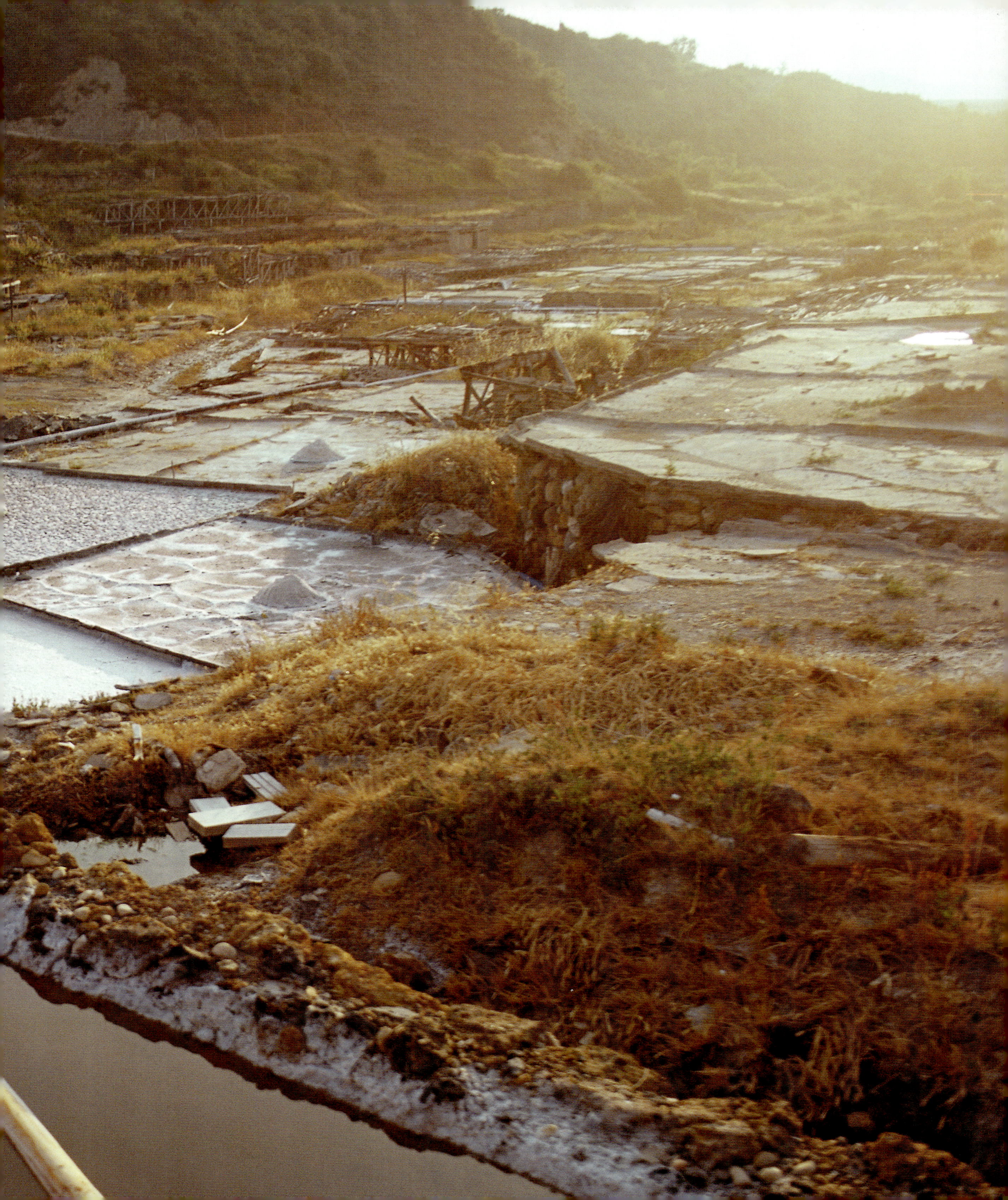

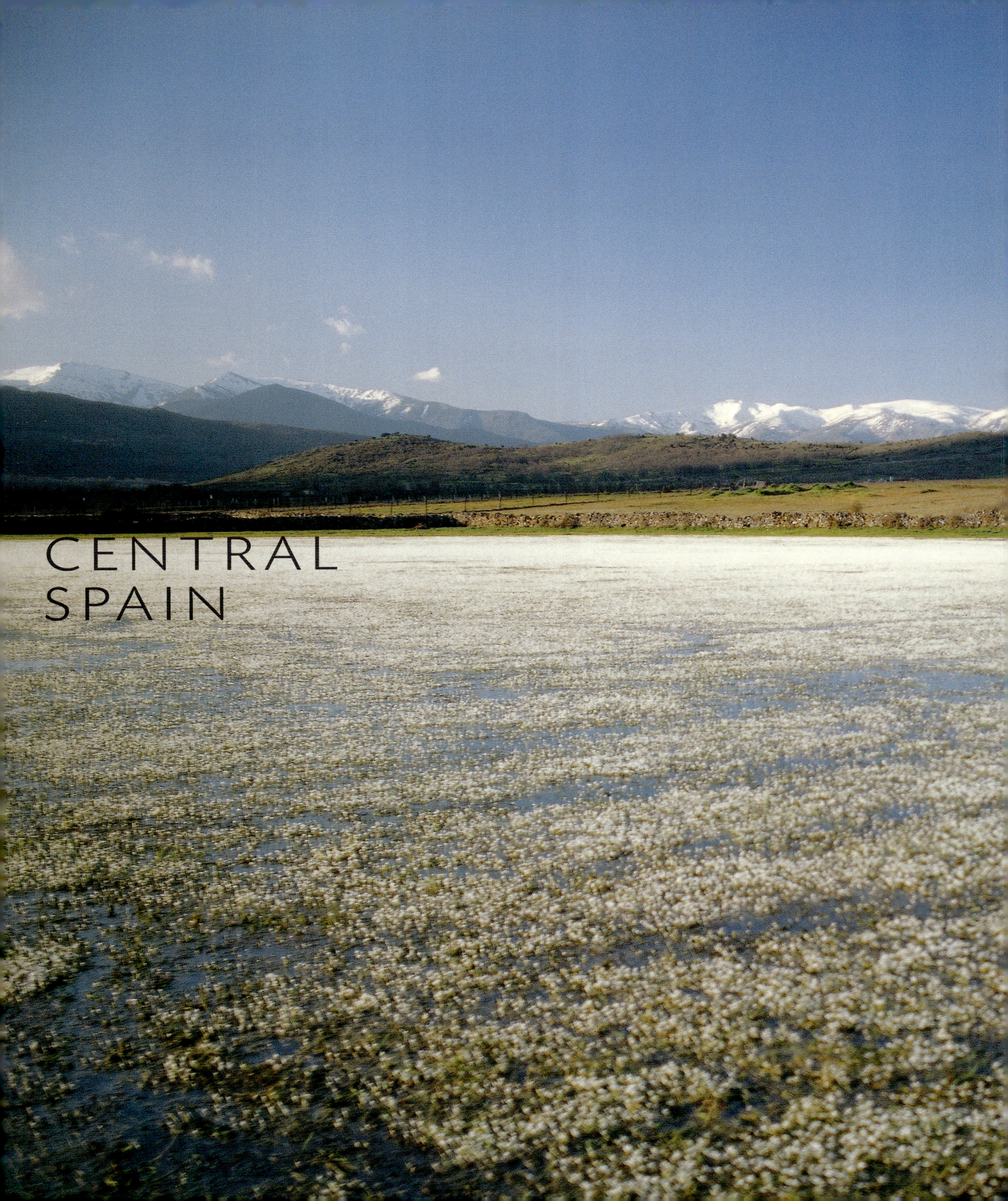

CENTRAL SPAIN

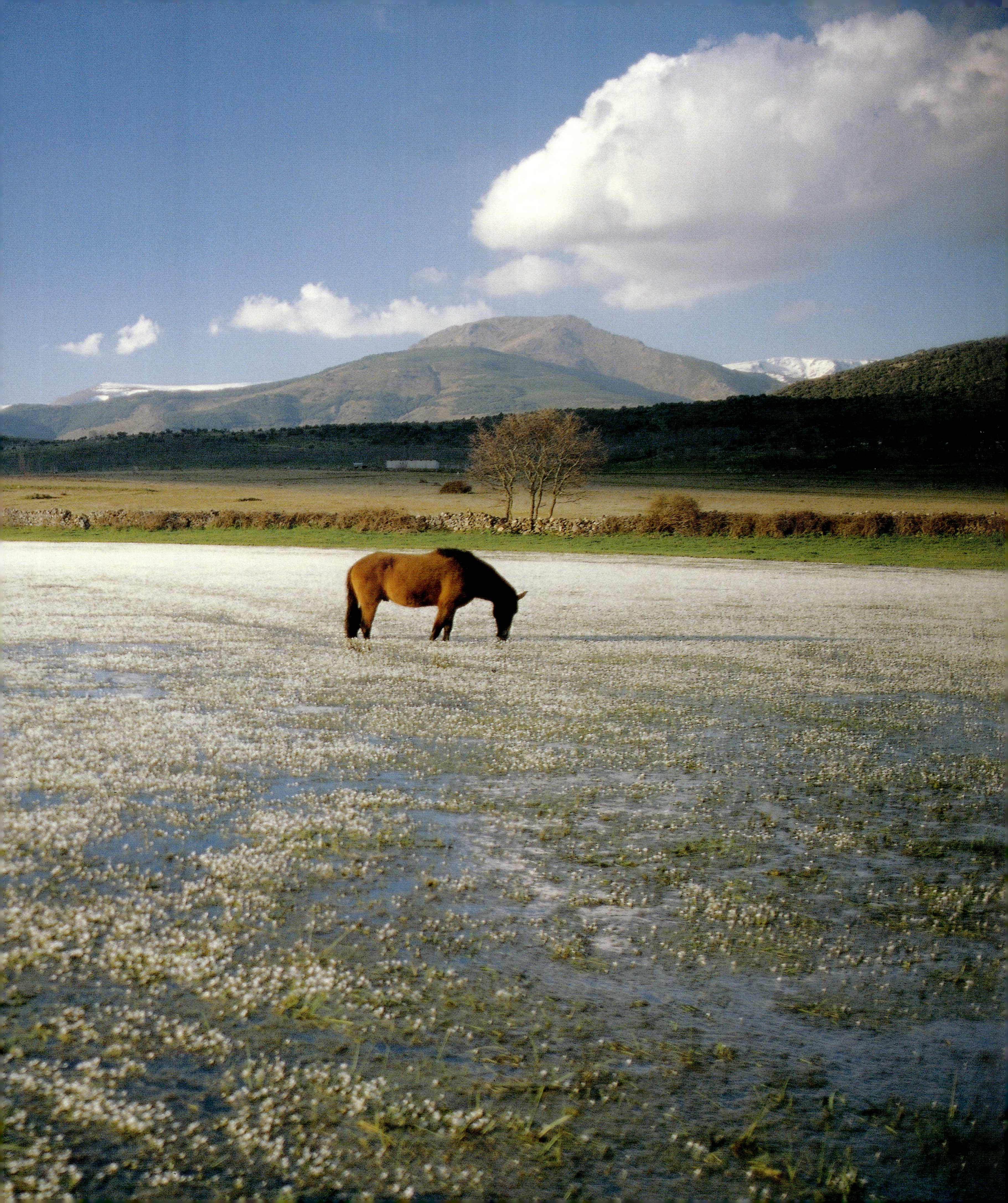

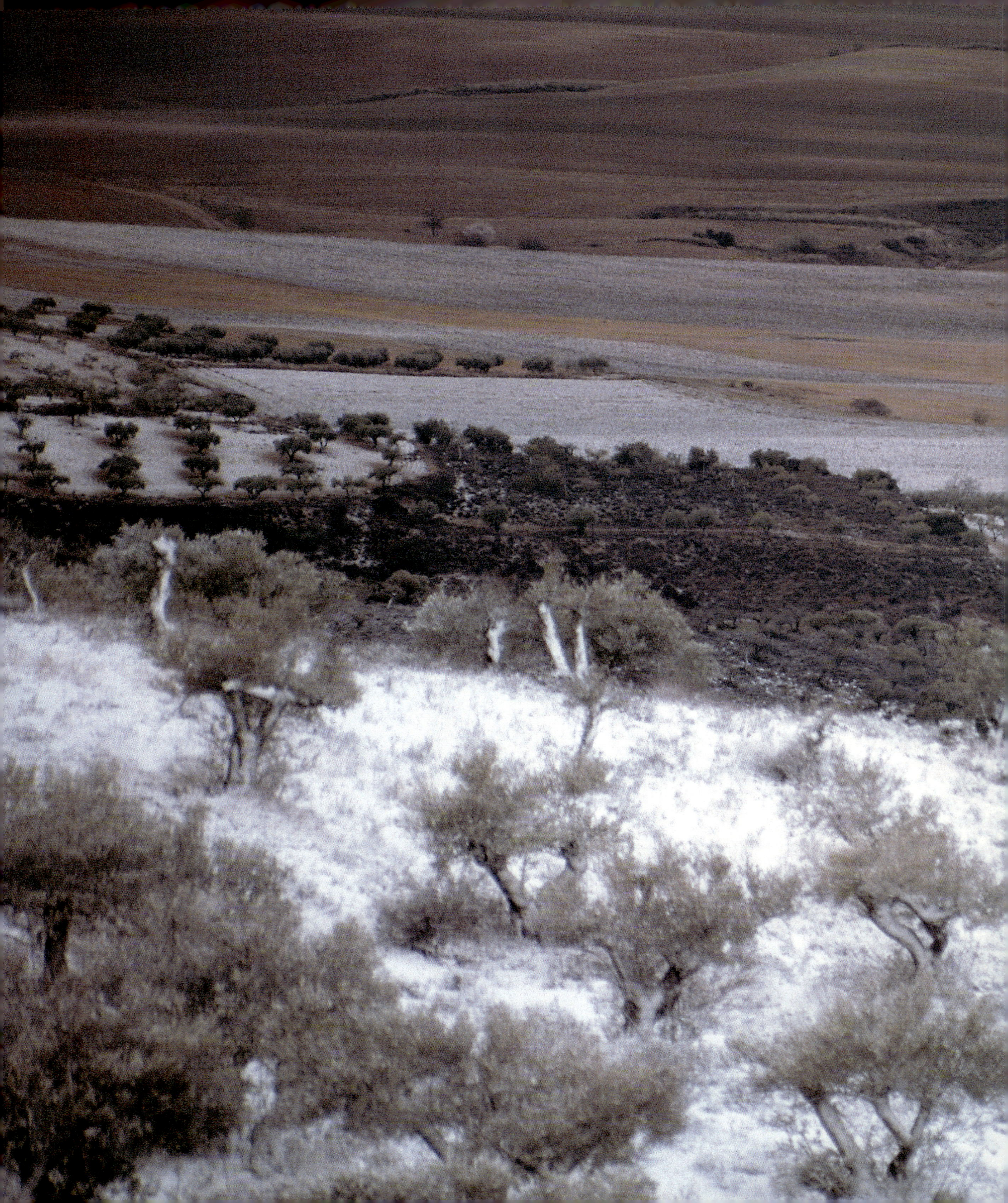

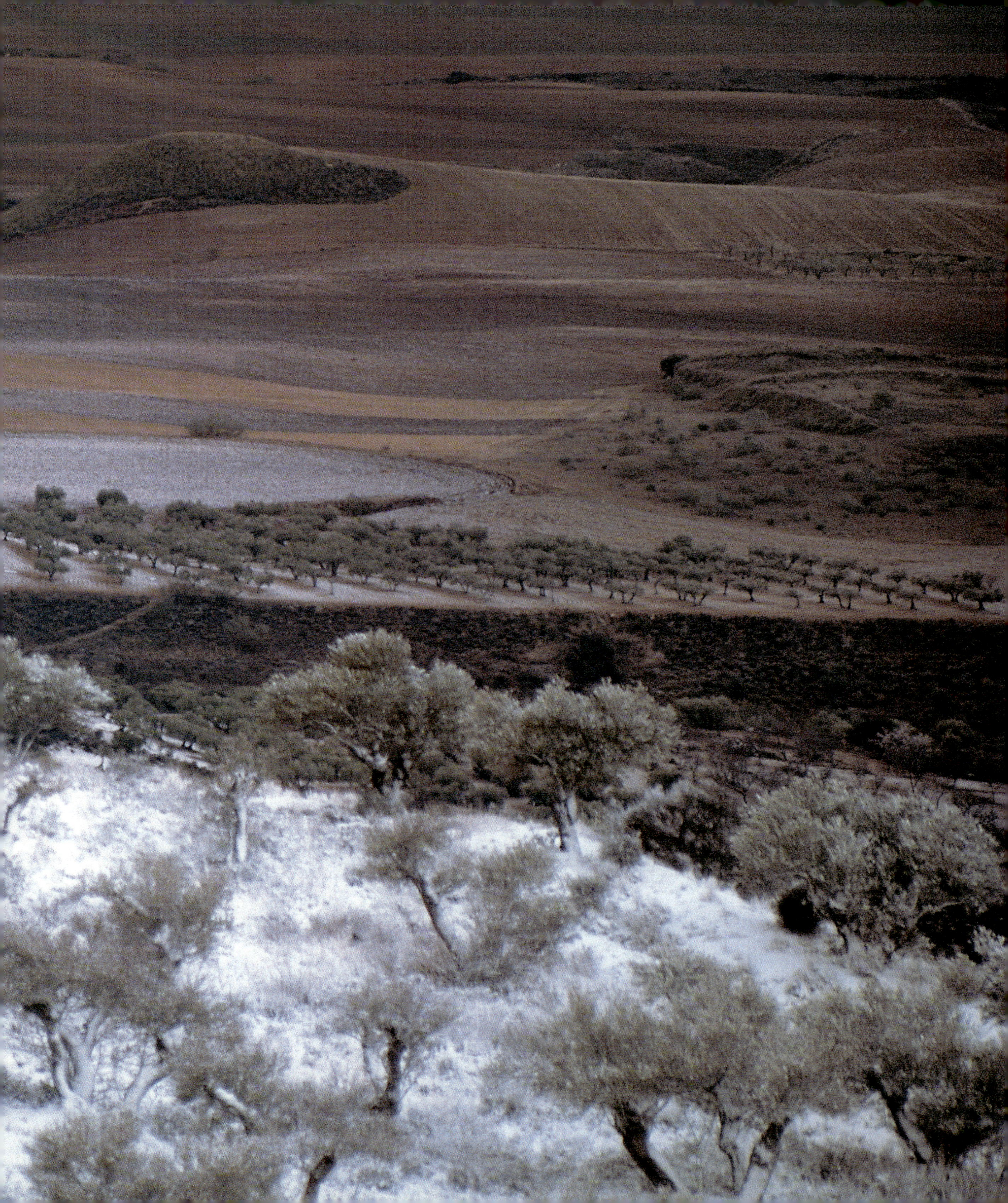

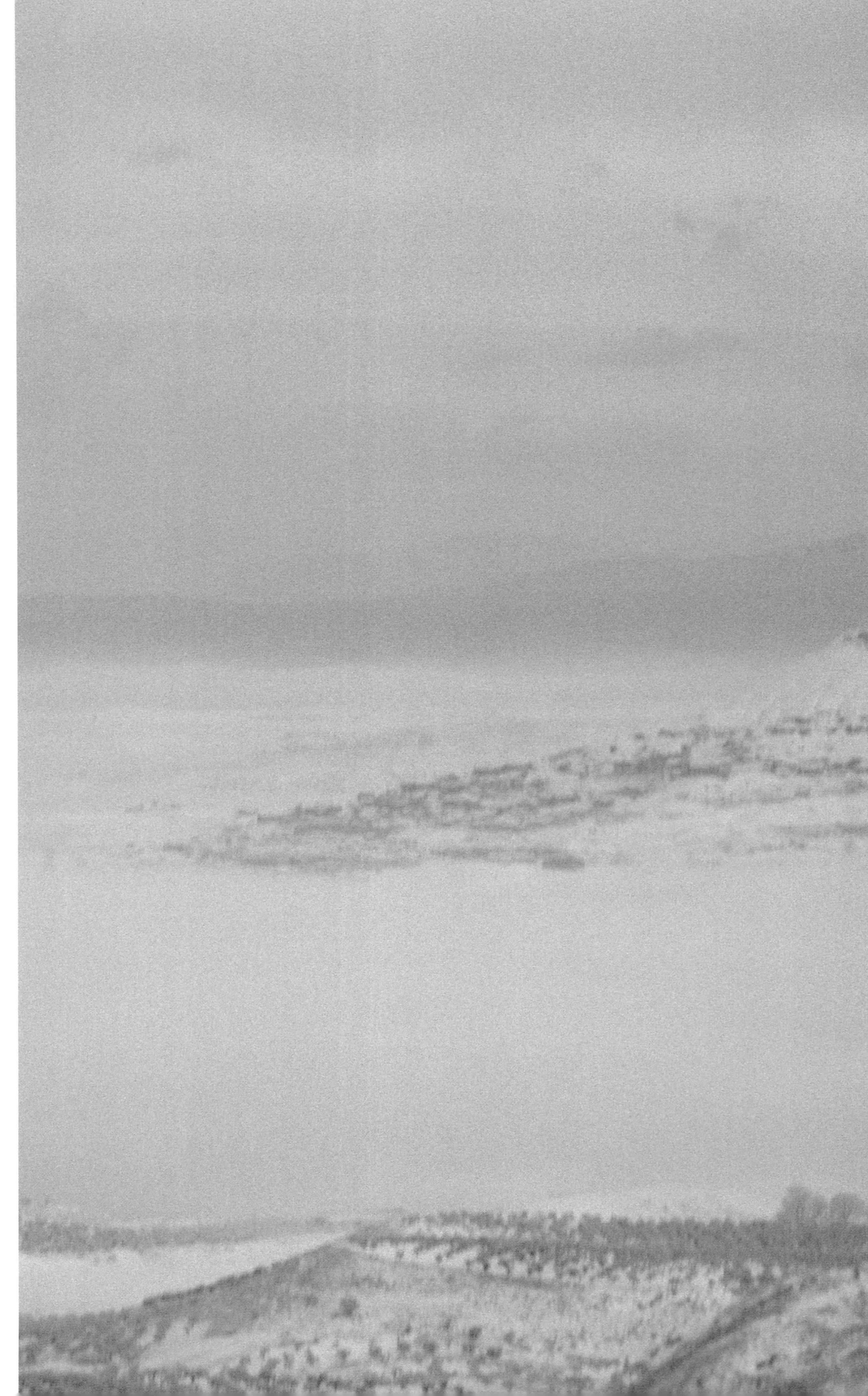

PREVIOUS PAGES
Guadalajara, Castilla-La Mancha, in January

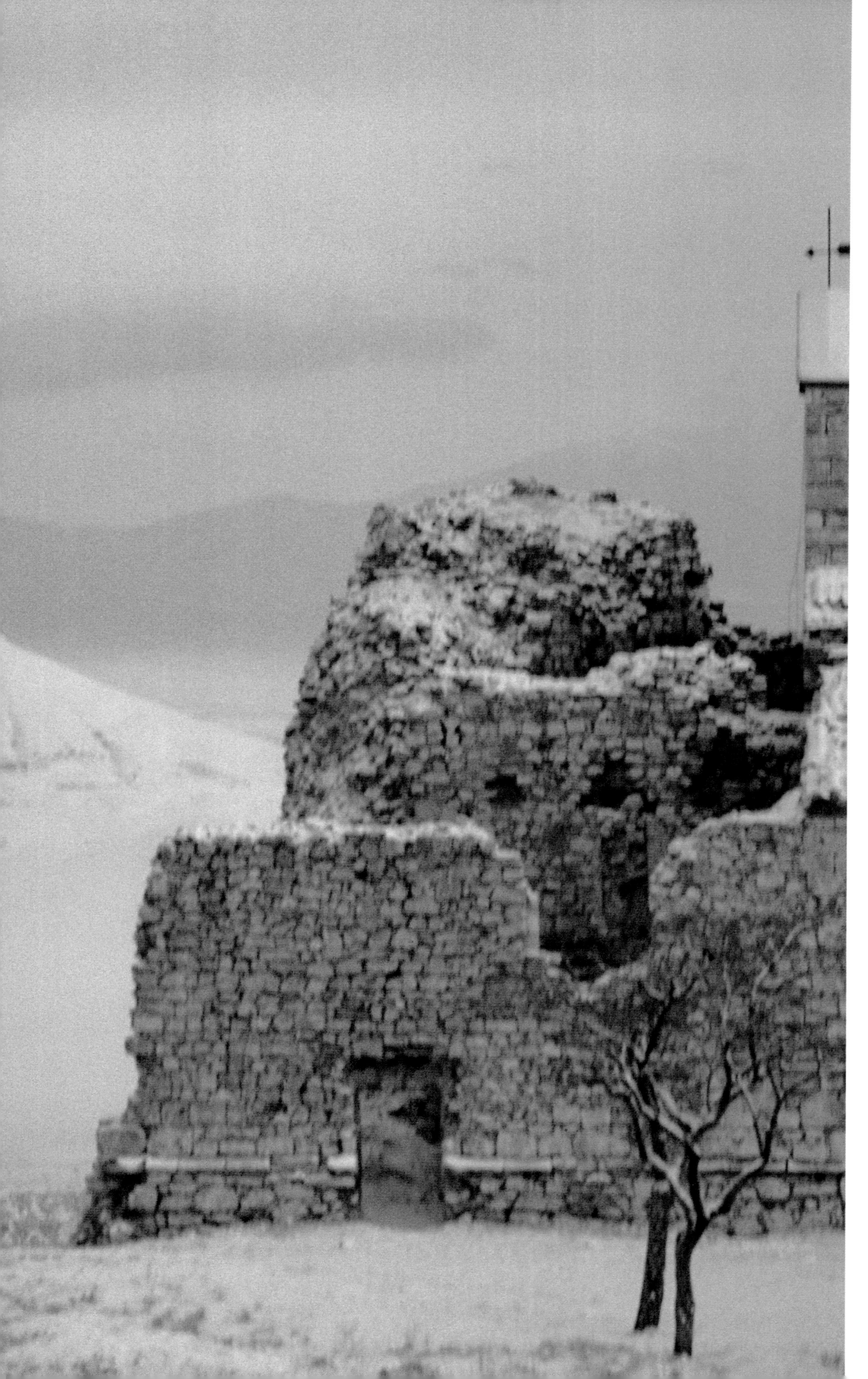

LEFT
Guadalajara, Castilla-La Mancha, in January

FOLLOWING PAGES
Burgos, Castilla y León, in February

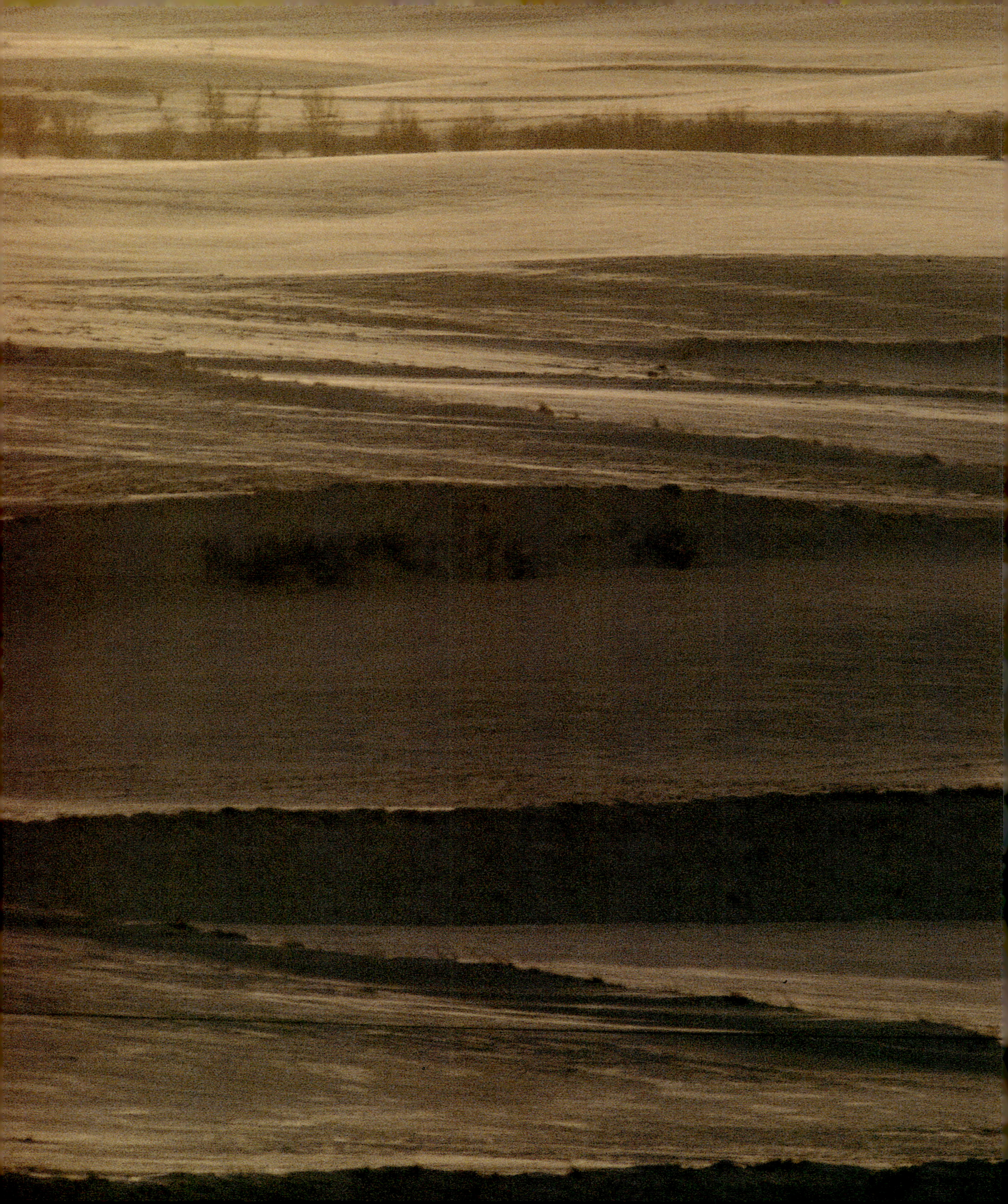

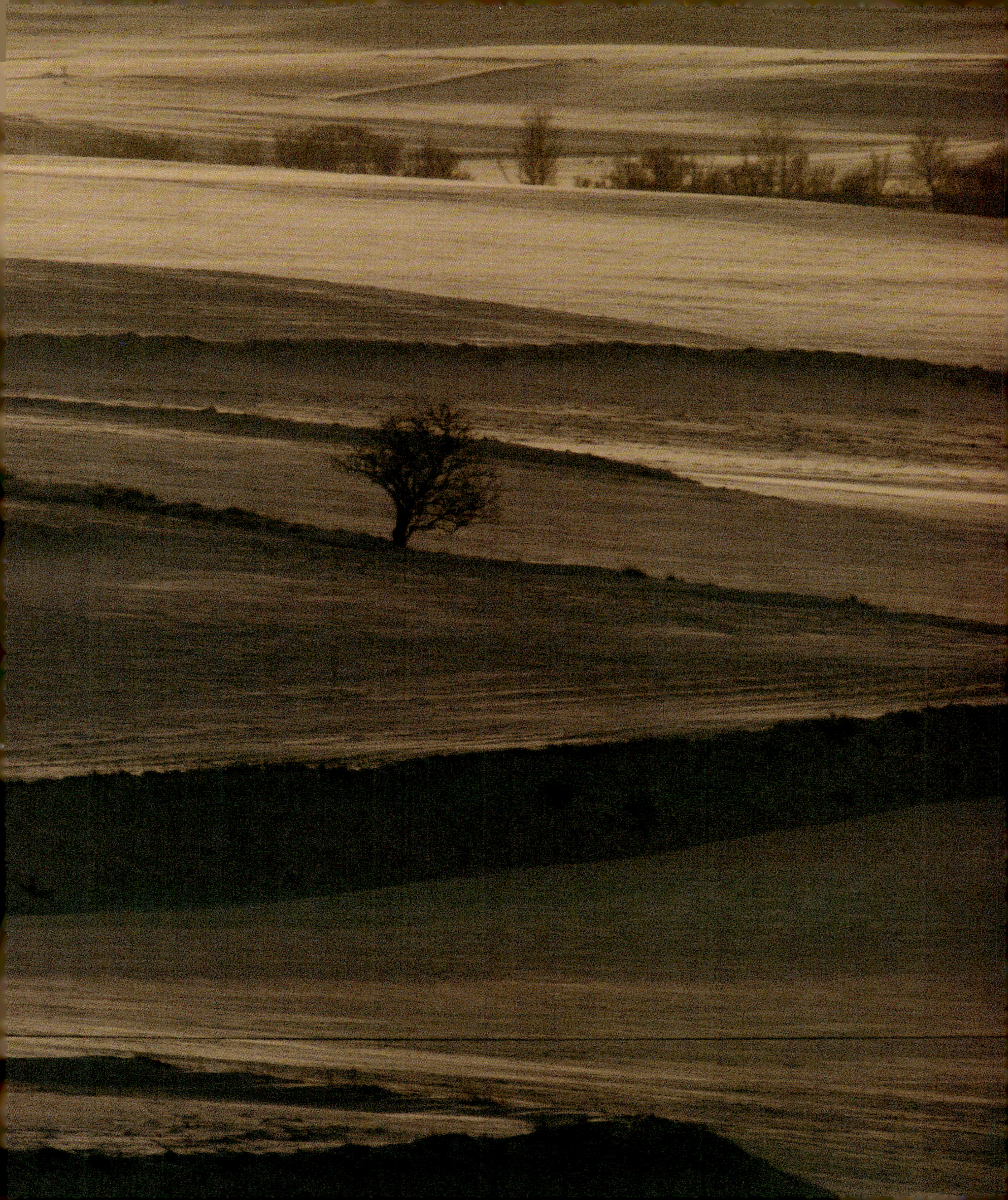

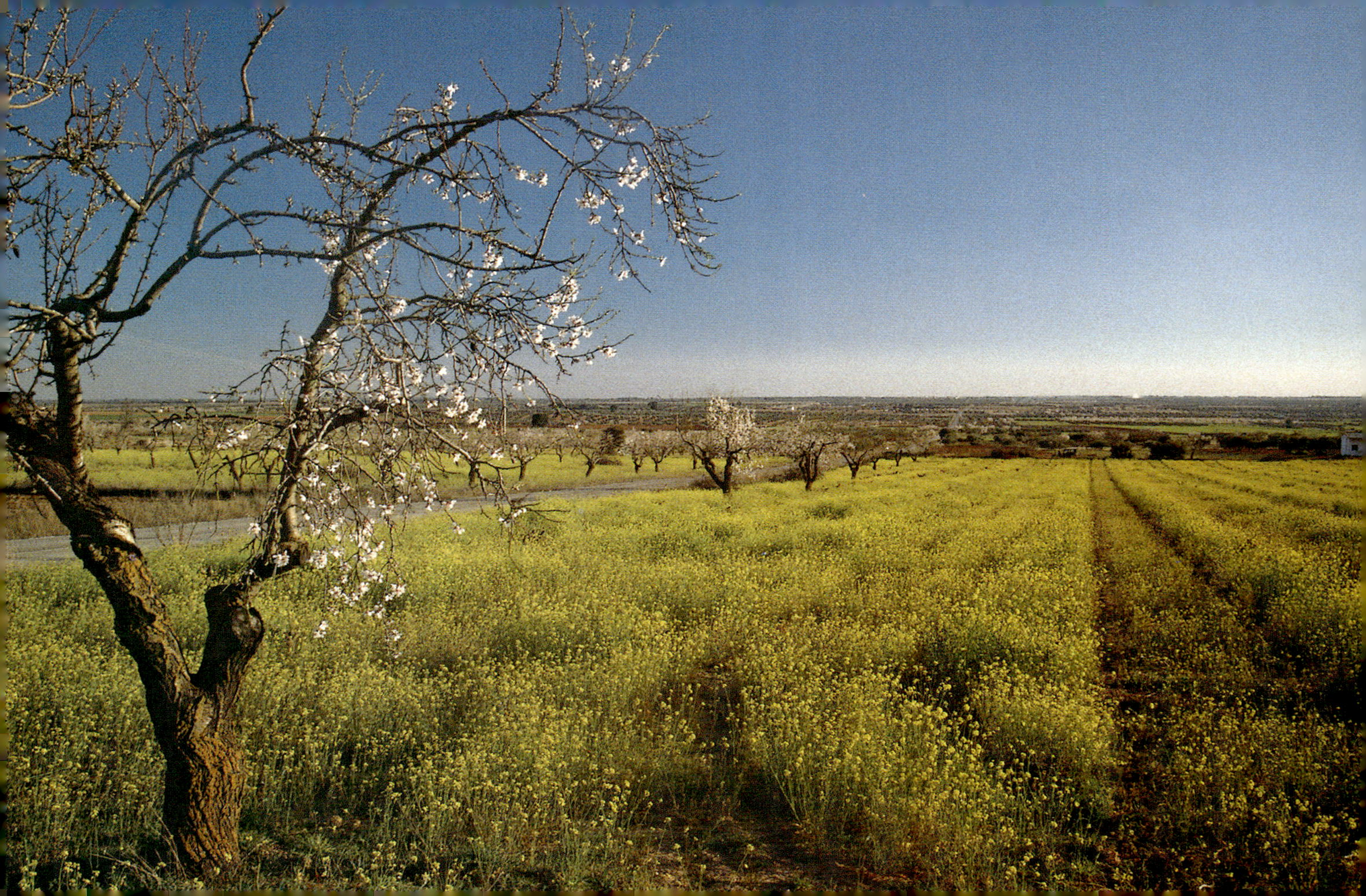

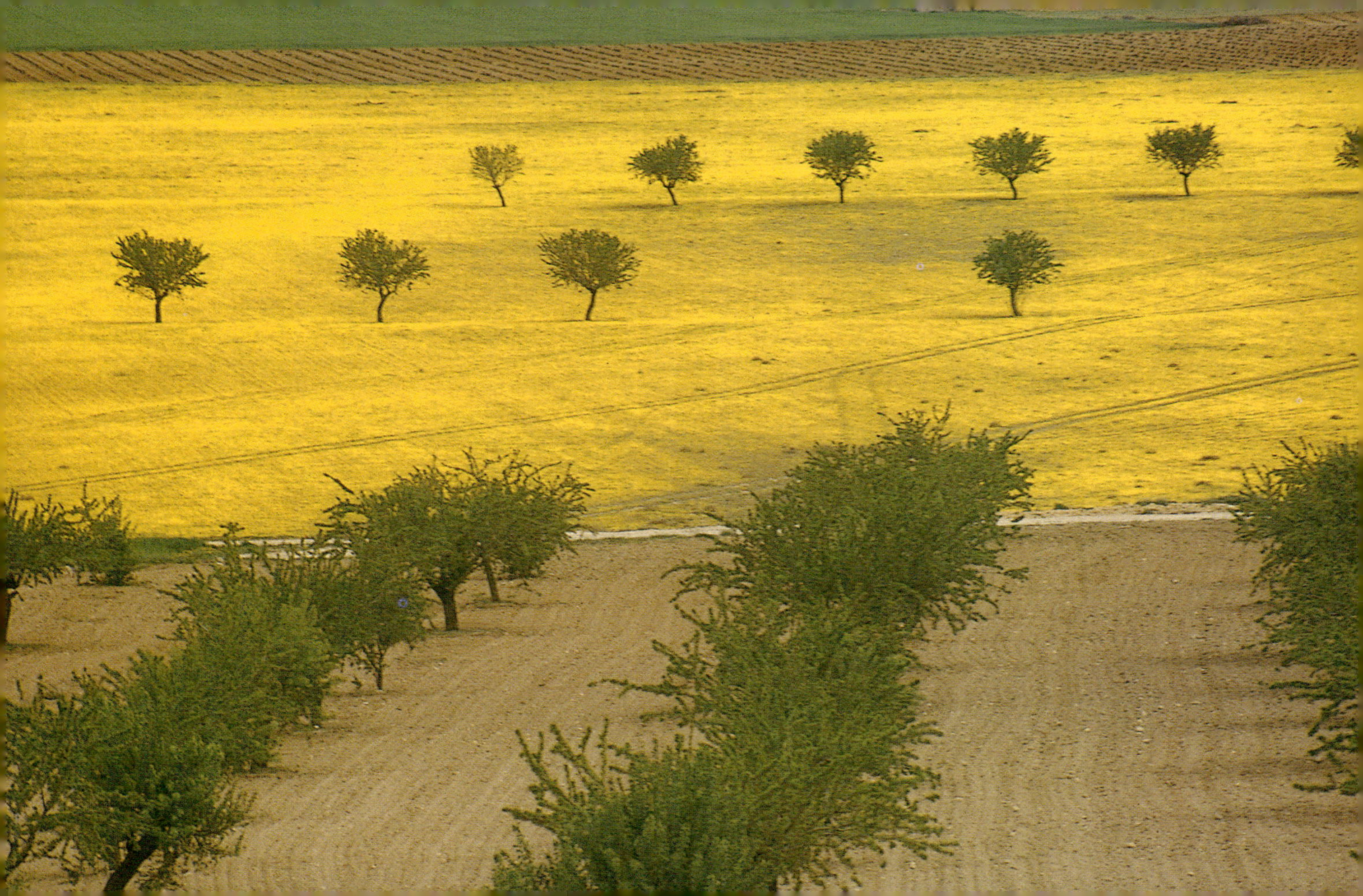

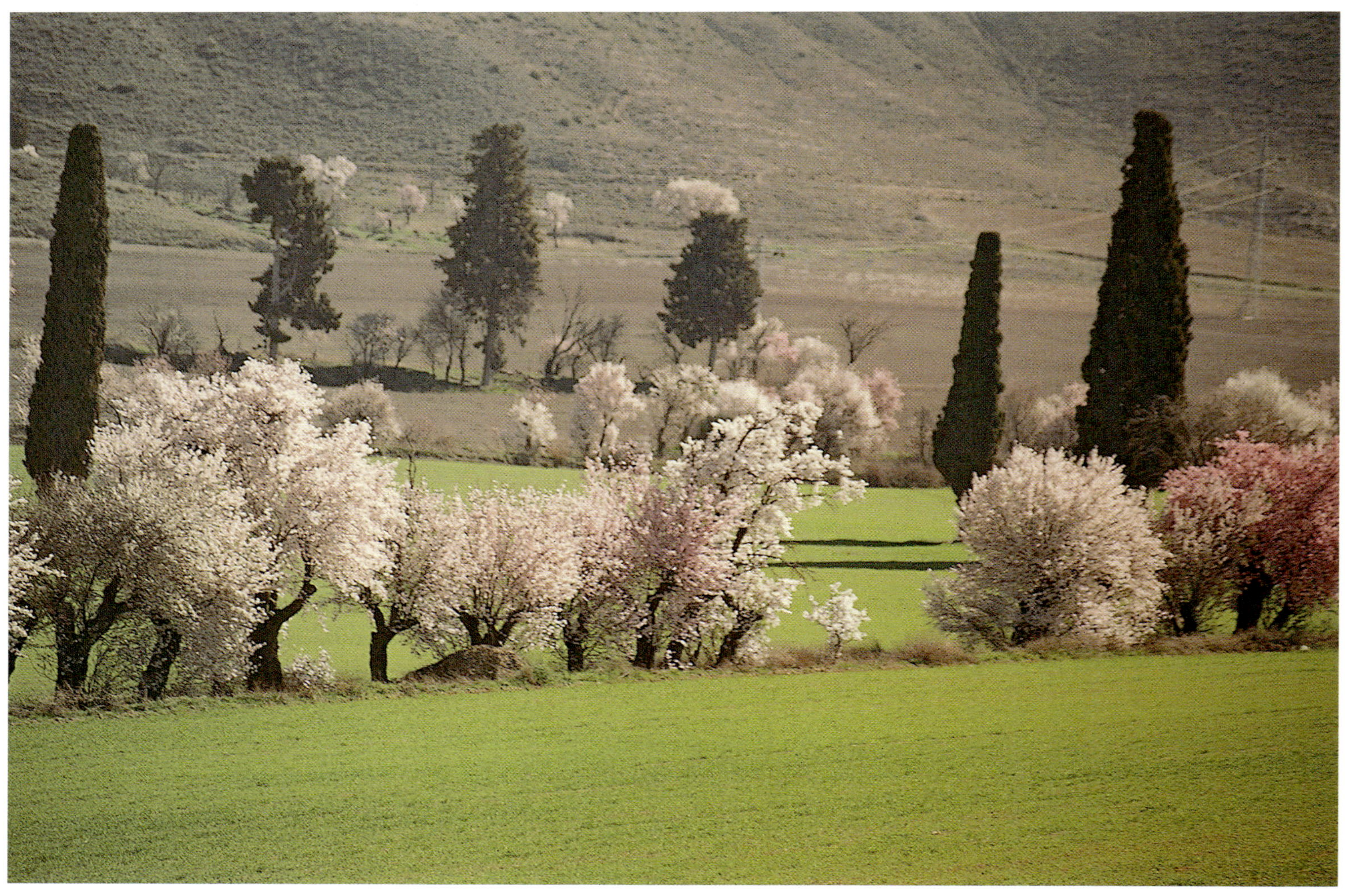

ABOVE LEFT AND RIGHT
Madrid in March

PREVIOUS PAGES
LEFT Cuenca in March
RIGHT Castilla-La Mancha in March

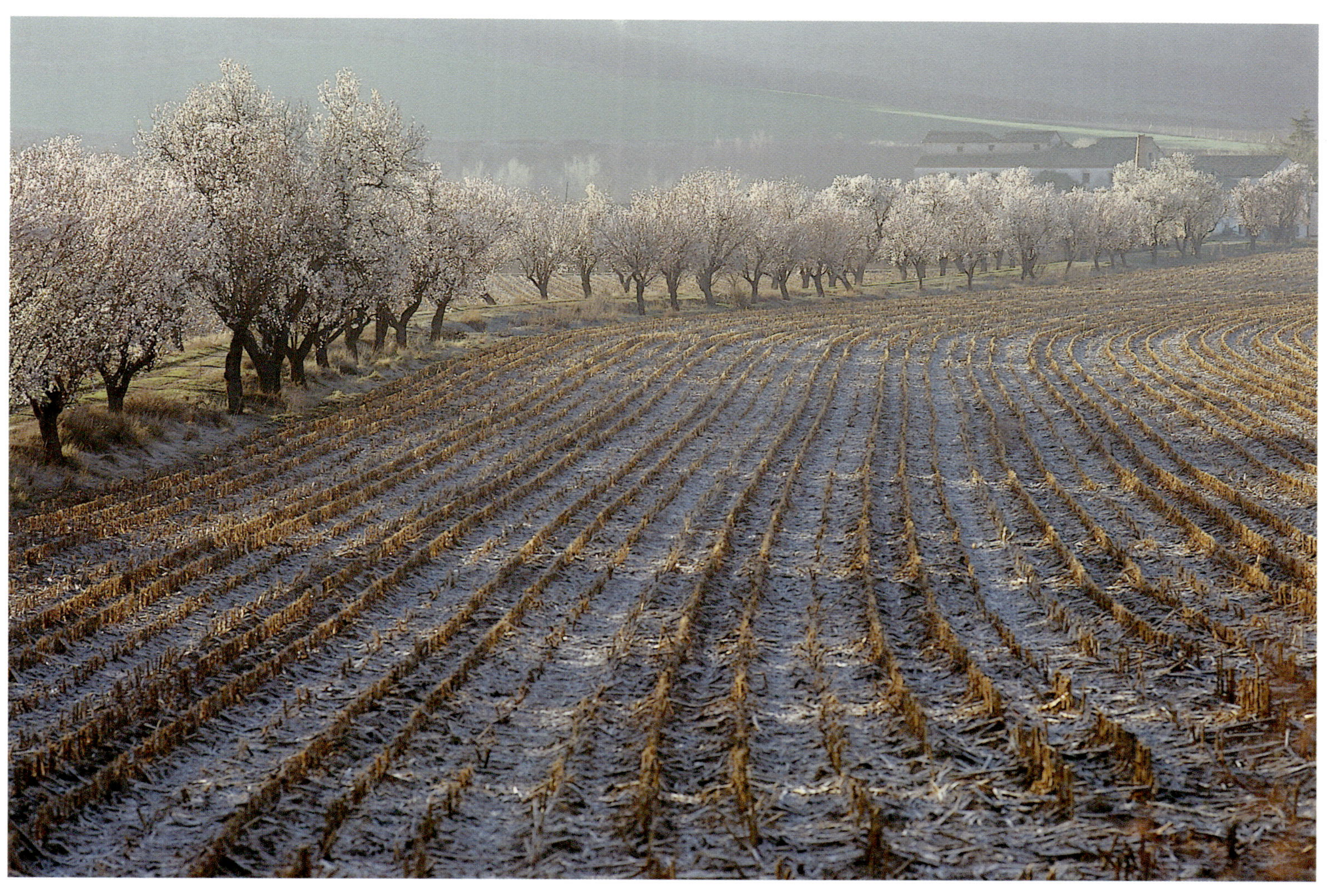

FOLLOWING PAGES
Cáceres, Extremadura, in March

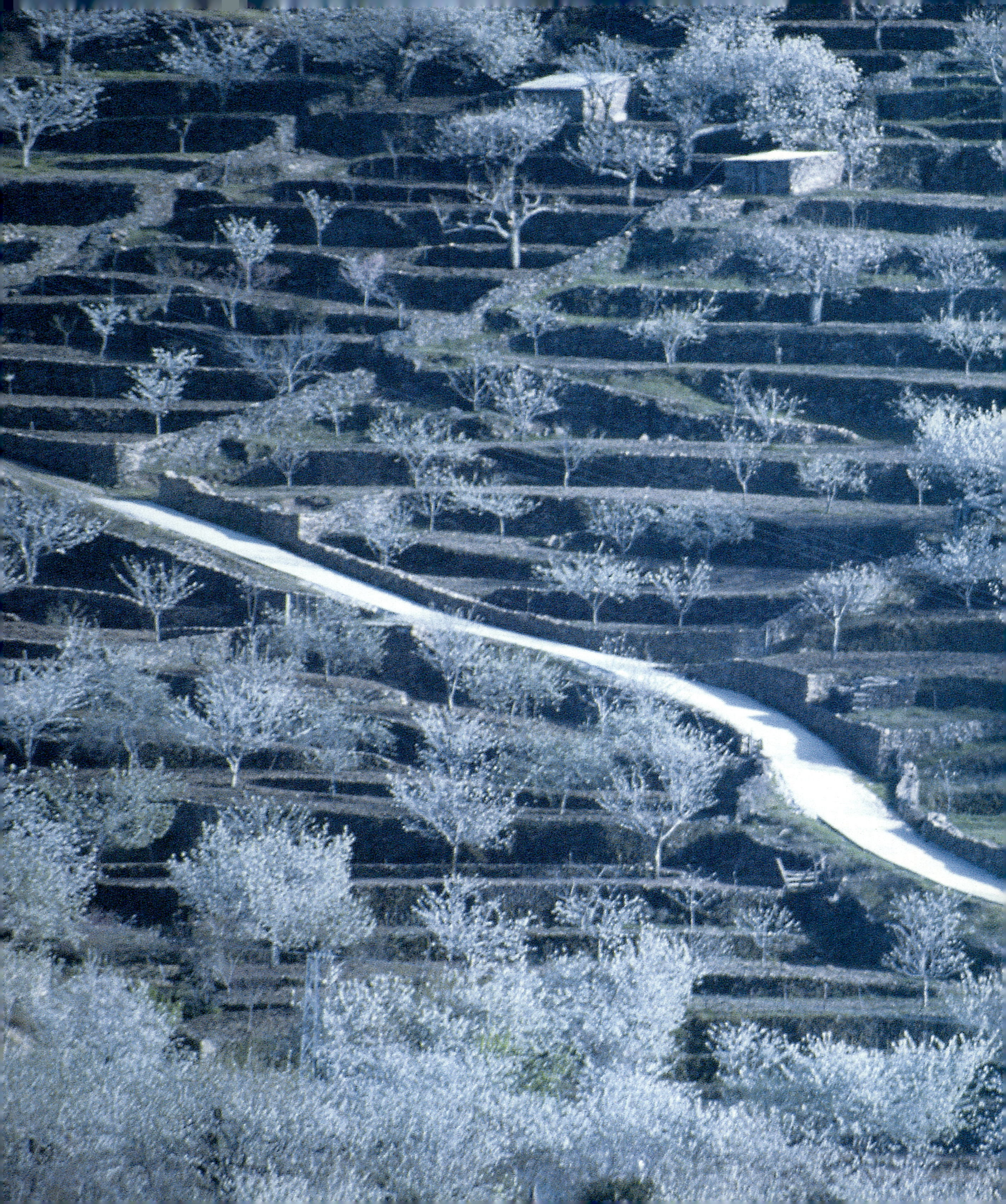

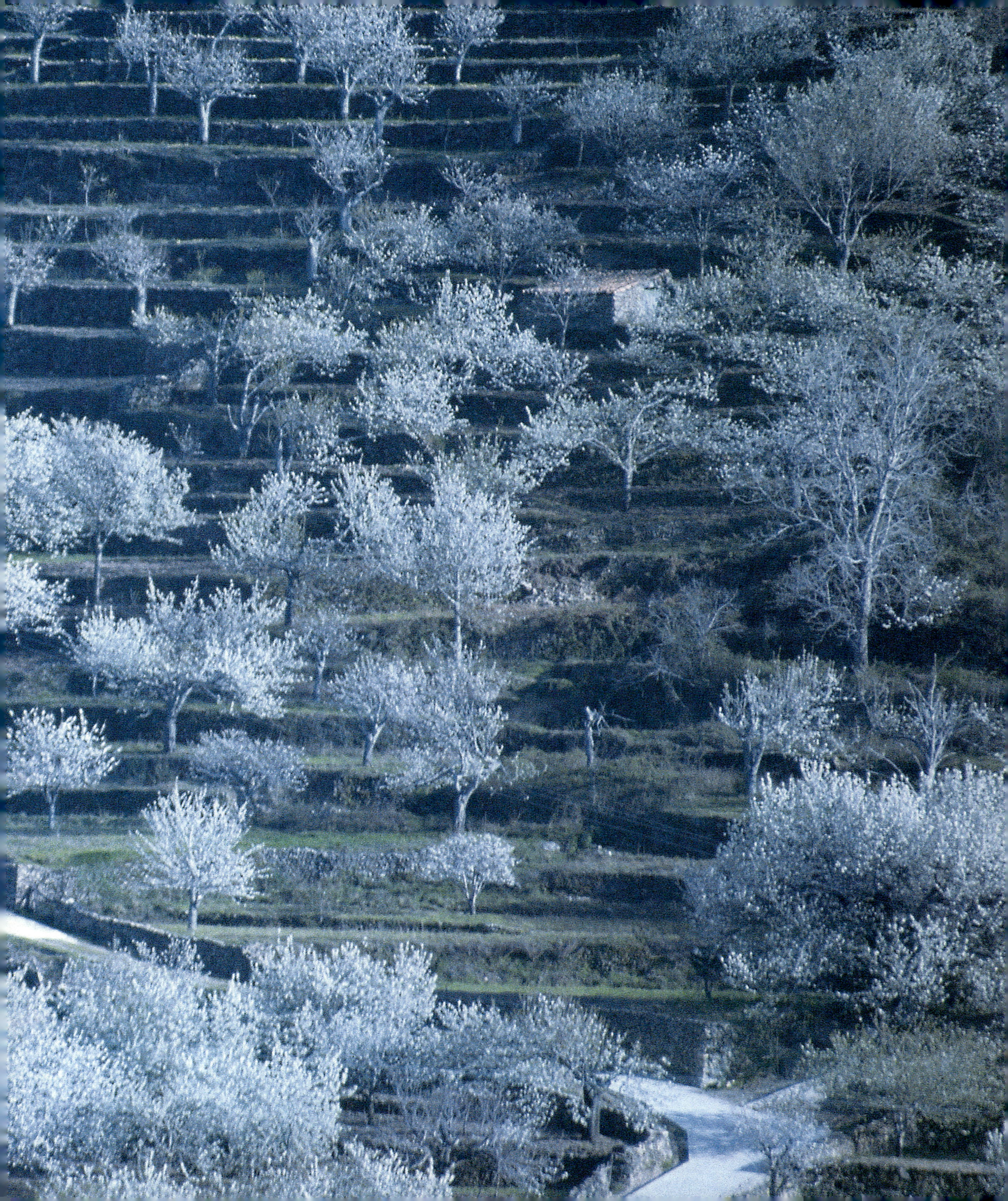

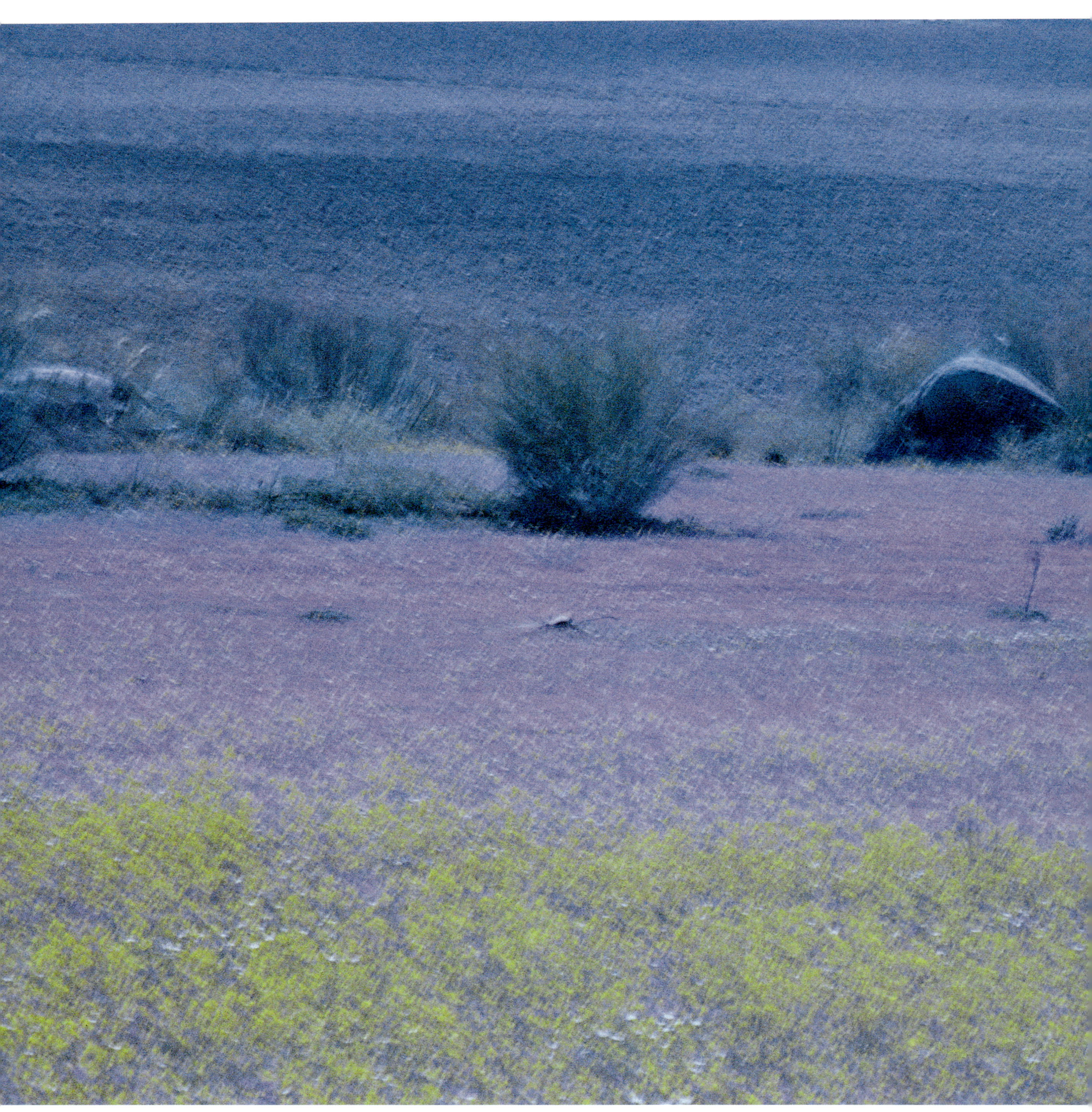

ABOVE
Toledo, Castilla-La Mancha, in May

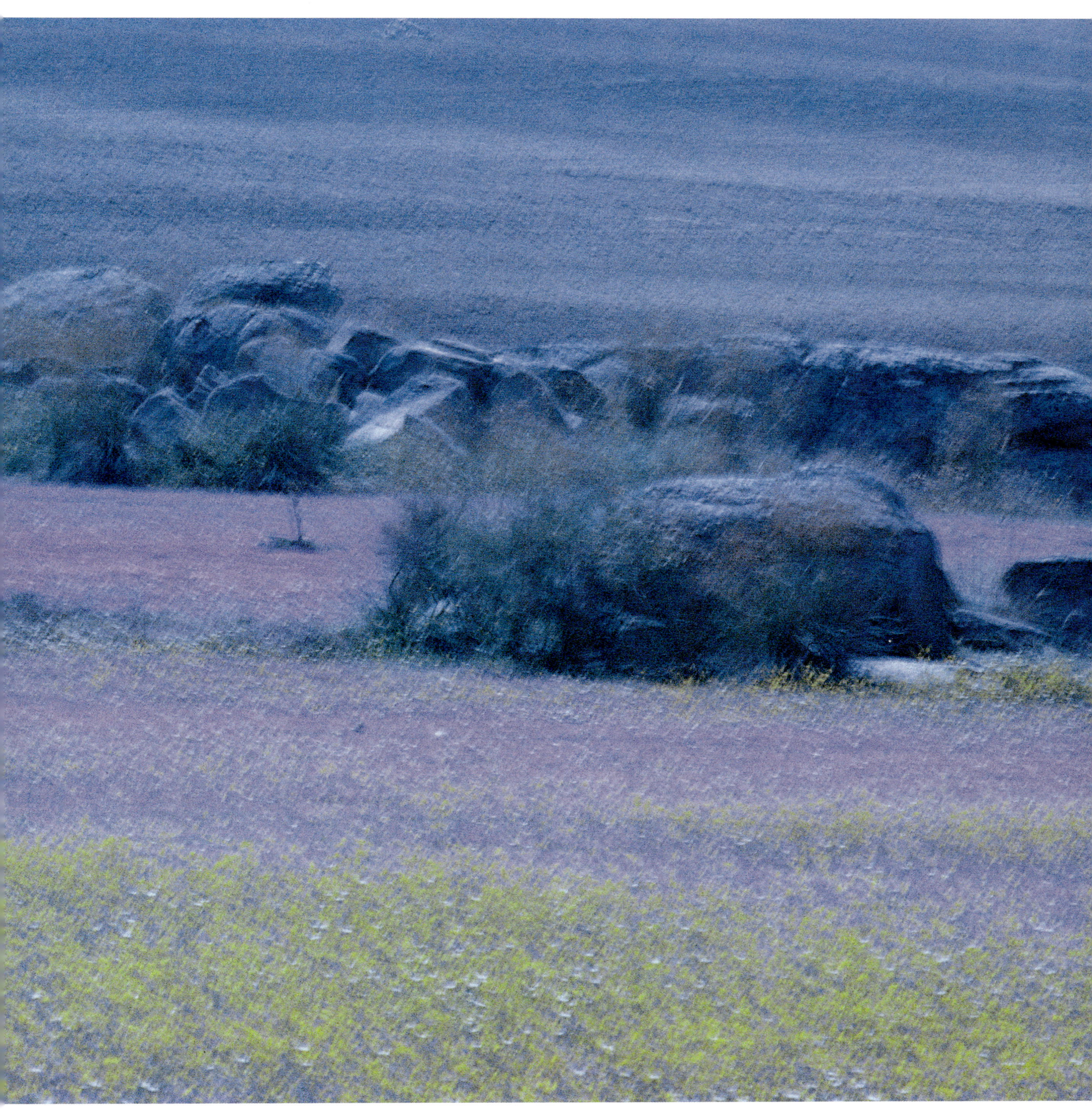

FOLLOWING PAGES
Cuenca, Castilla-La Mancha, in June

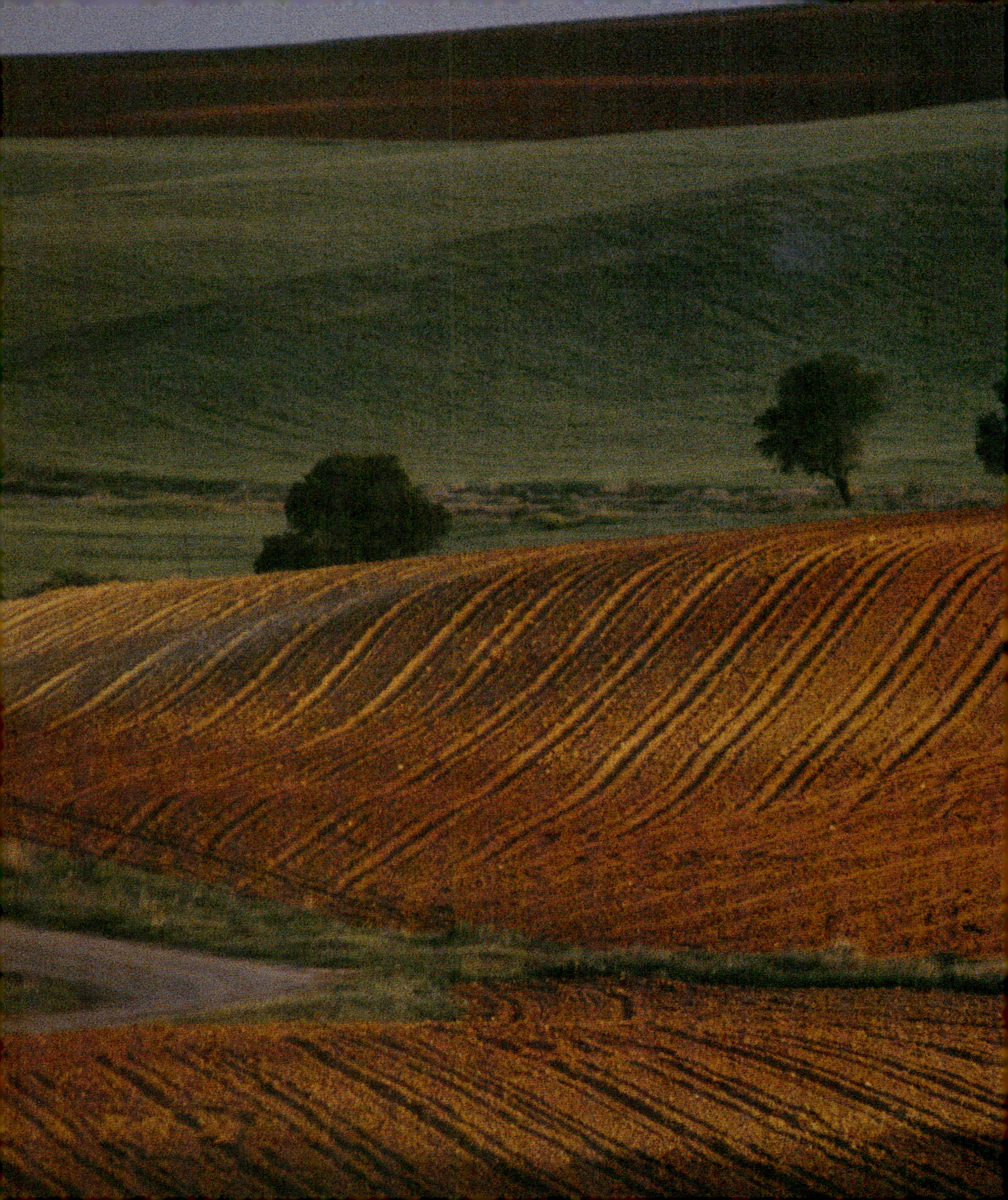

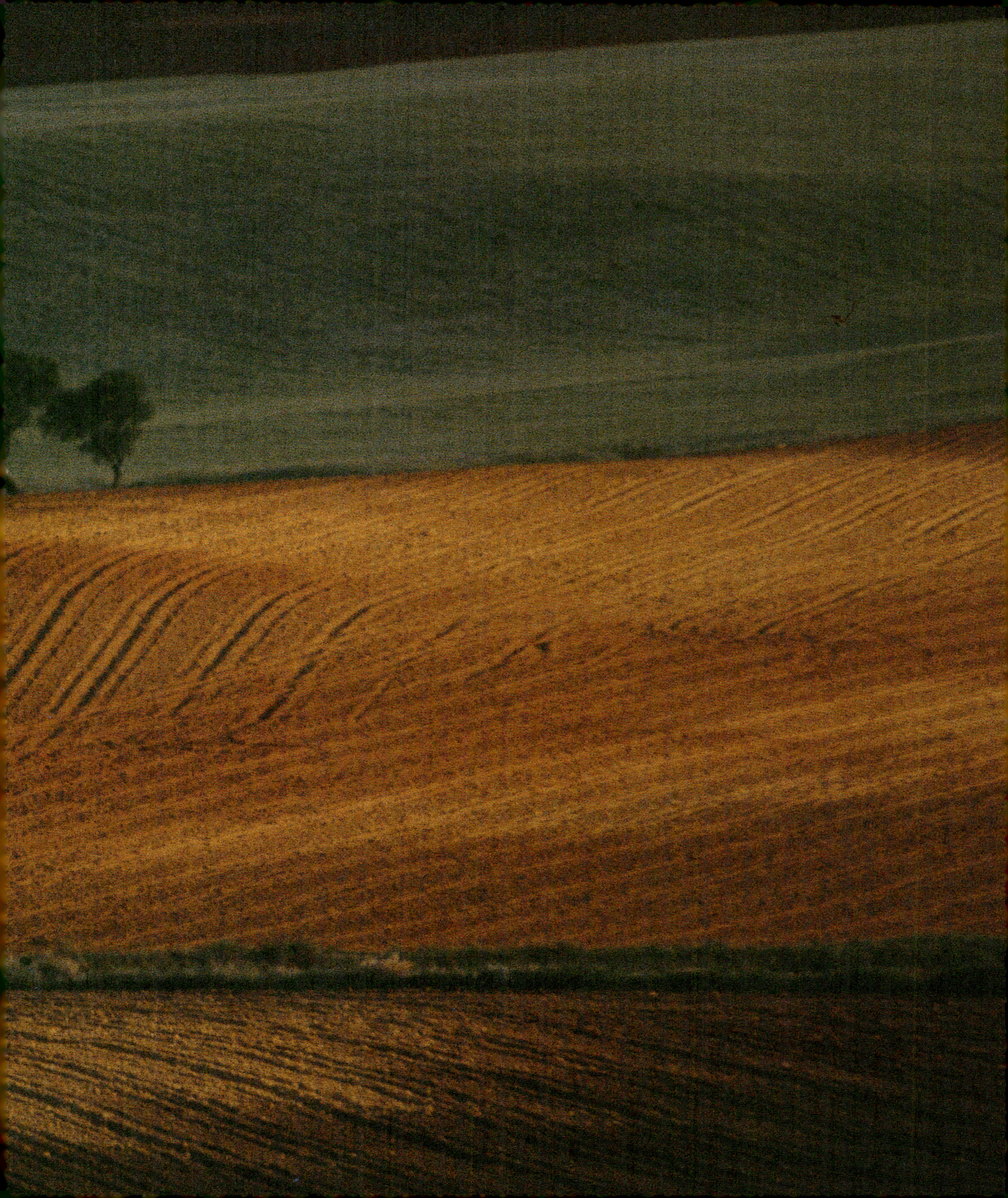

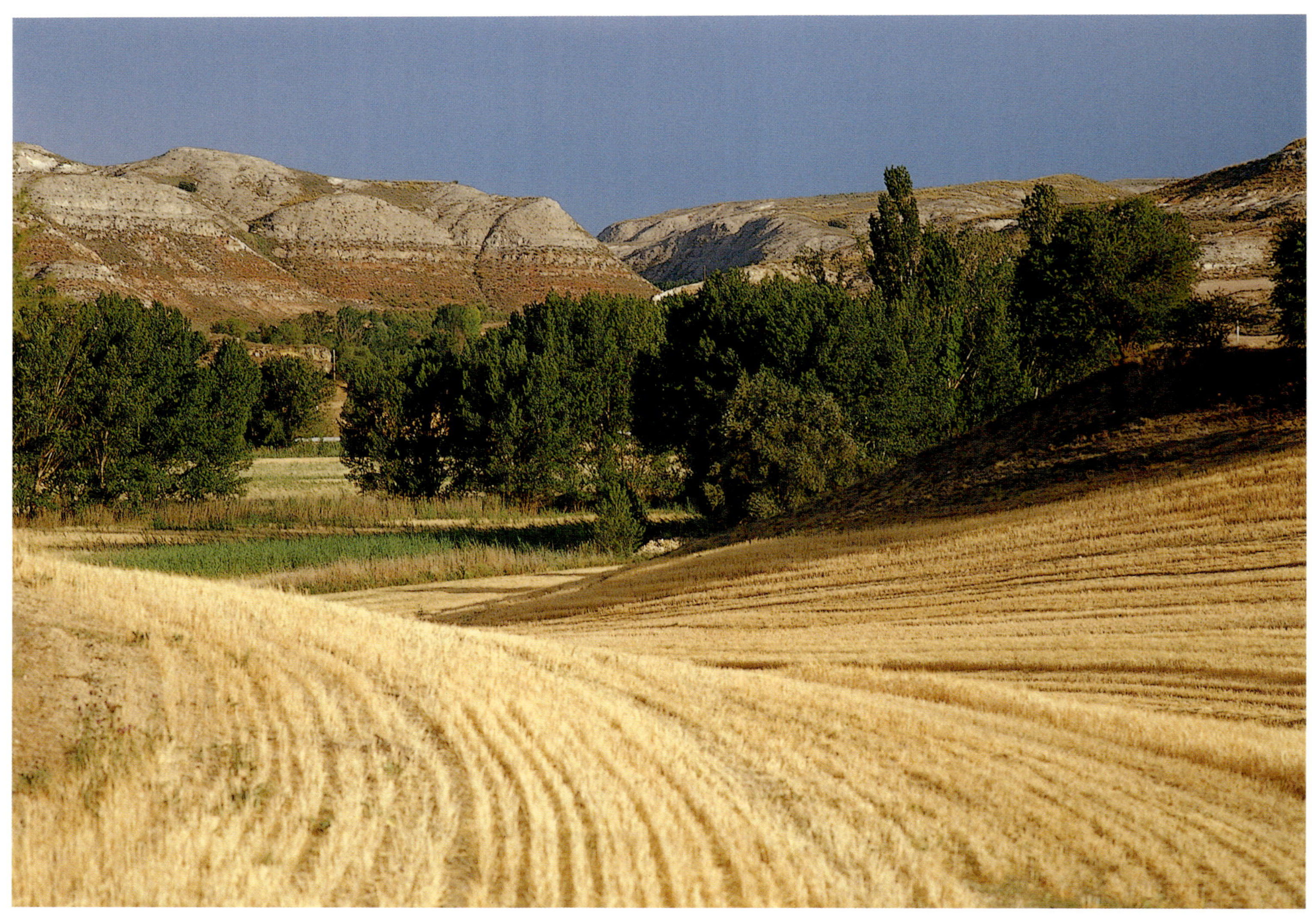

ABOVE
Cuenca, Castilla-La Mancha, in July

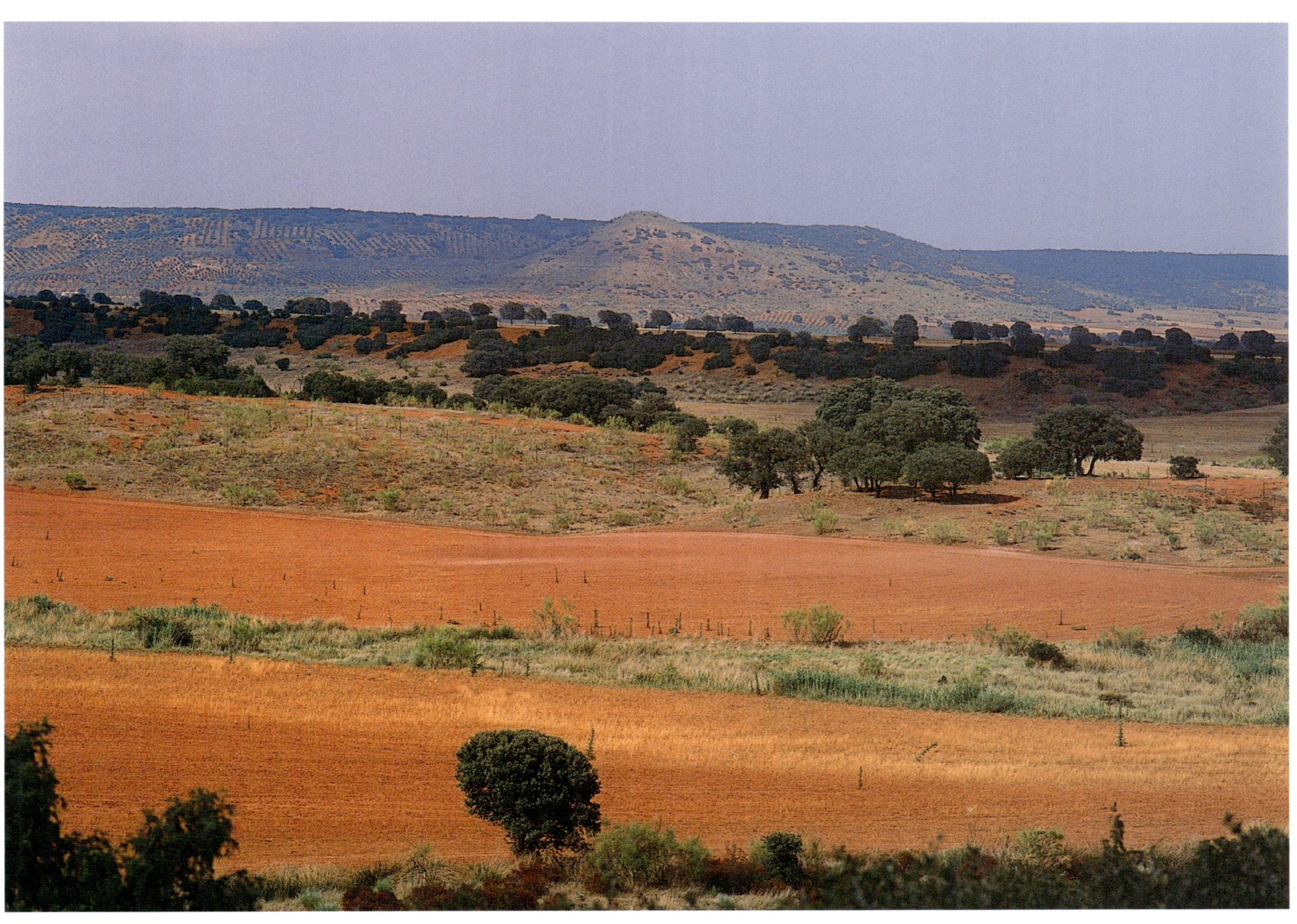

ABOVE
Albacete, Castilla-La Mancha, in July

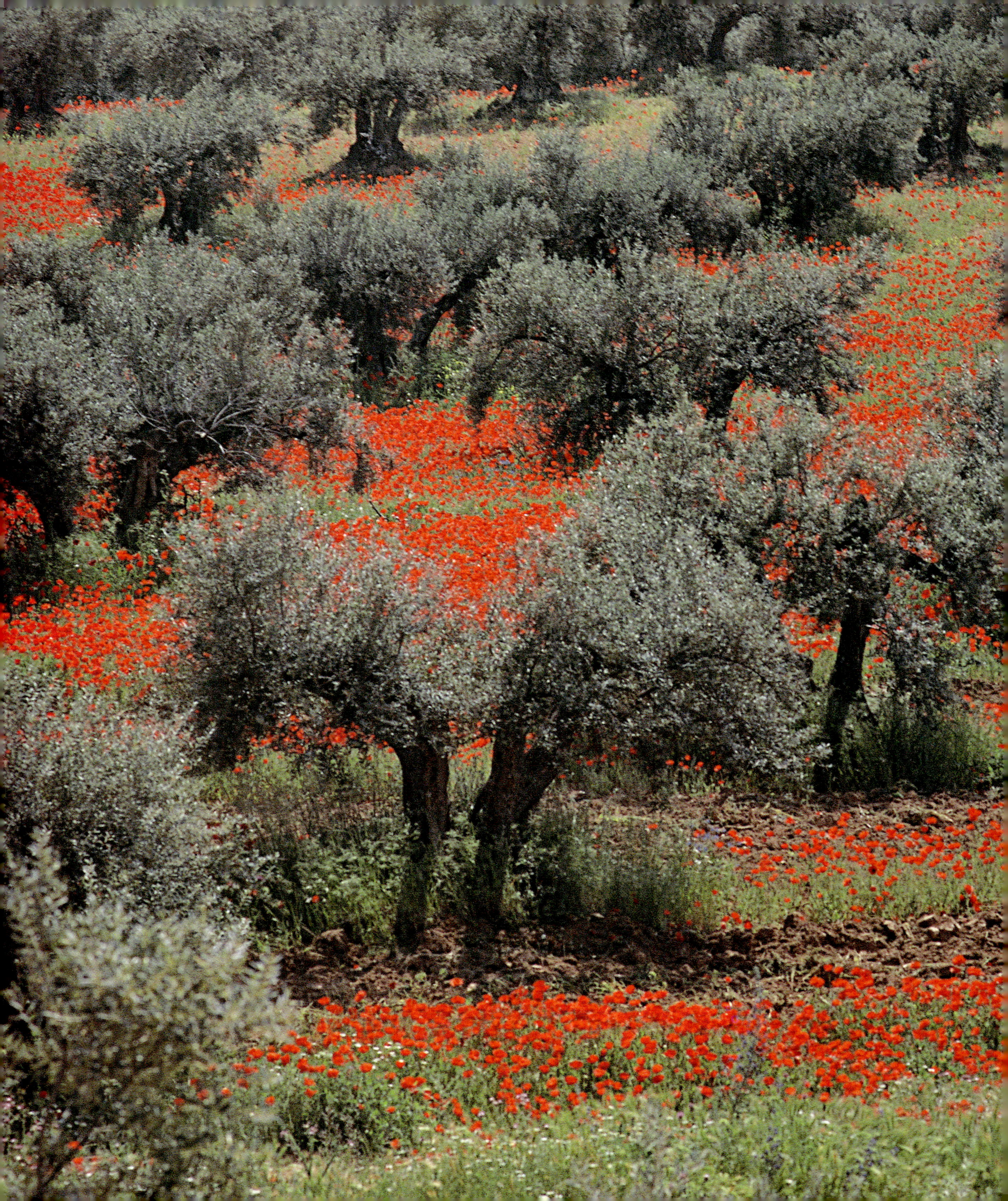

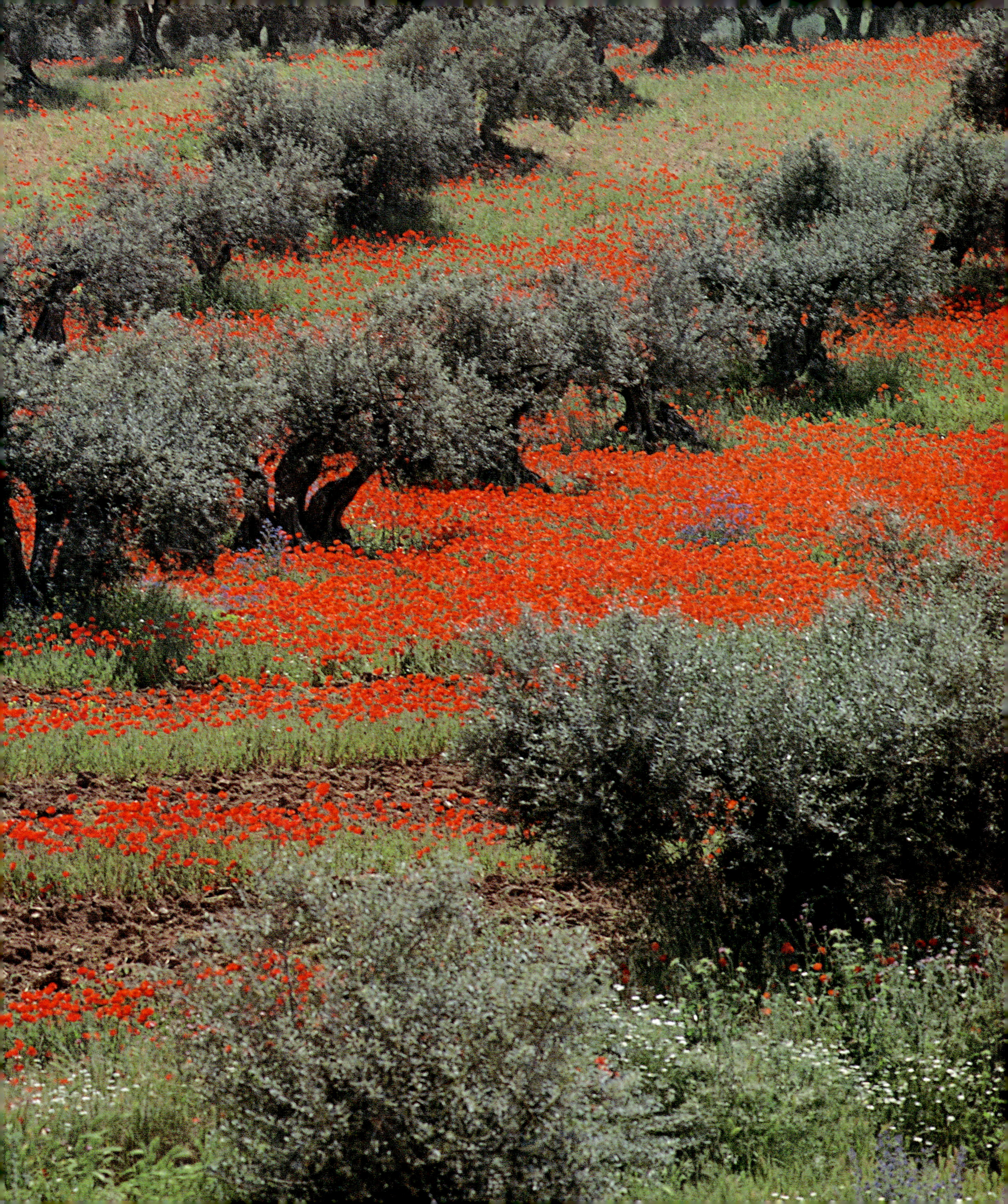

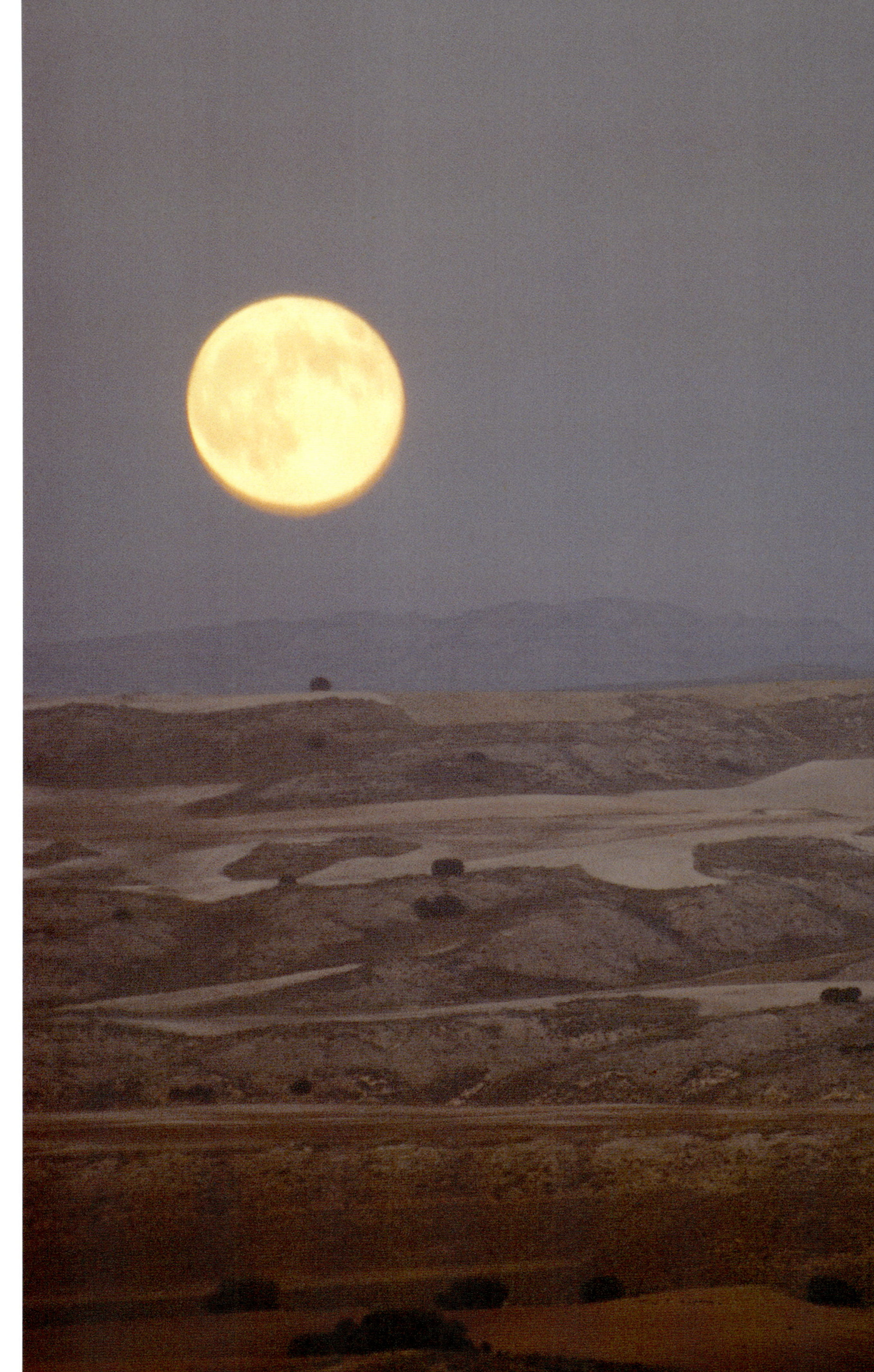

PREVIOUS PAGES
Guadalajara, Castilla-La Mancha, in July

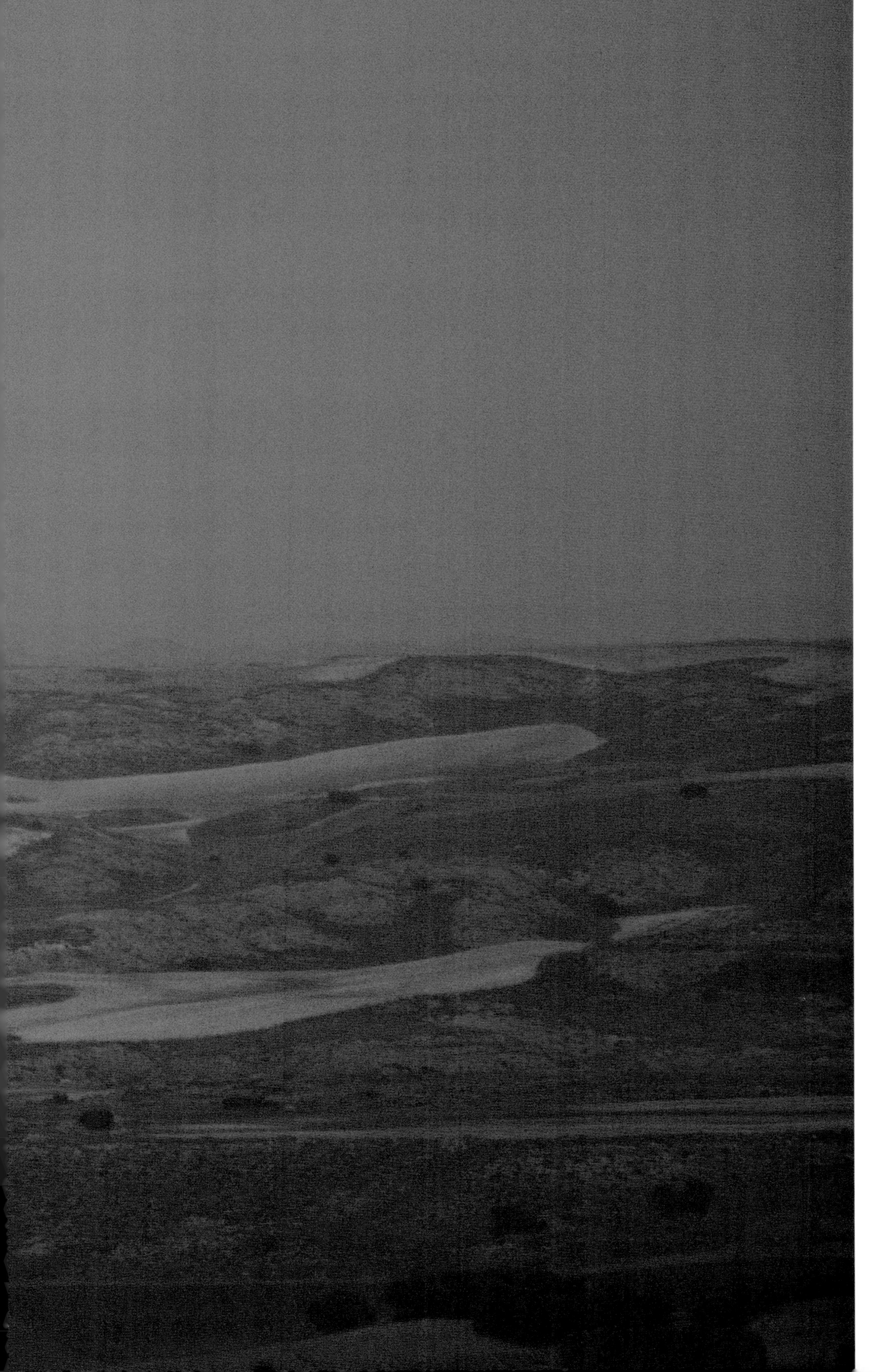

LEFT
Cuenca, Castilla-La Mancha, in July

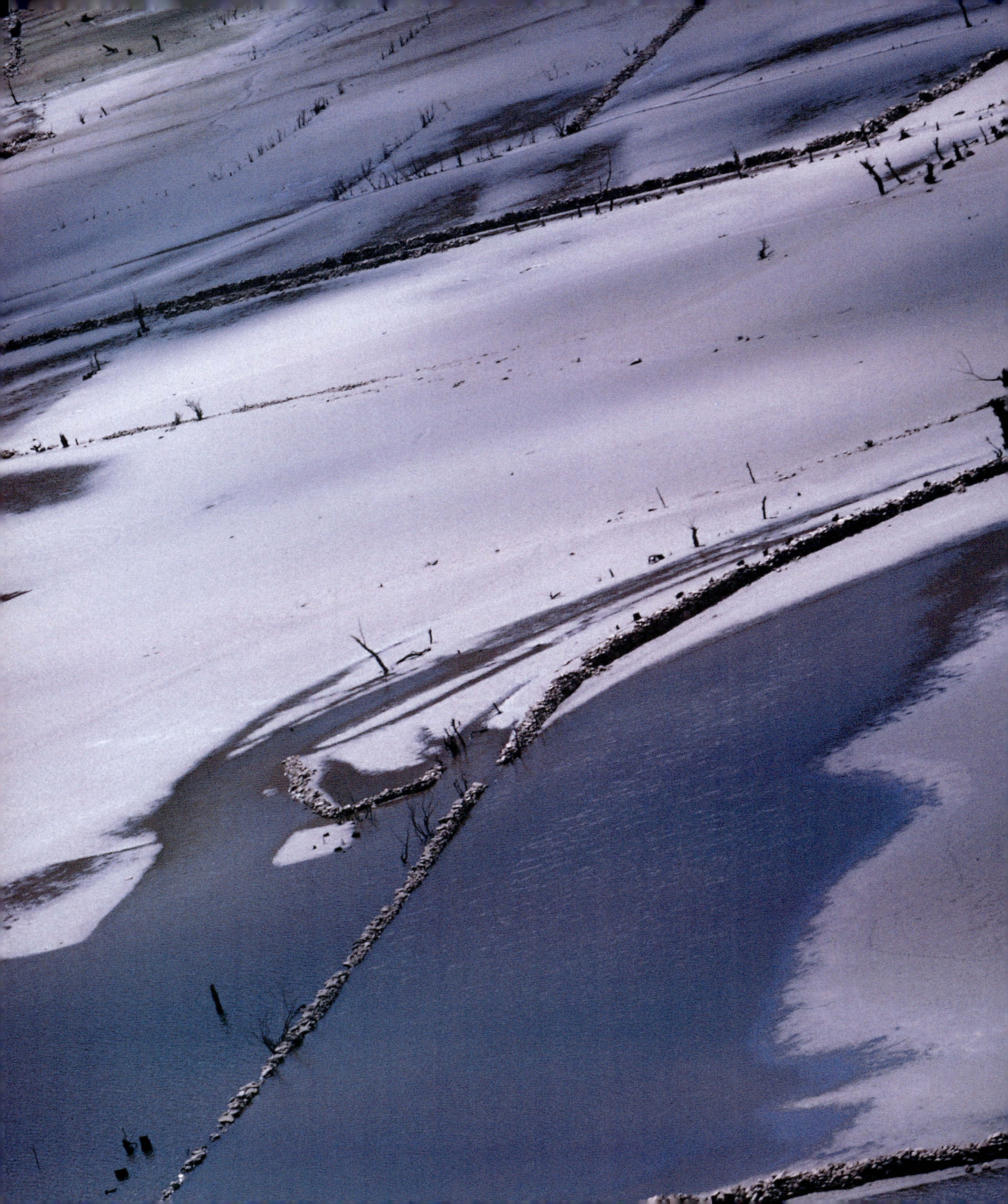

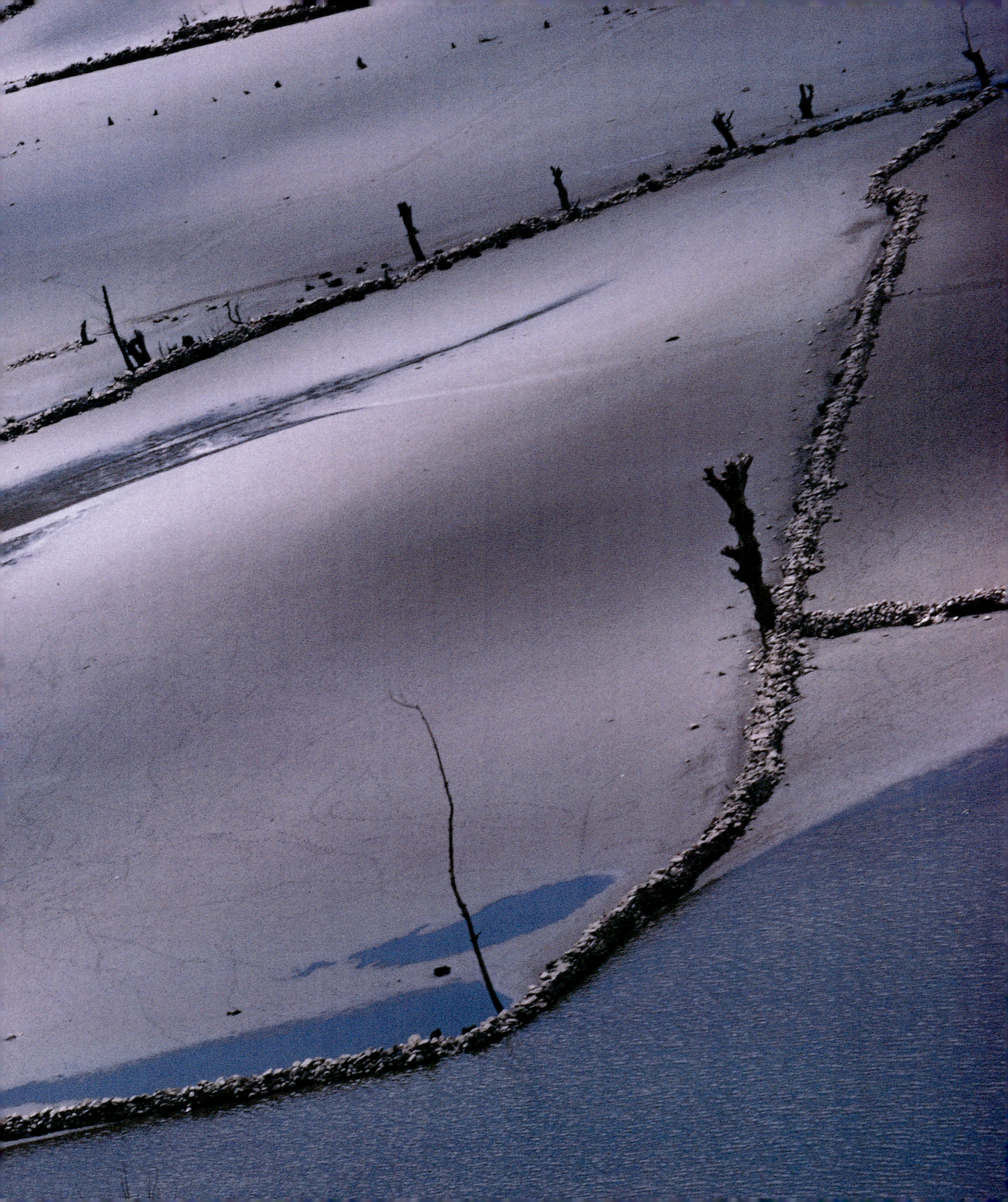

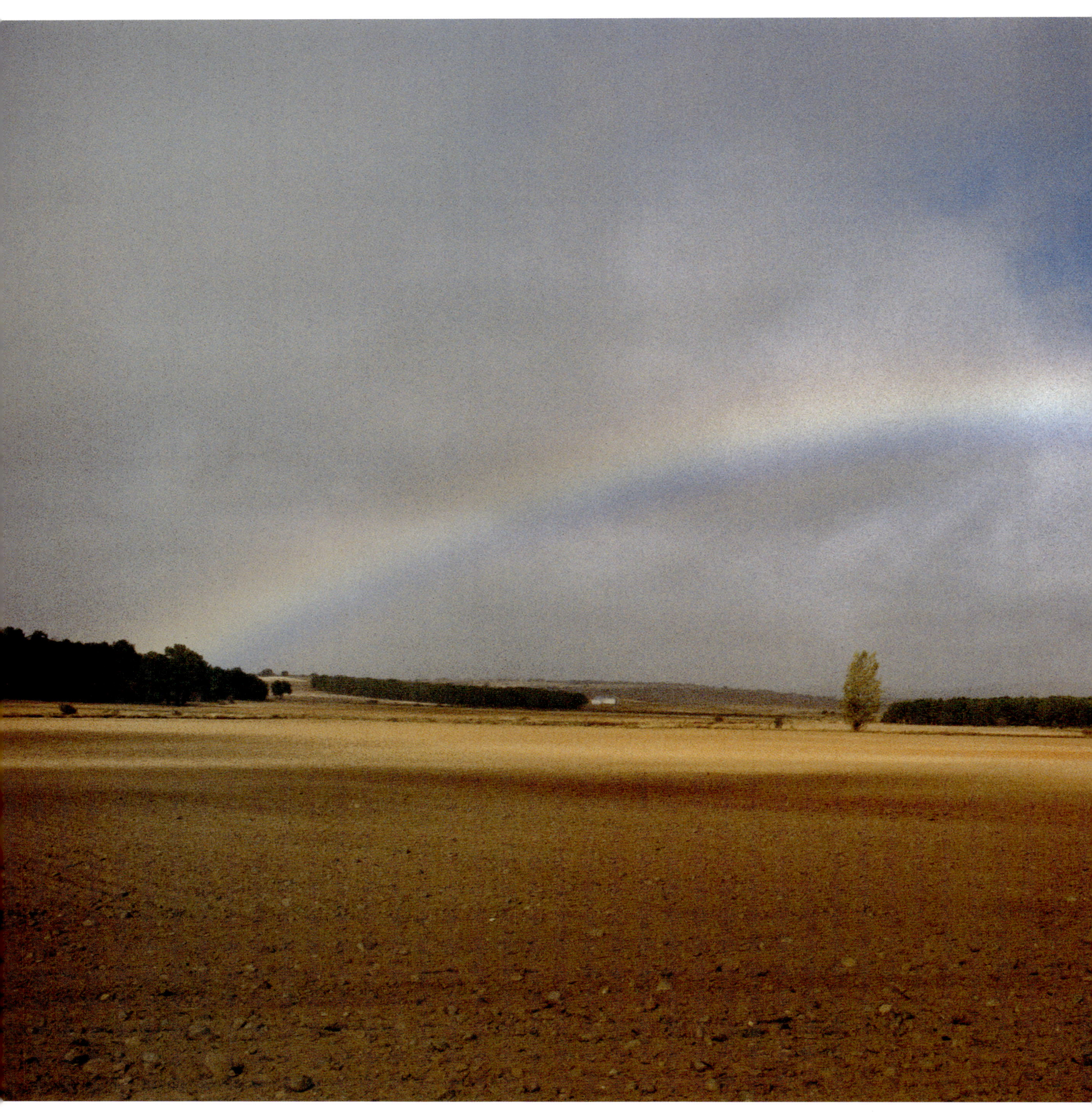

PREVIOUS PAGES
León, Castilla y León, in August

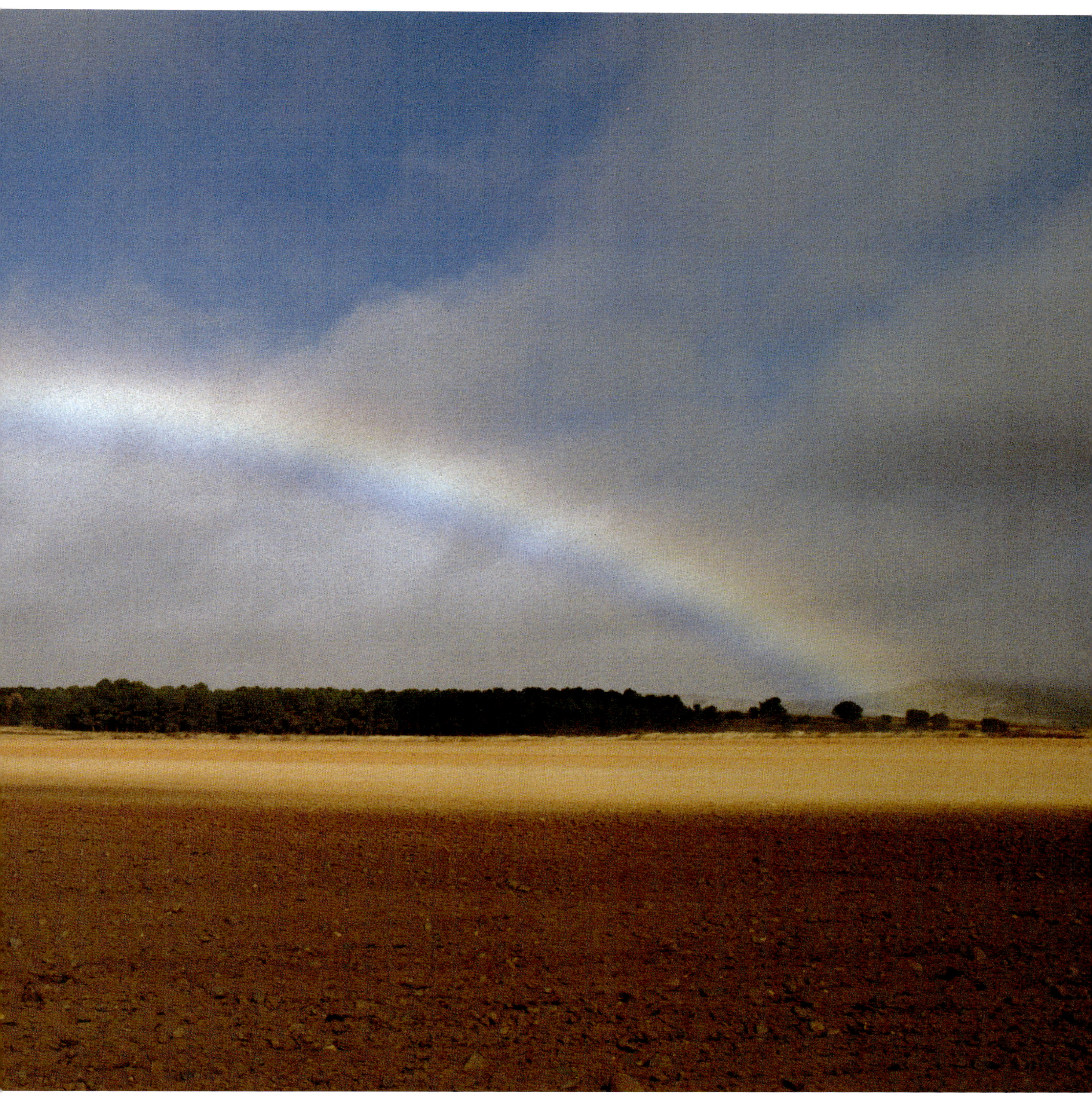

ABOVE
Soria, Castilla y León, in November

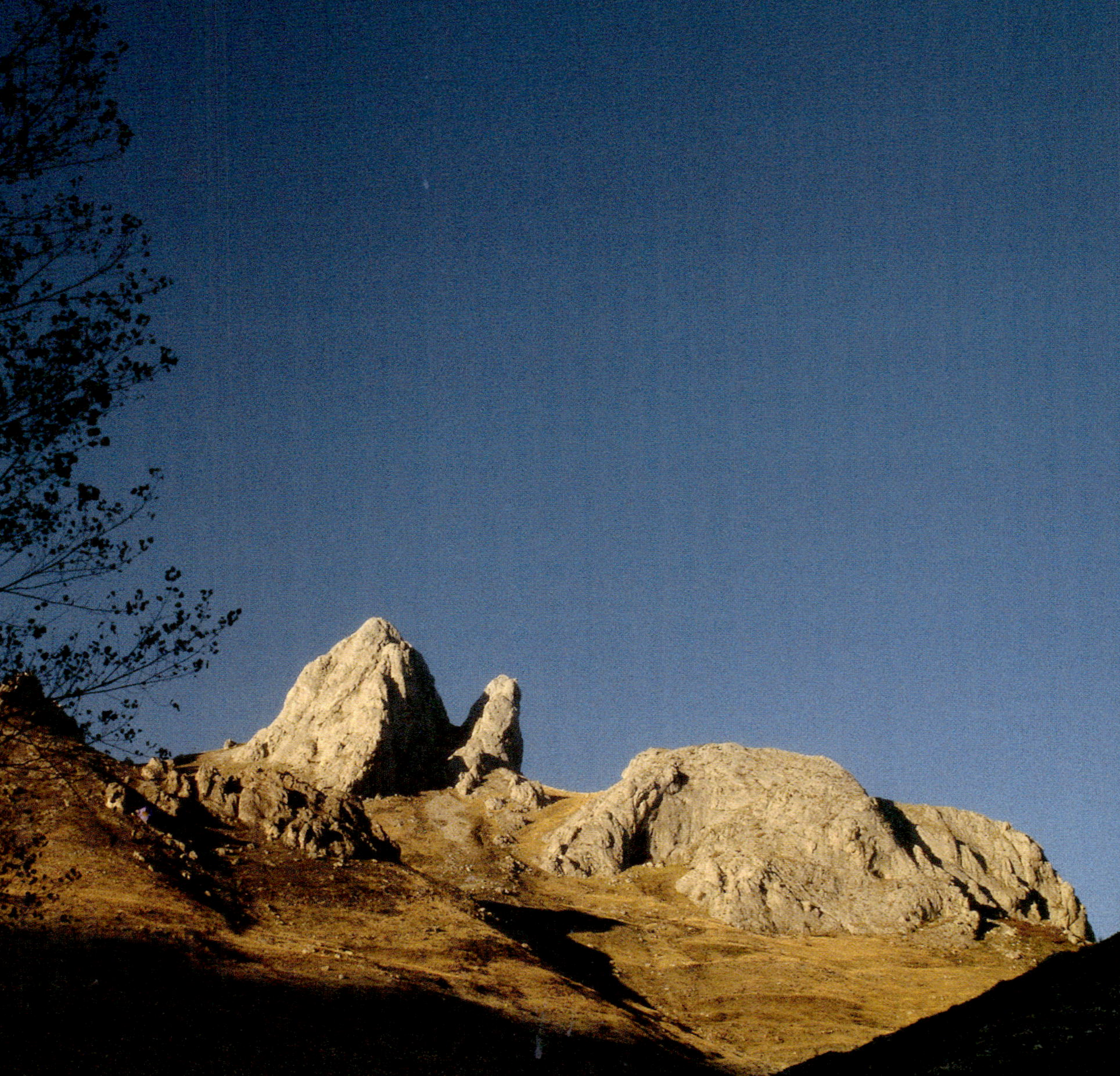

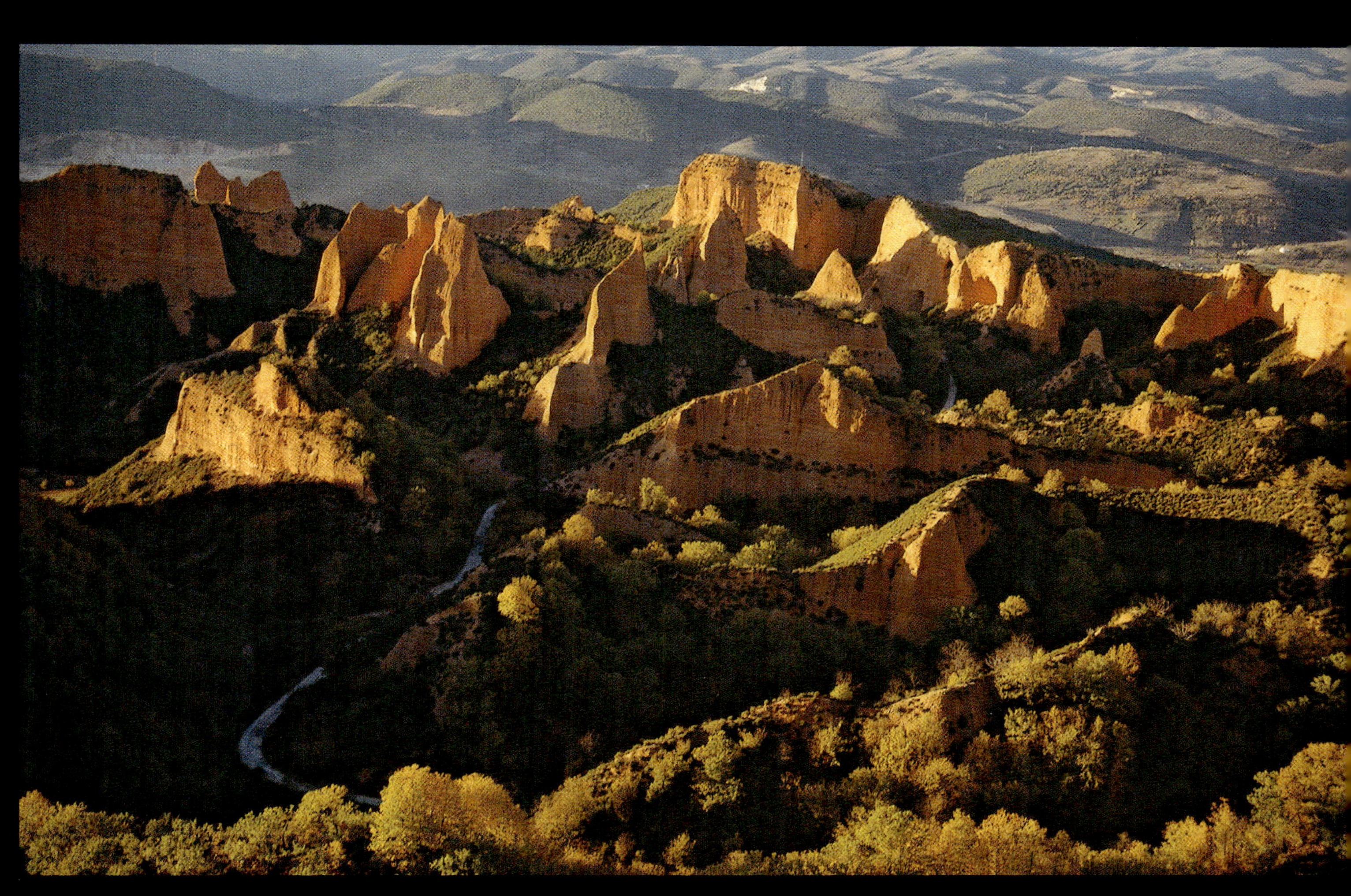

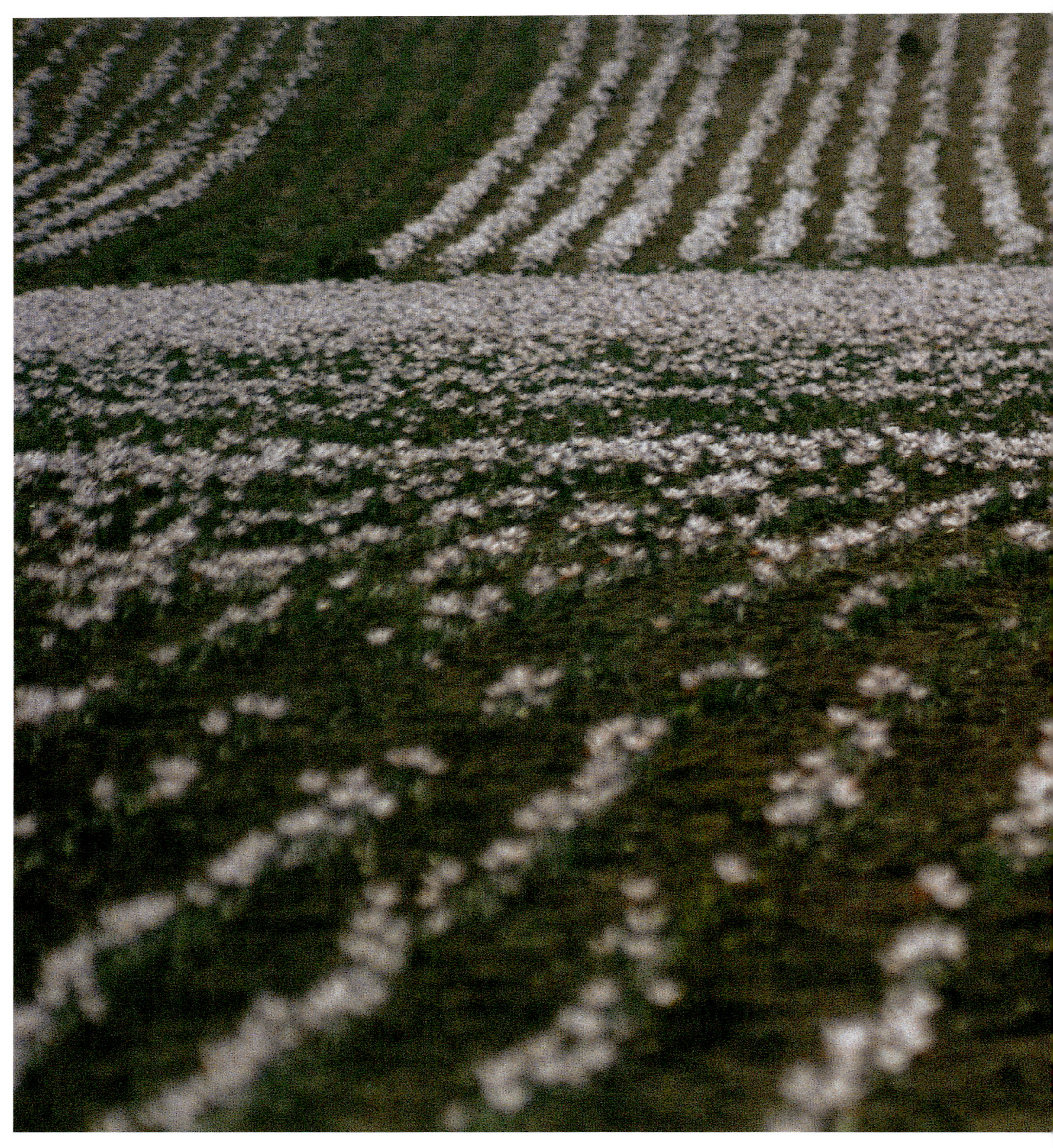

PREVIOUS PAGES
LEFT AND RIGHT León, Castilla y León, in November

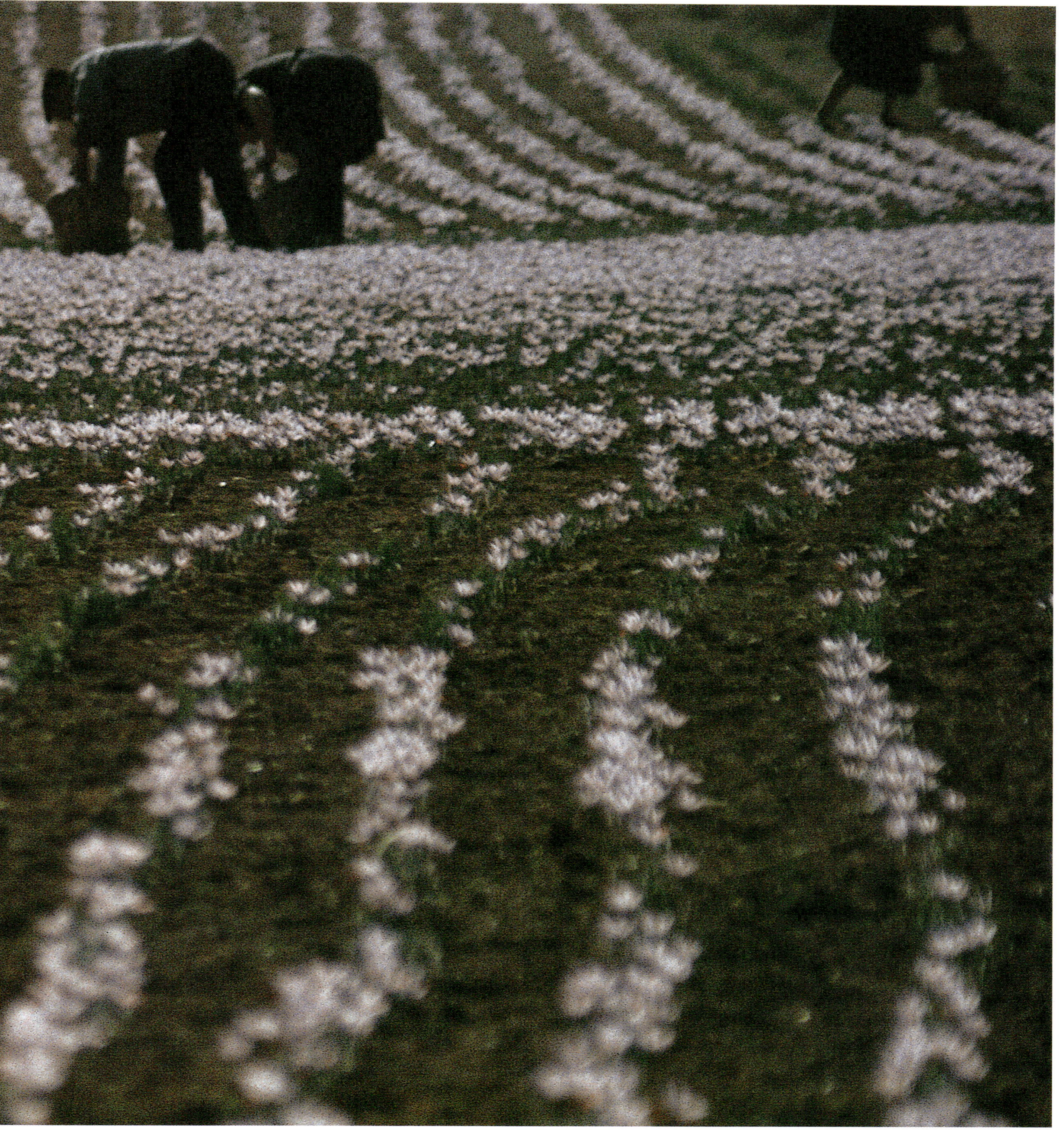

ABOVE
Ciudad Real, Castilla-La Mancha, in November

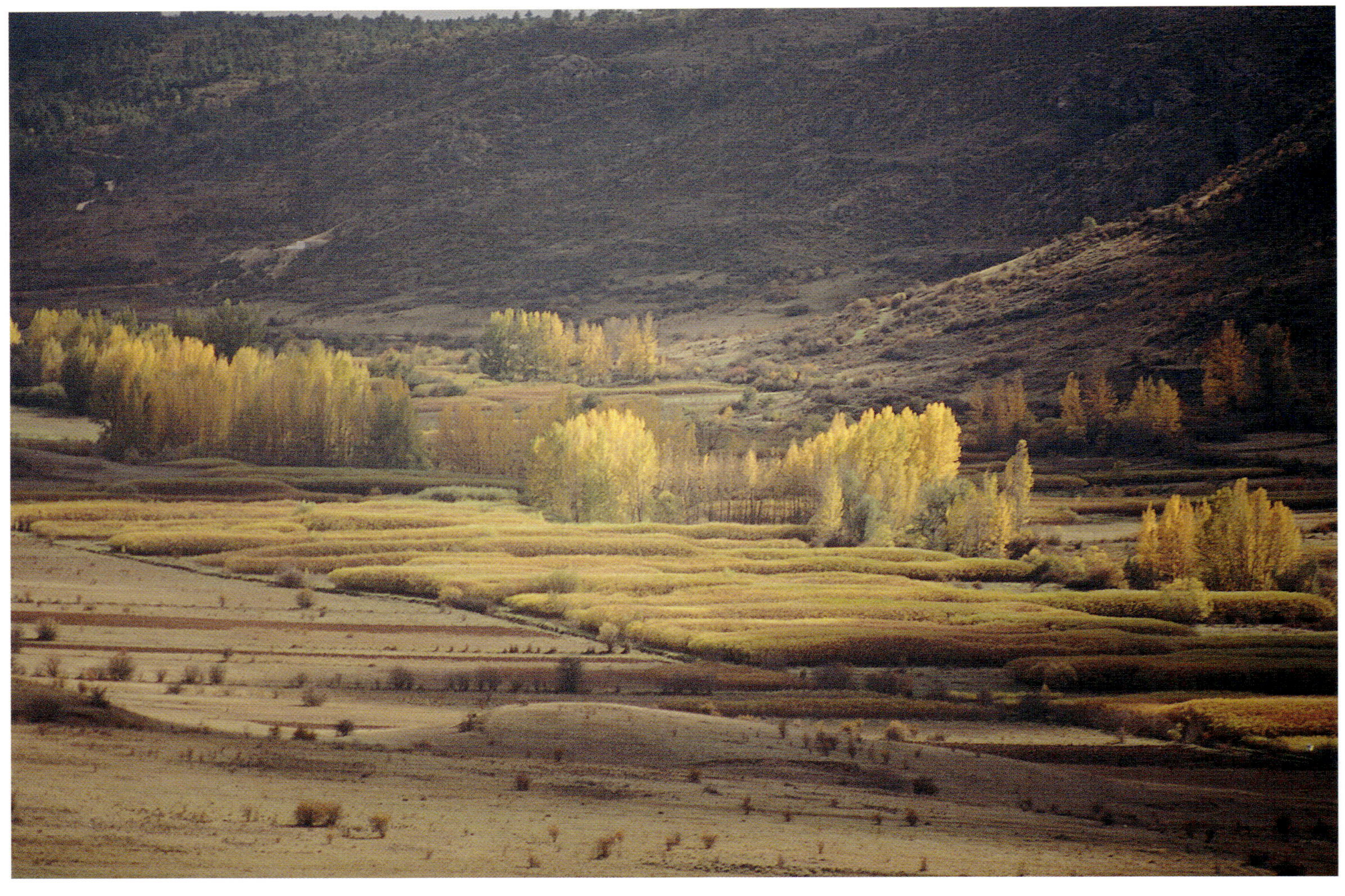

ABOVE LEFT AND RIGHT
Cuenca, Castilla-La Mancha, in November

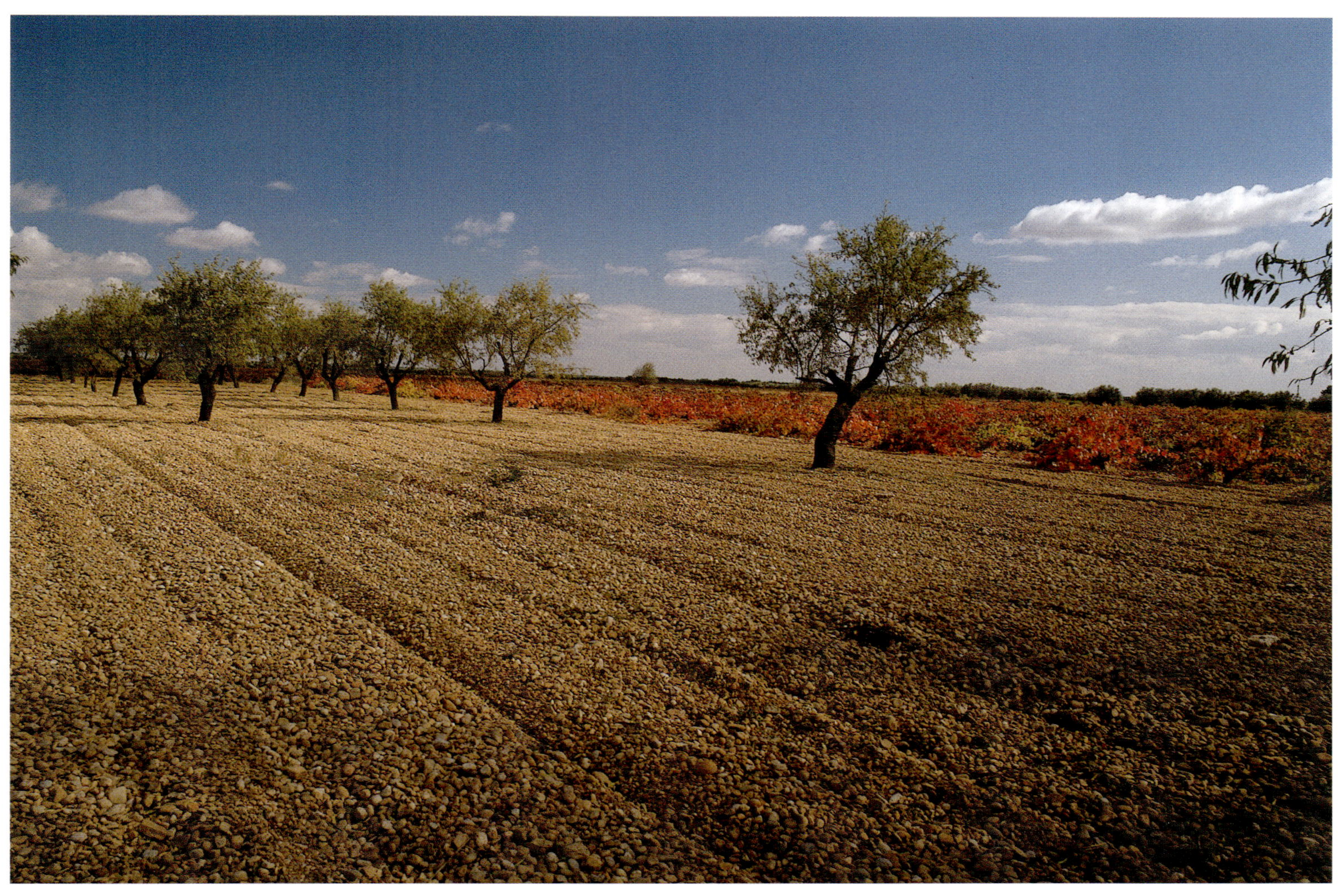

FOLLOWING PAGES
Zaragoza, Aragón,
in November

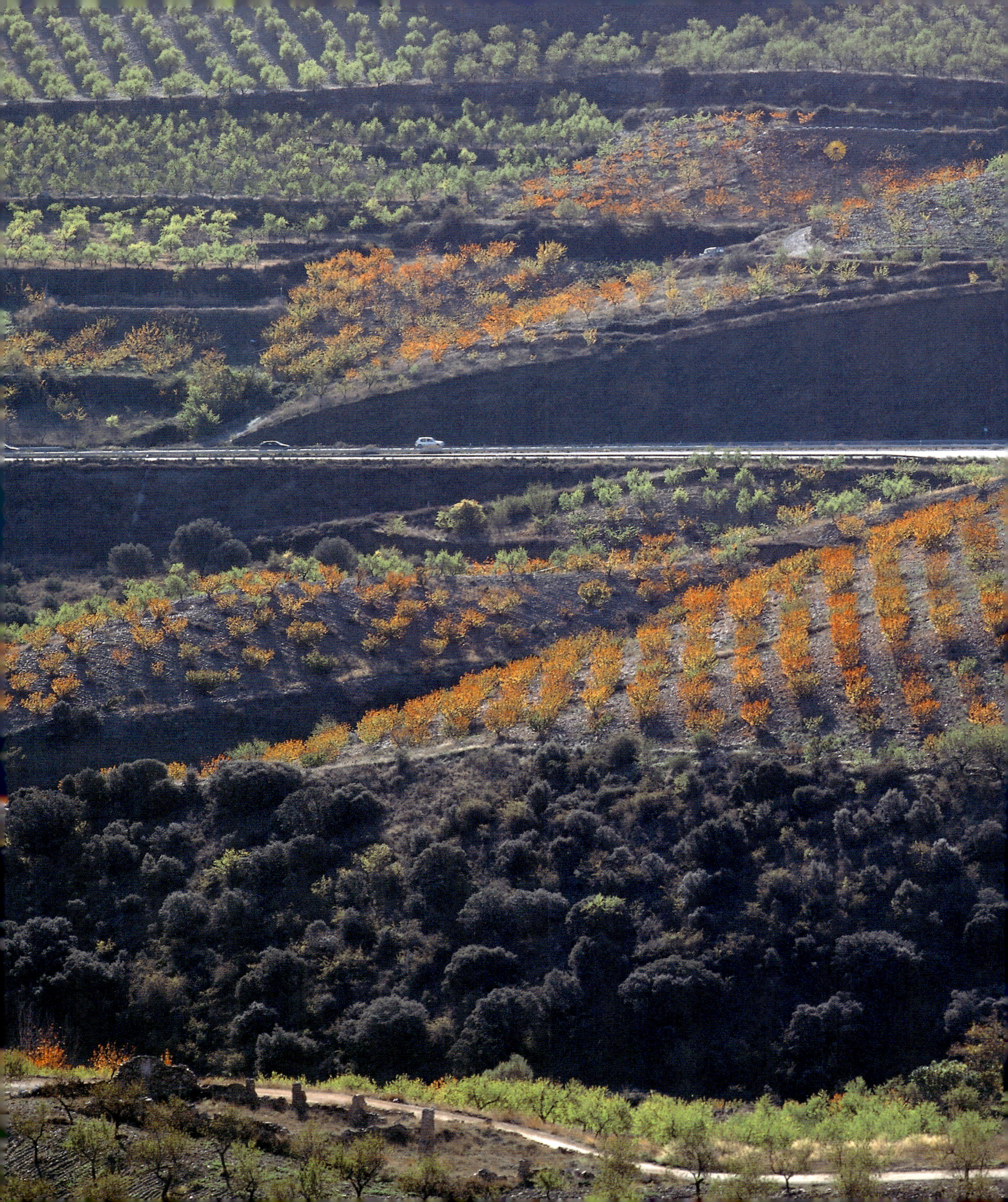

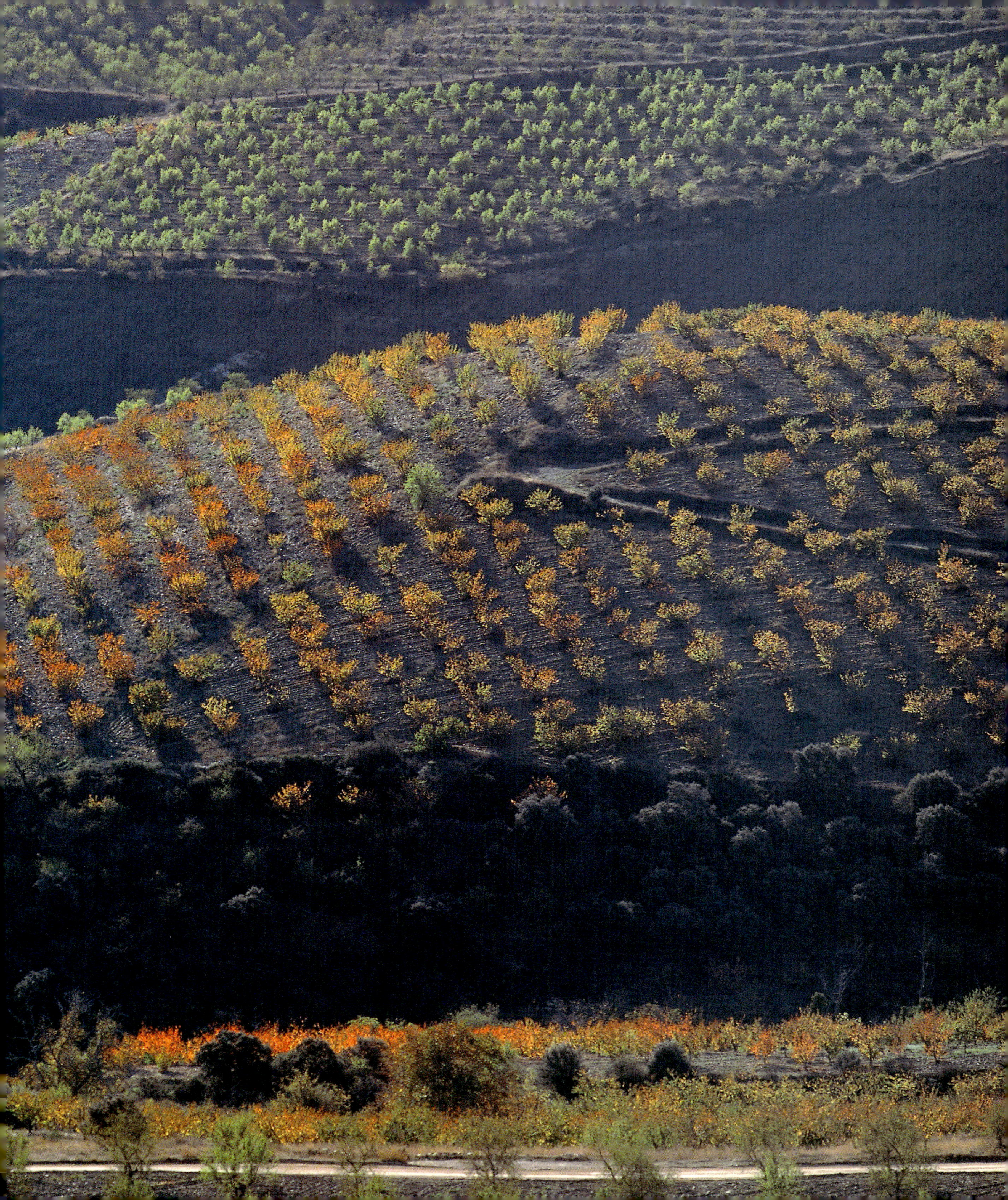

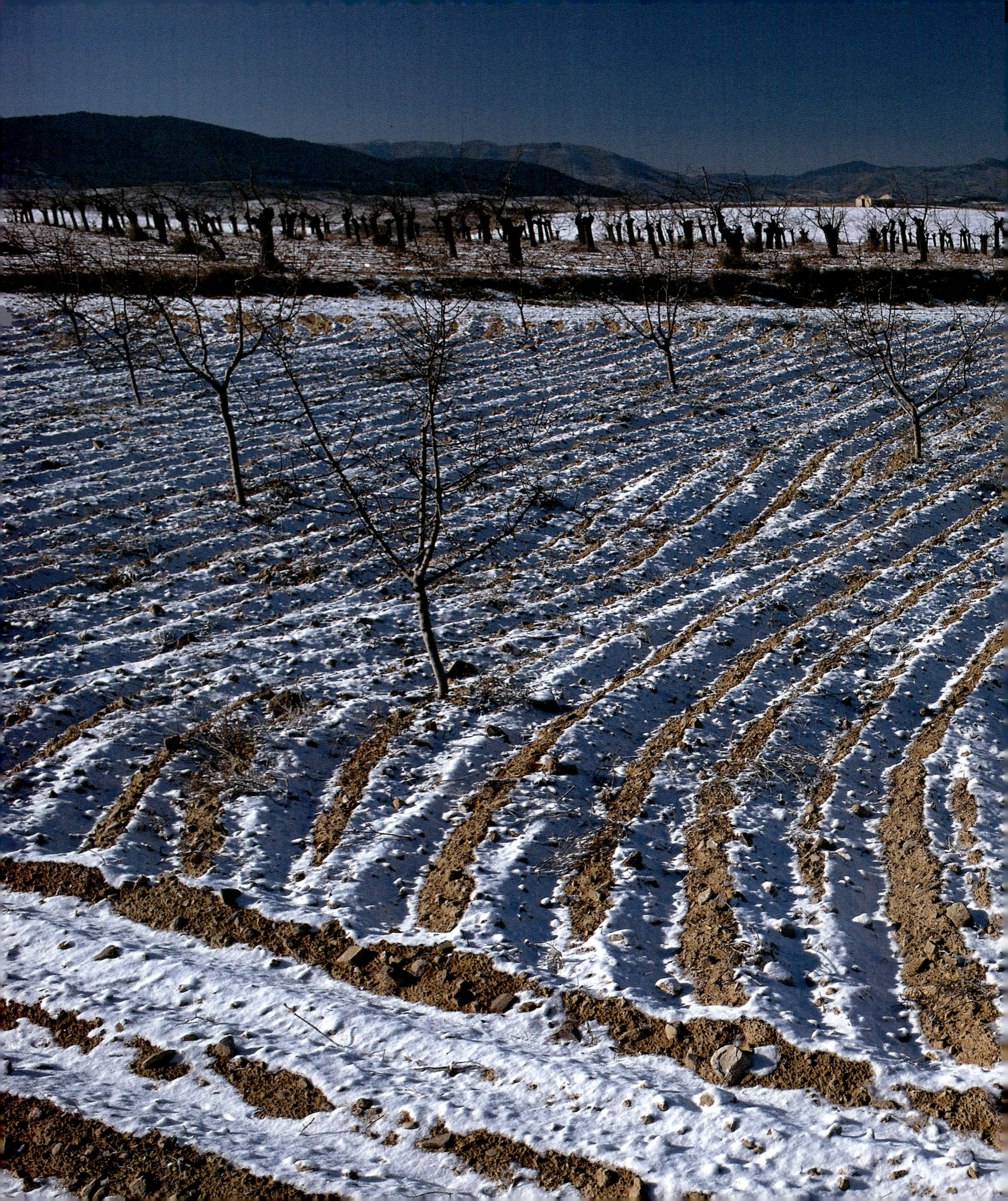

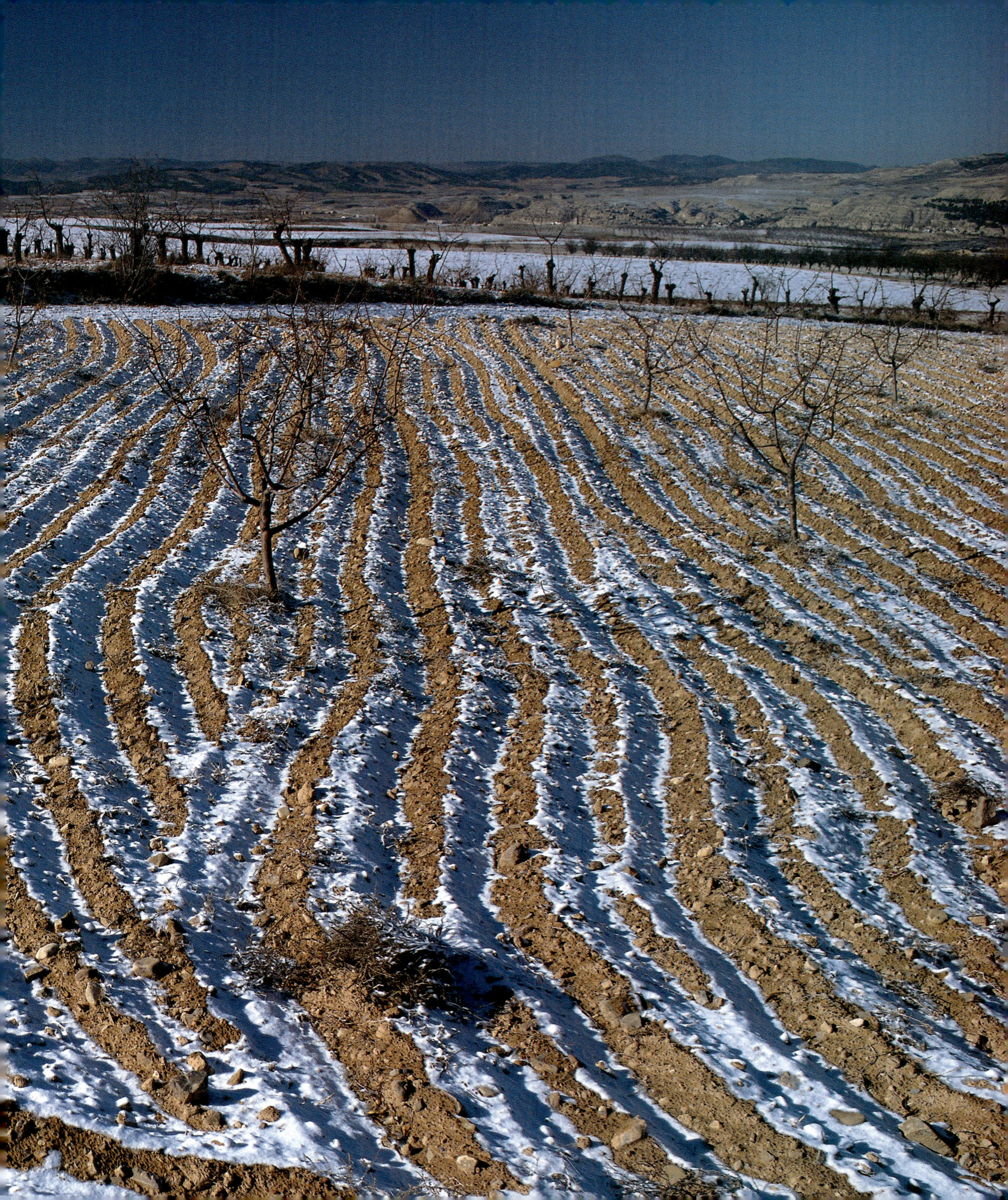

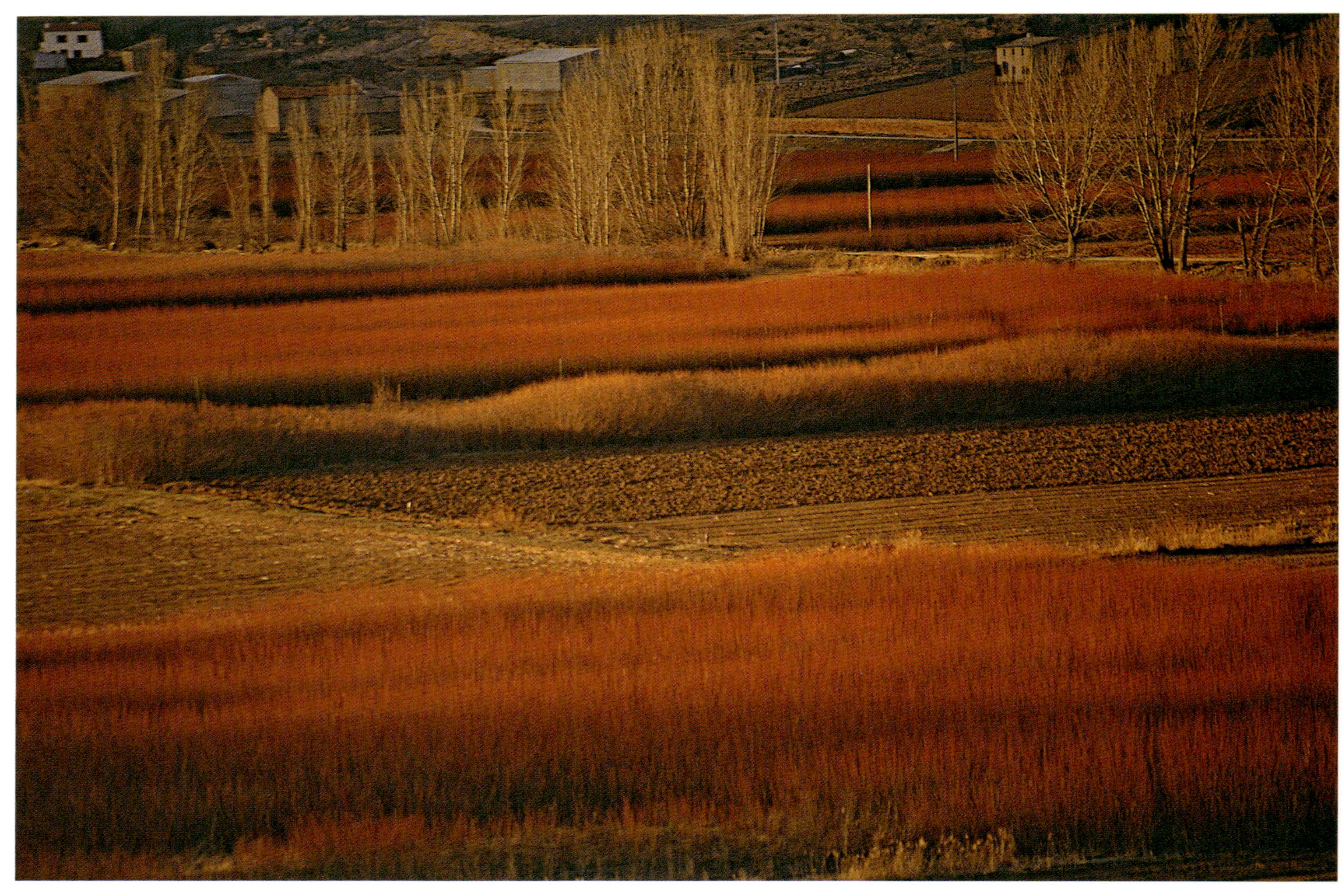

ABOVE
Cuenca, Castilla-La Mancha,
in November

PREVIOUS PAGES
Zaragoza, Aragón,
in December

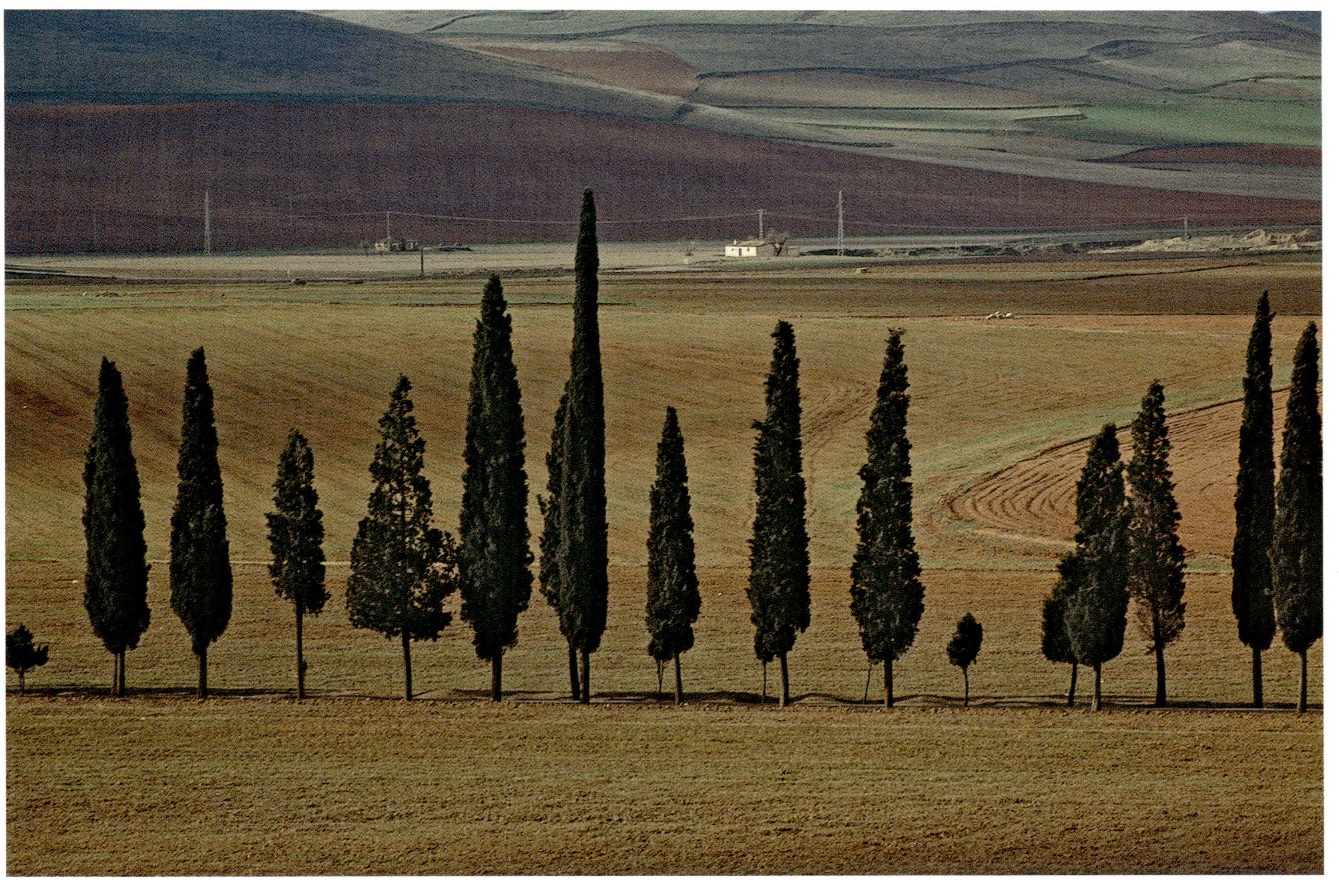

ABOVE
Ciudad Real, Castilla-La Mancha,
in November

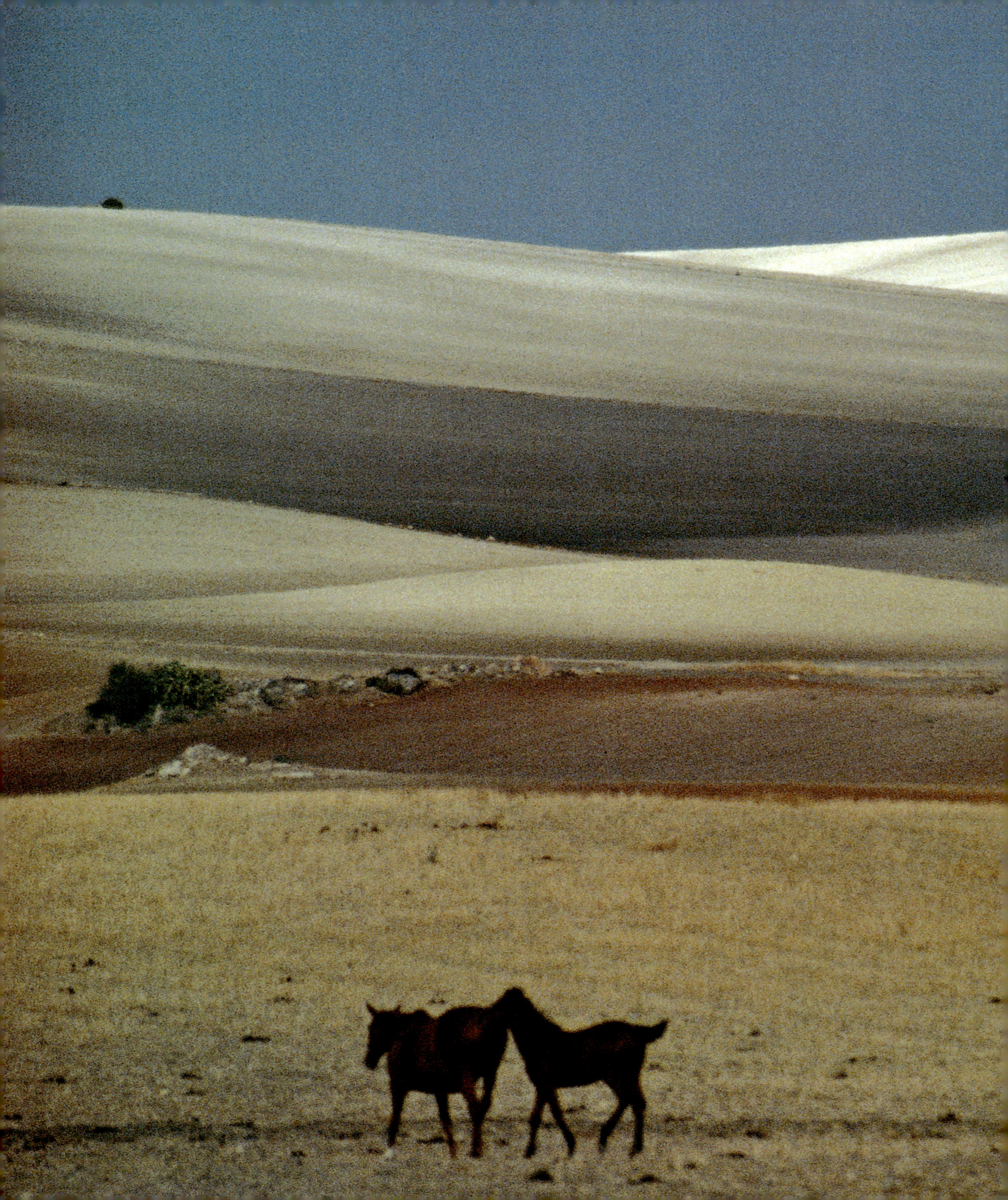

THE SOUTH

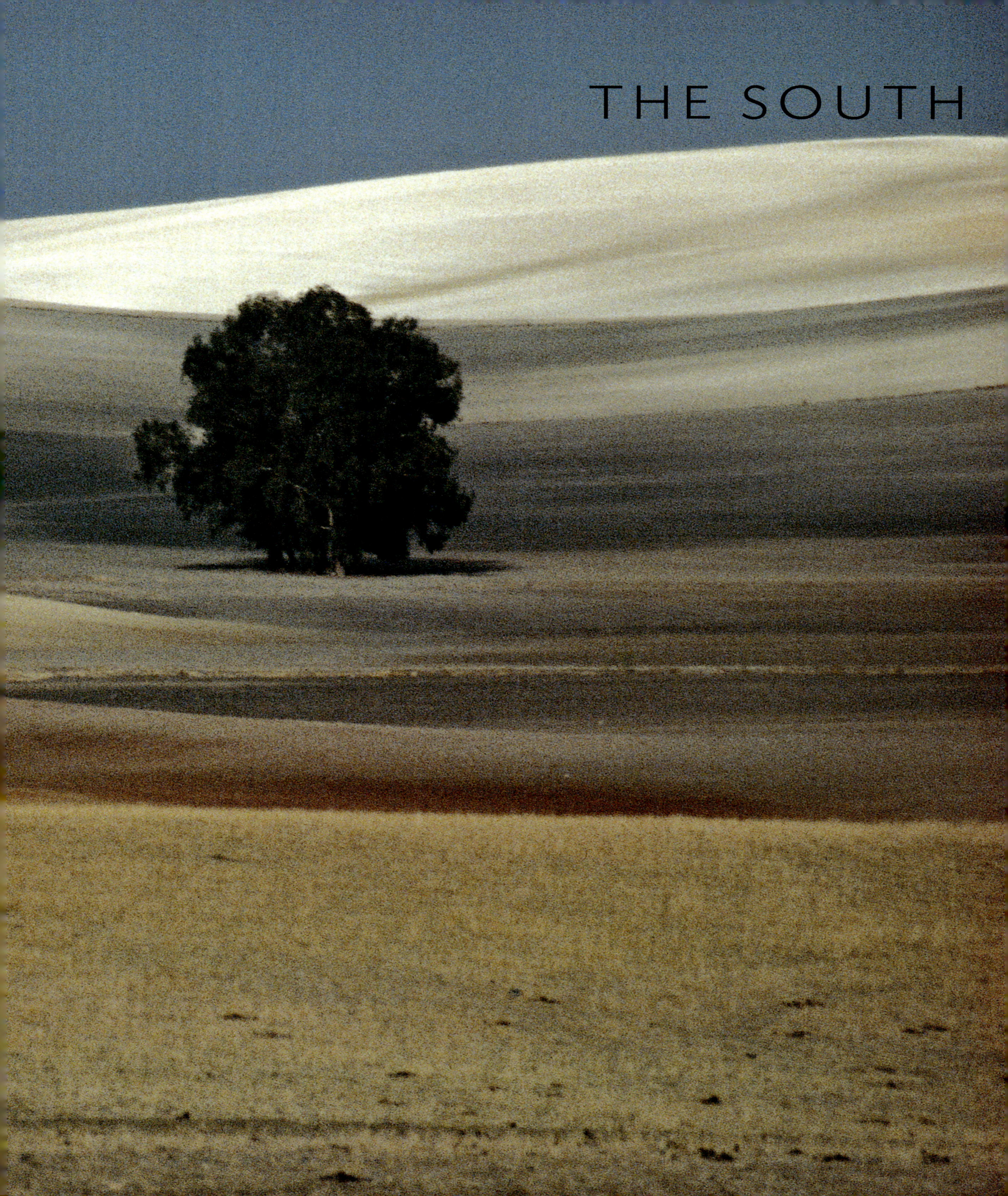

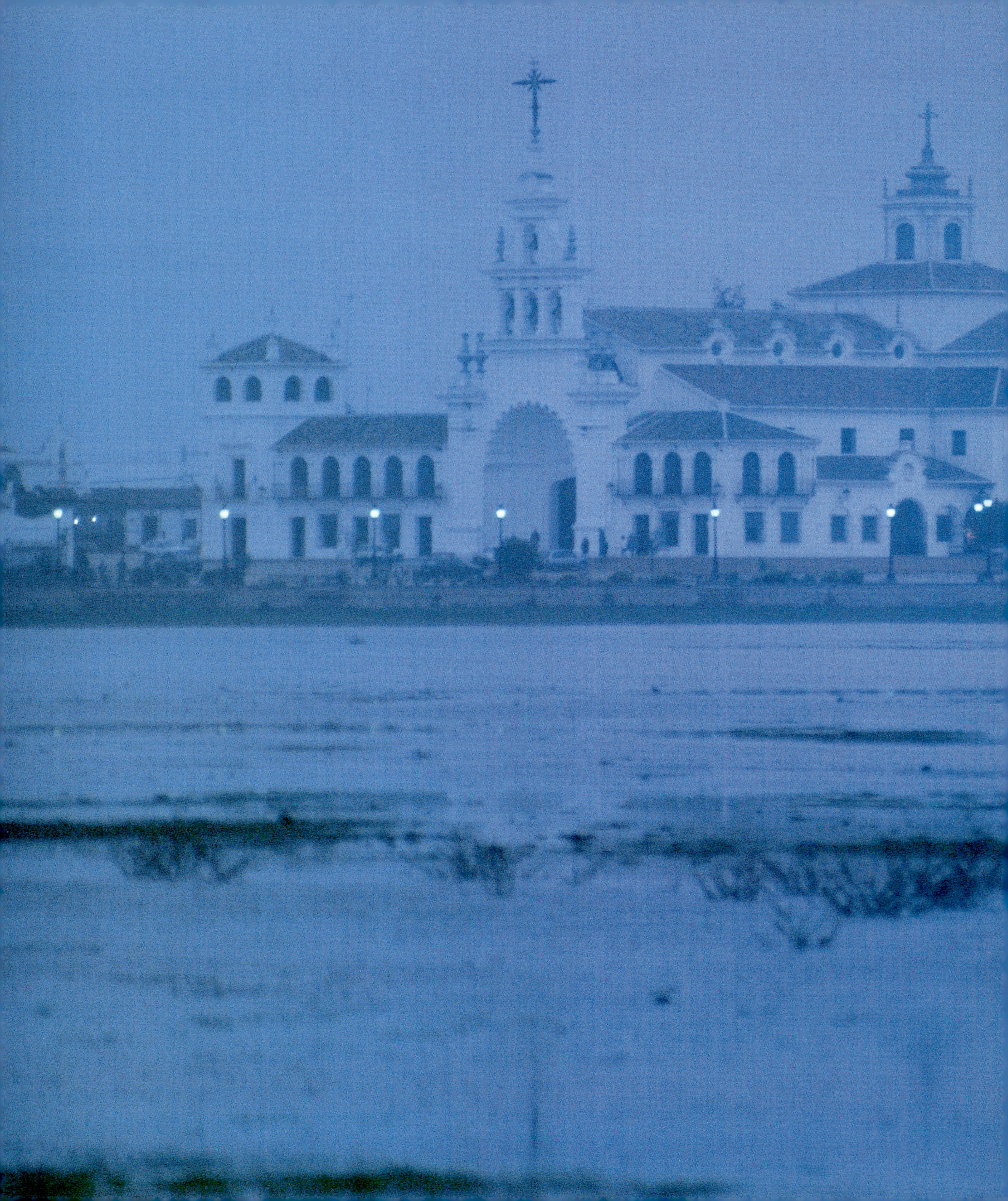

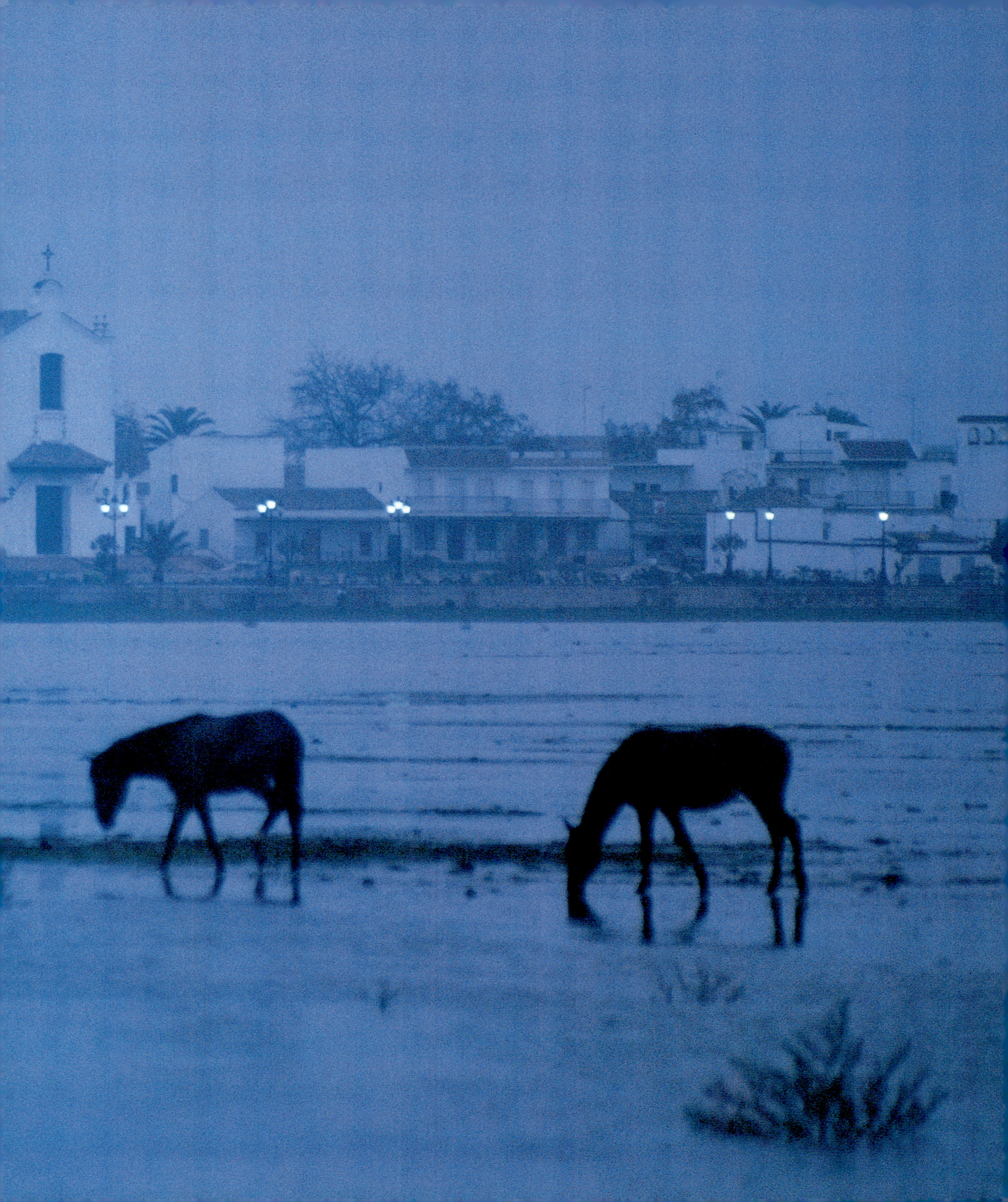

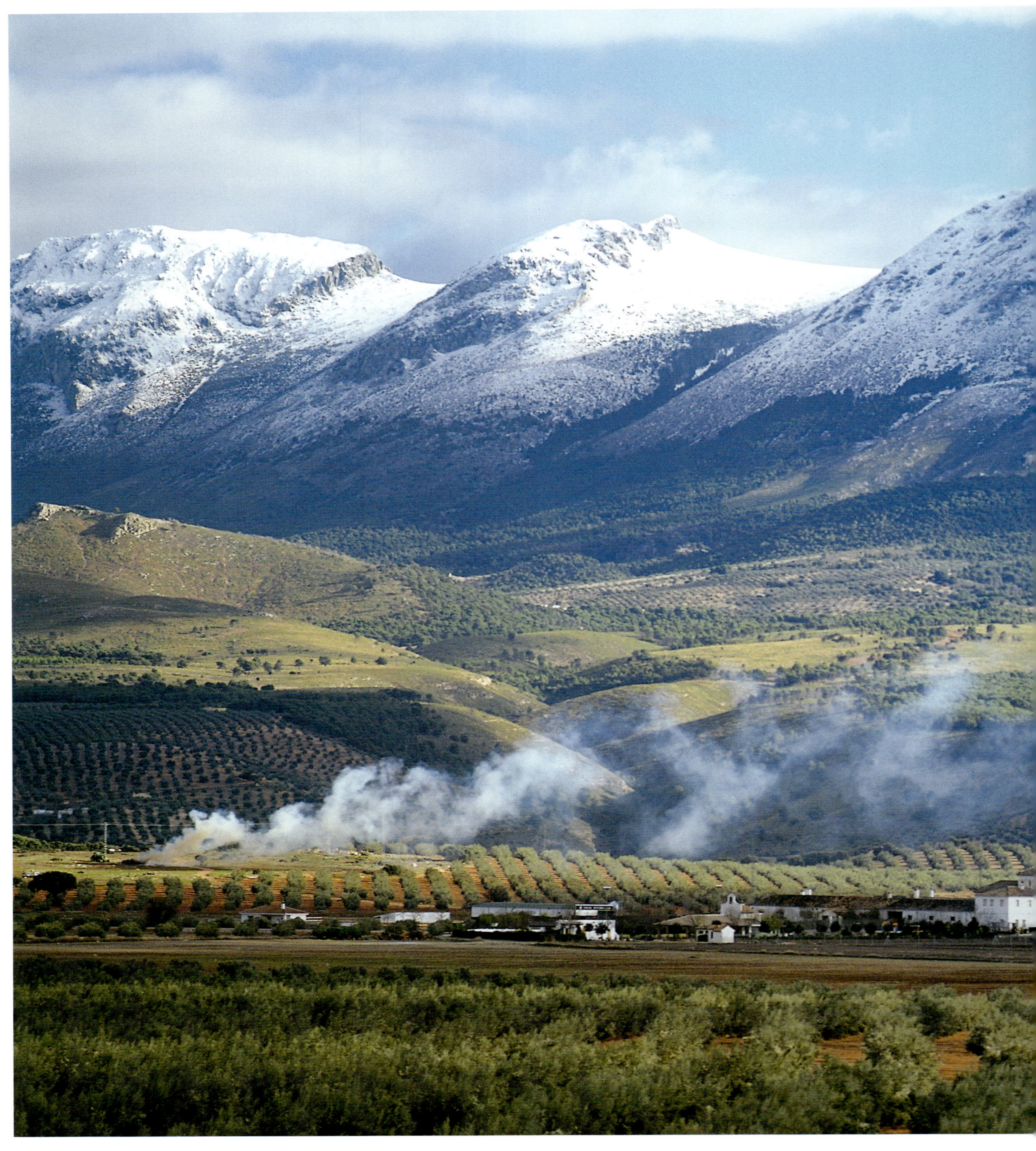

PREVIOUS PAGES
Huelva, Andalucía, in January

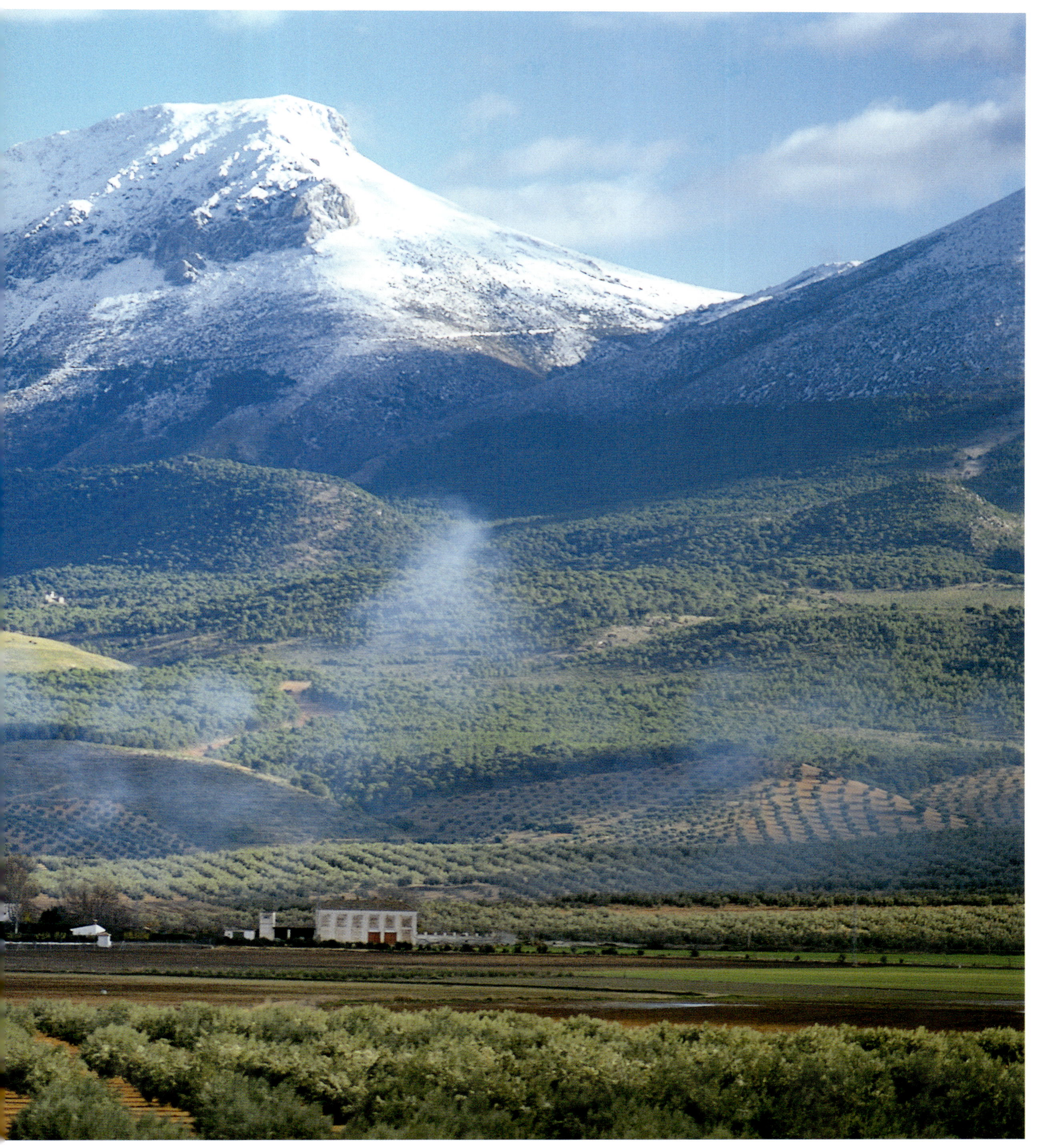

ABOVE
Granada, Andalucía, in January

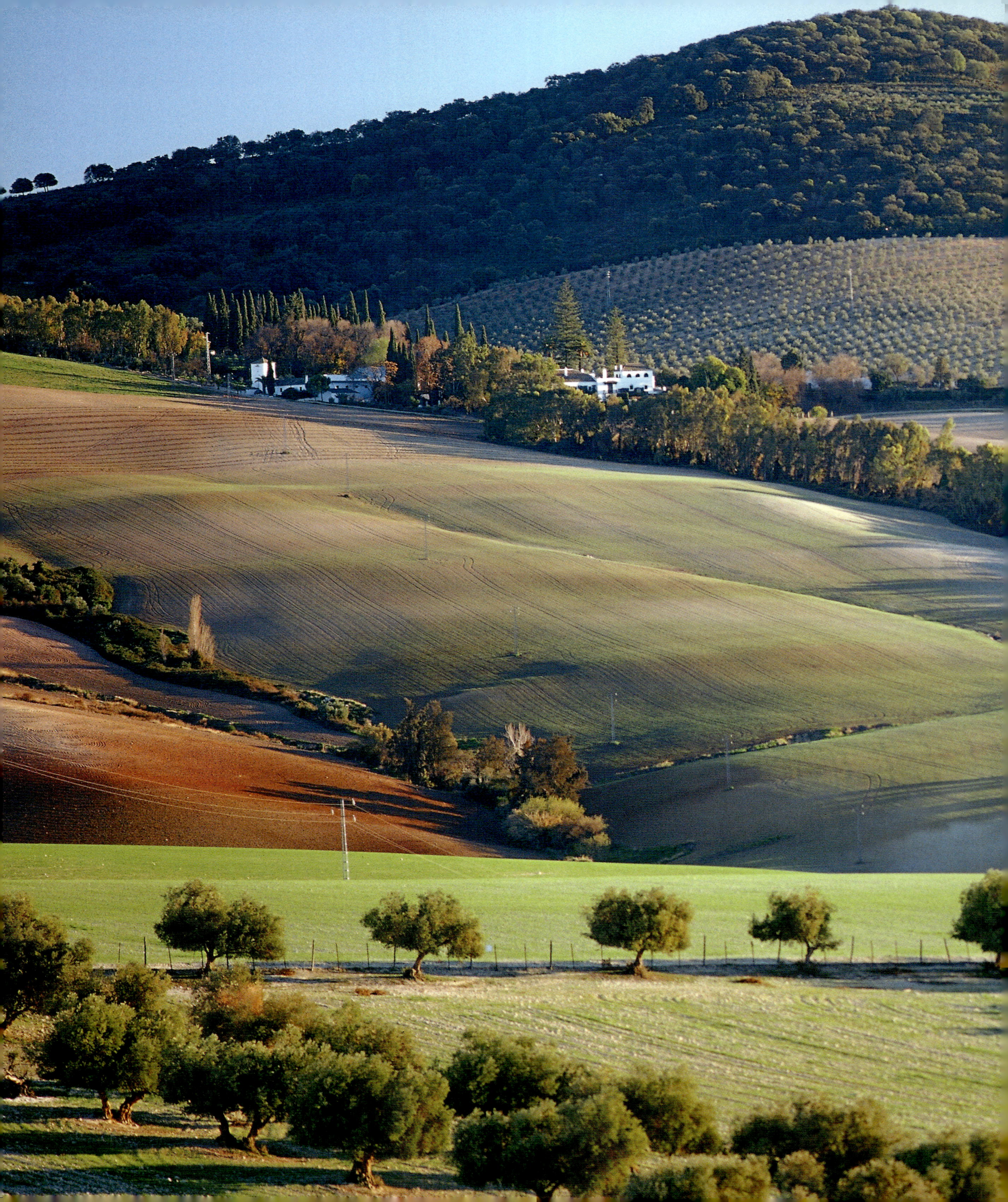

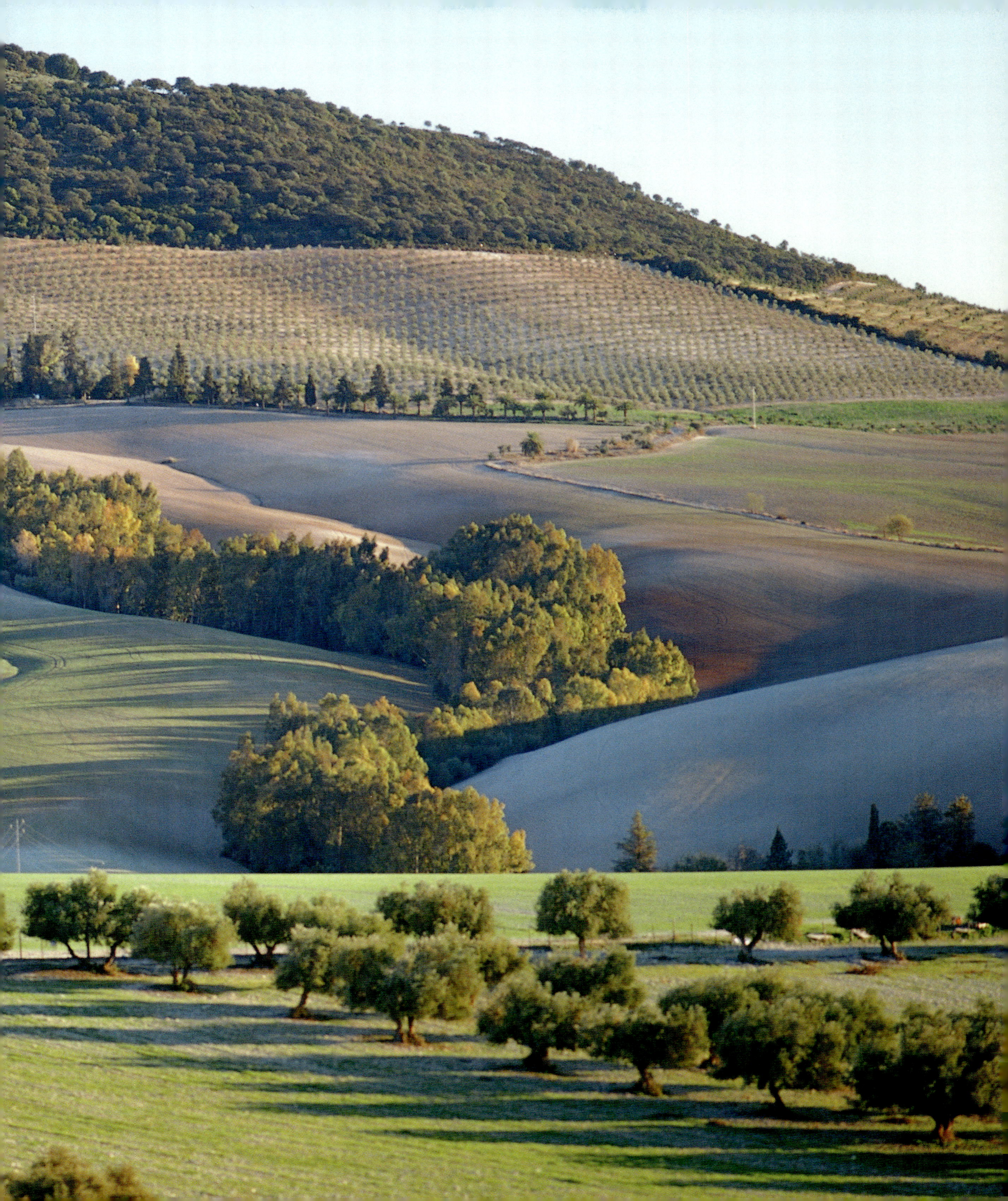

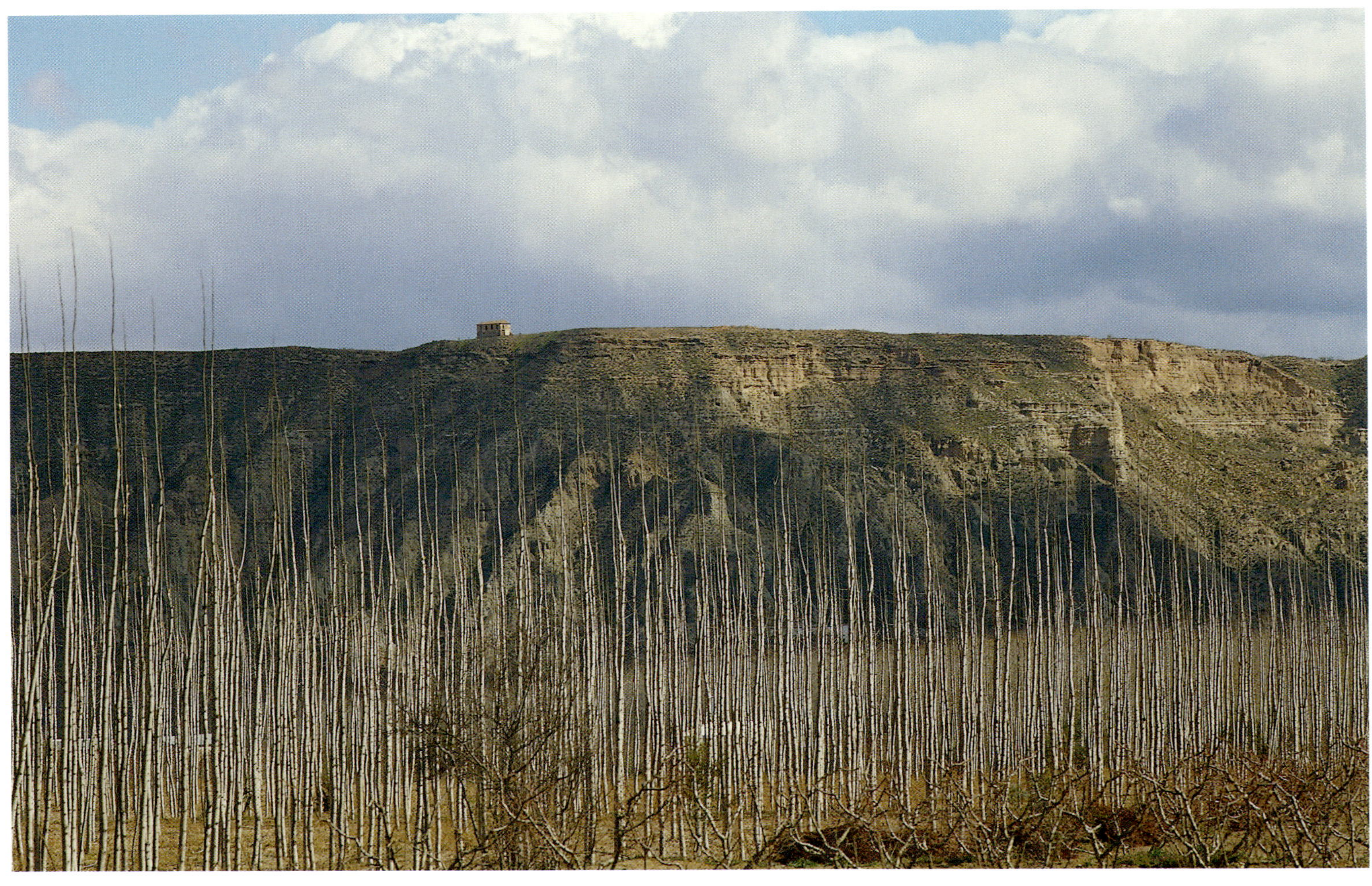

ABOVE
Granada, Andalucía, in January

PREVIOUS PAGES
Cádiz, Andalucía, in January

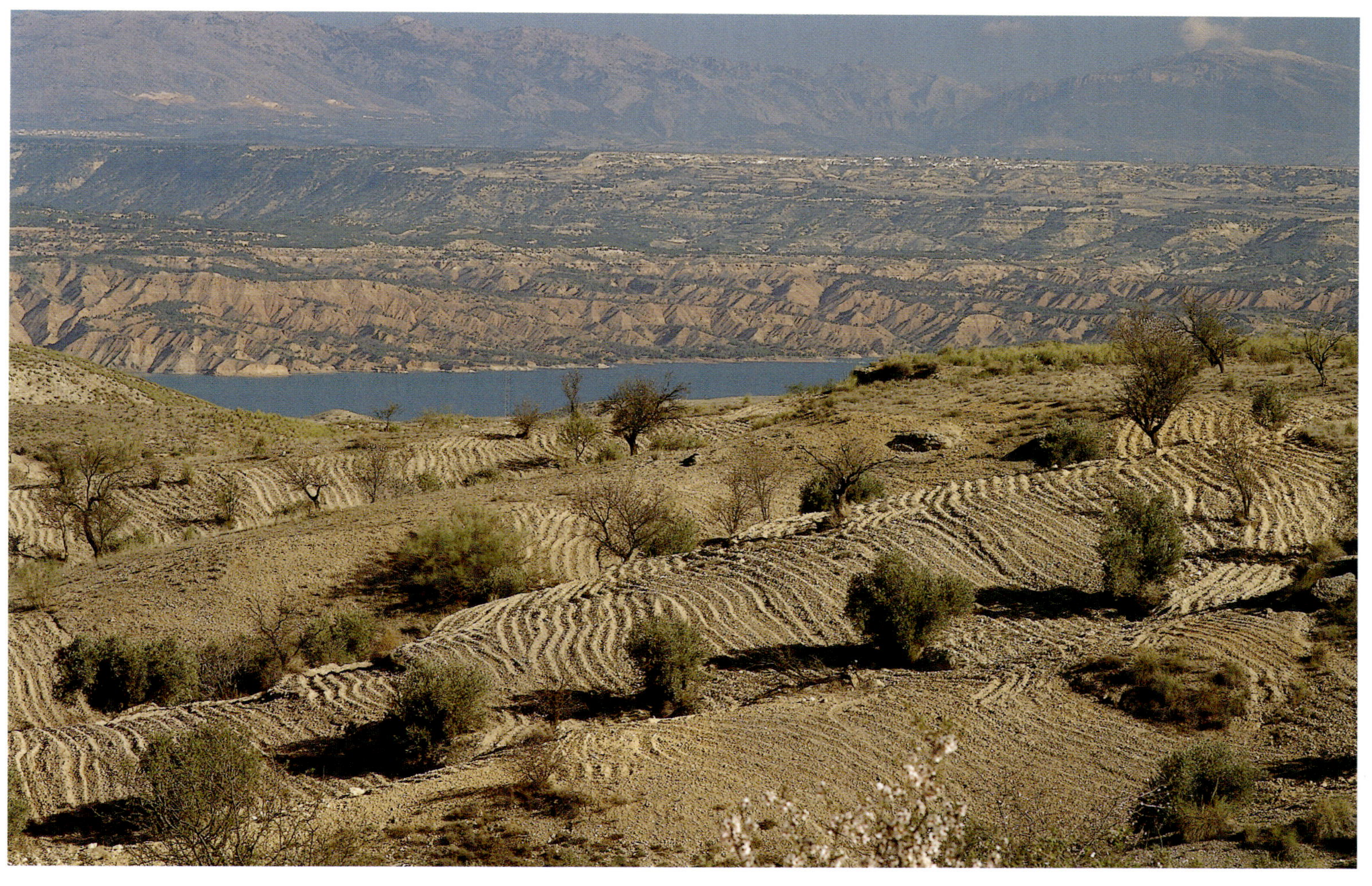

ABOVE
Granada, Andalucía, in February

FOLLOWING PAGES LEFT AND RIGHT
Granada, Andalucía, in February

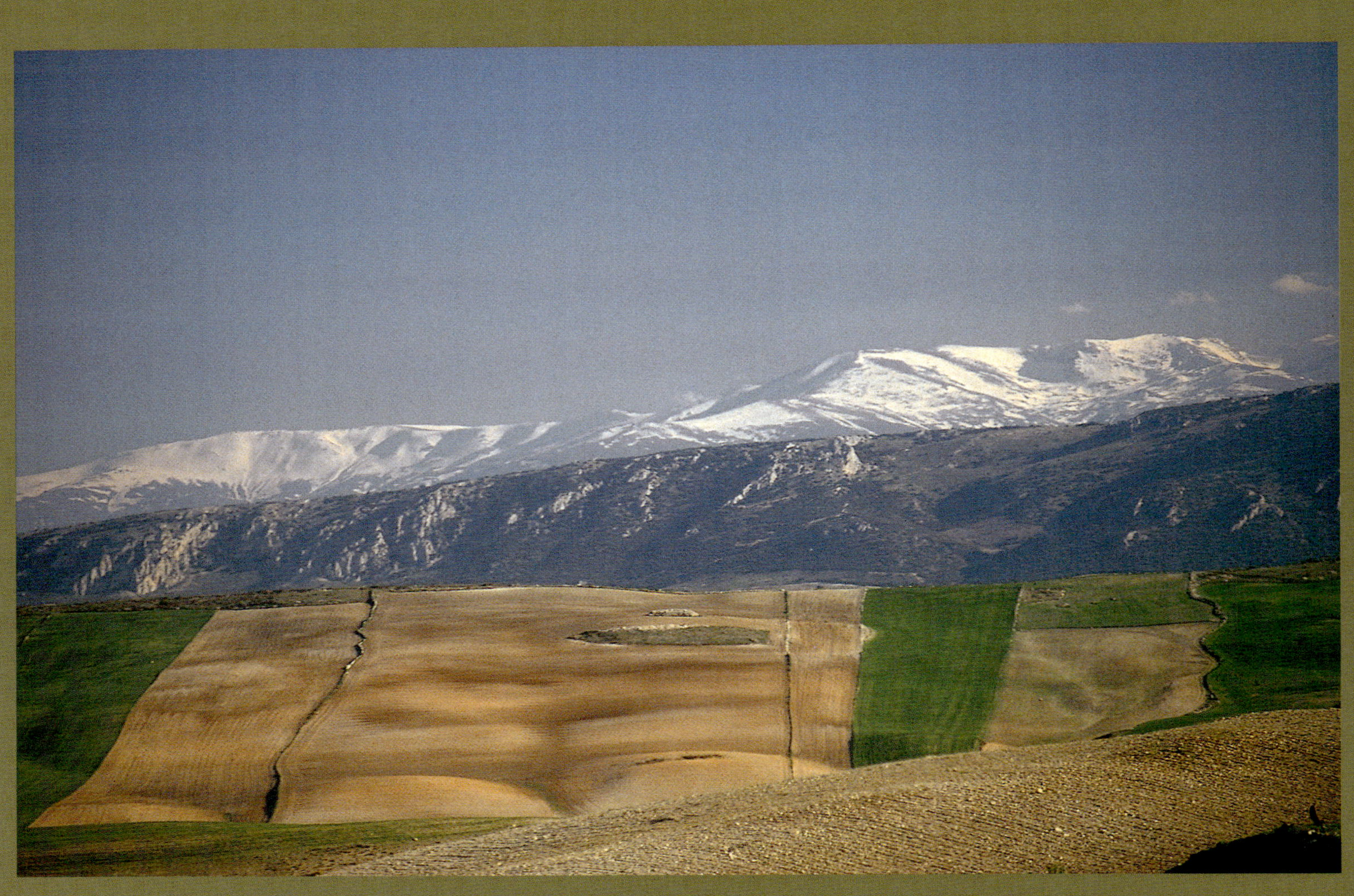

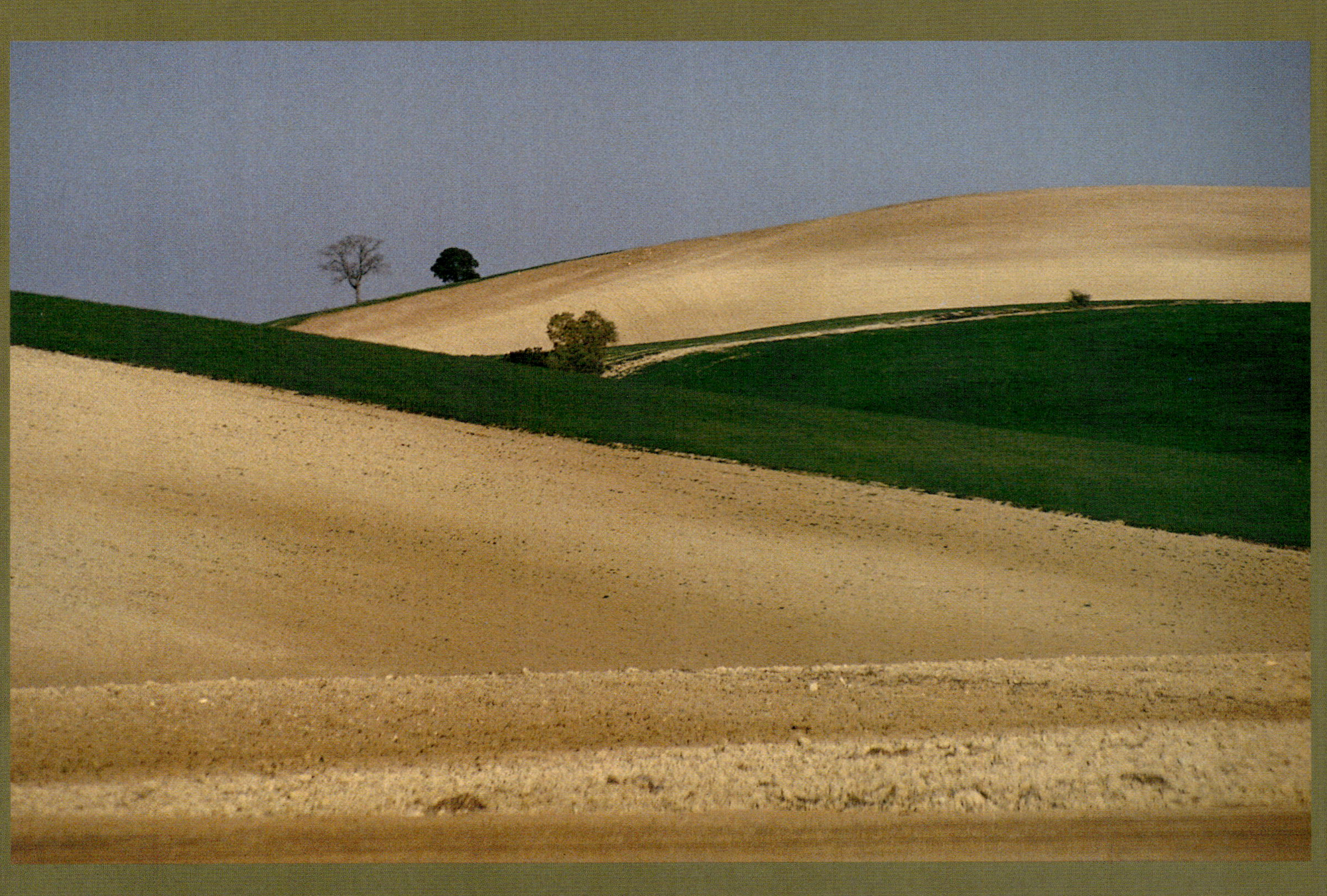

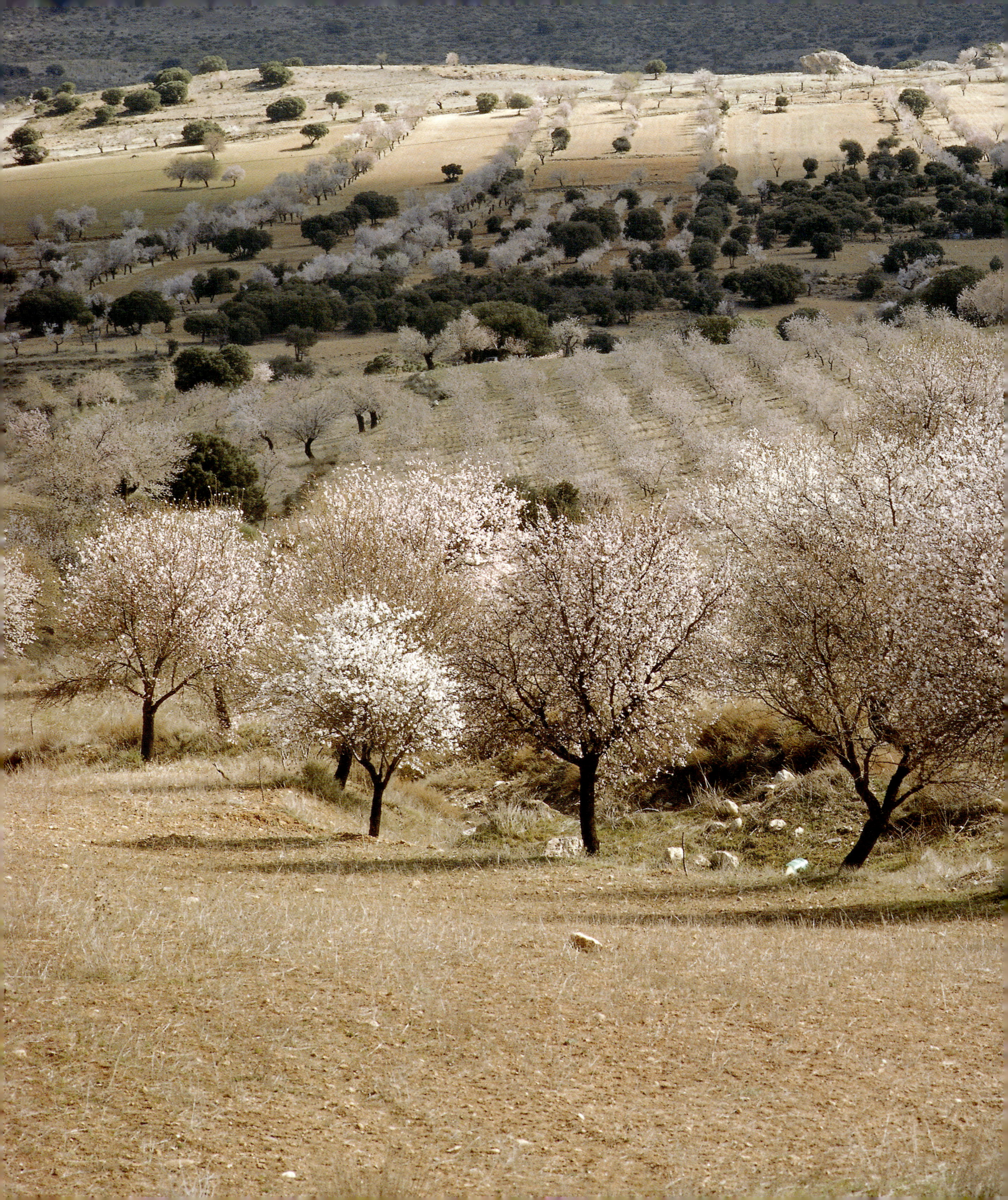

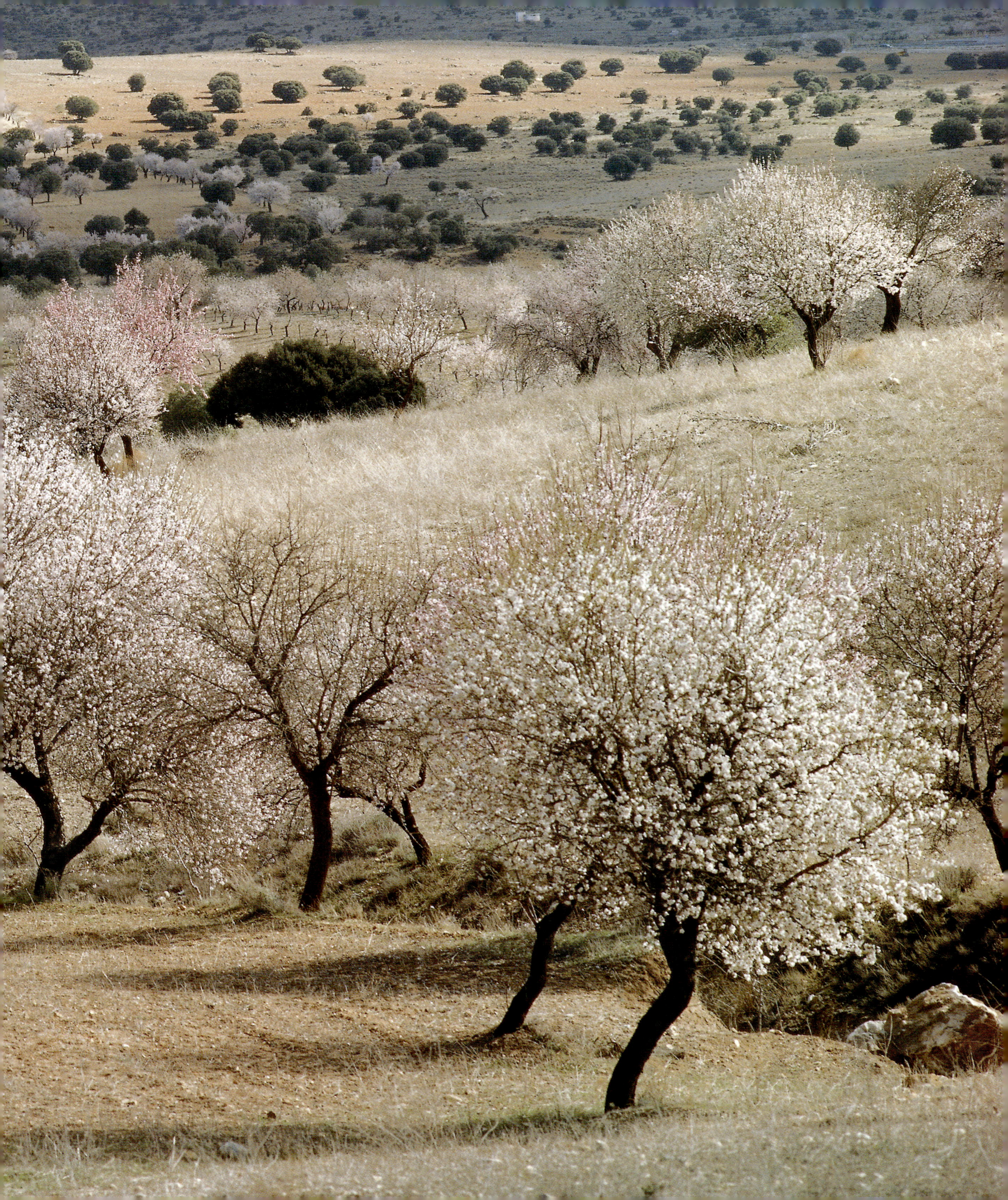

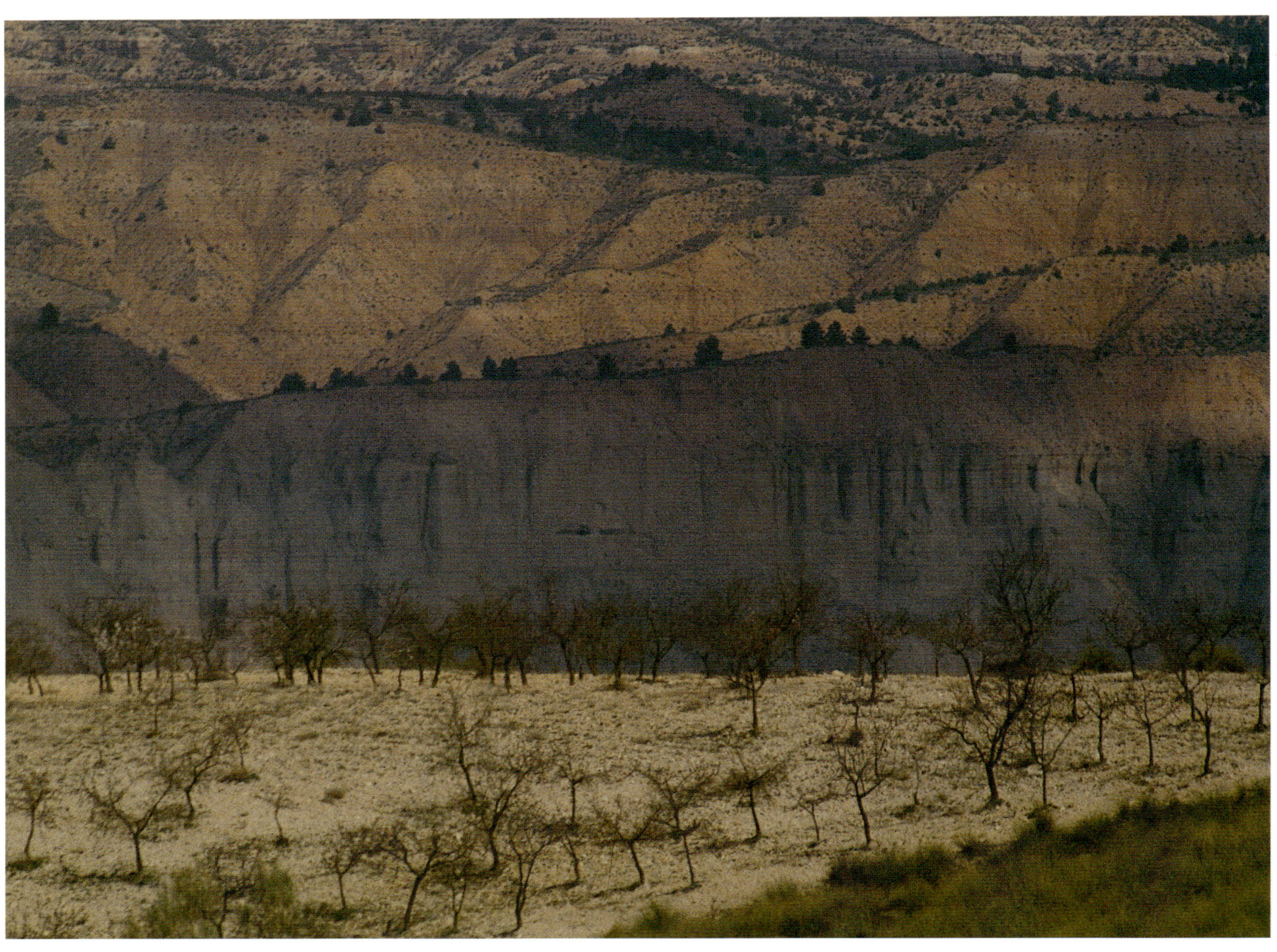

ABOVE AND PREVIOUS PAGES
Granada, Andalucía, in February

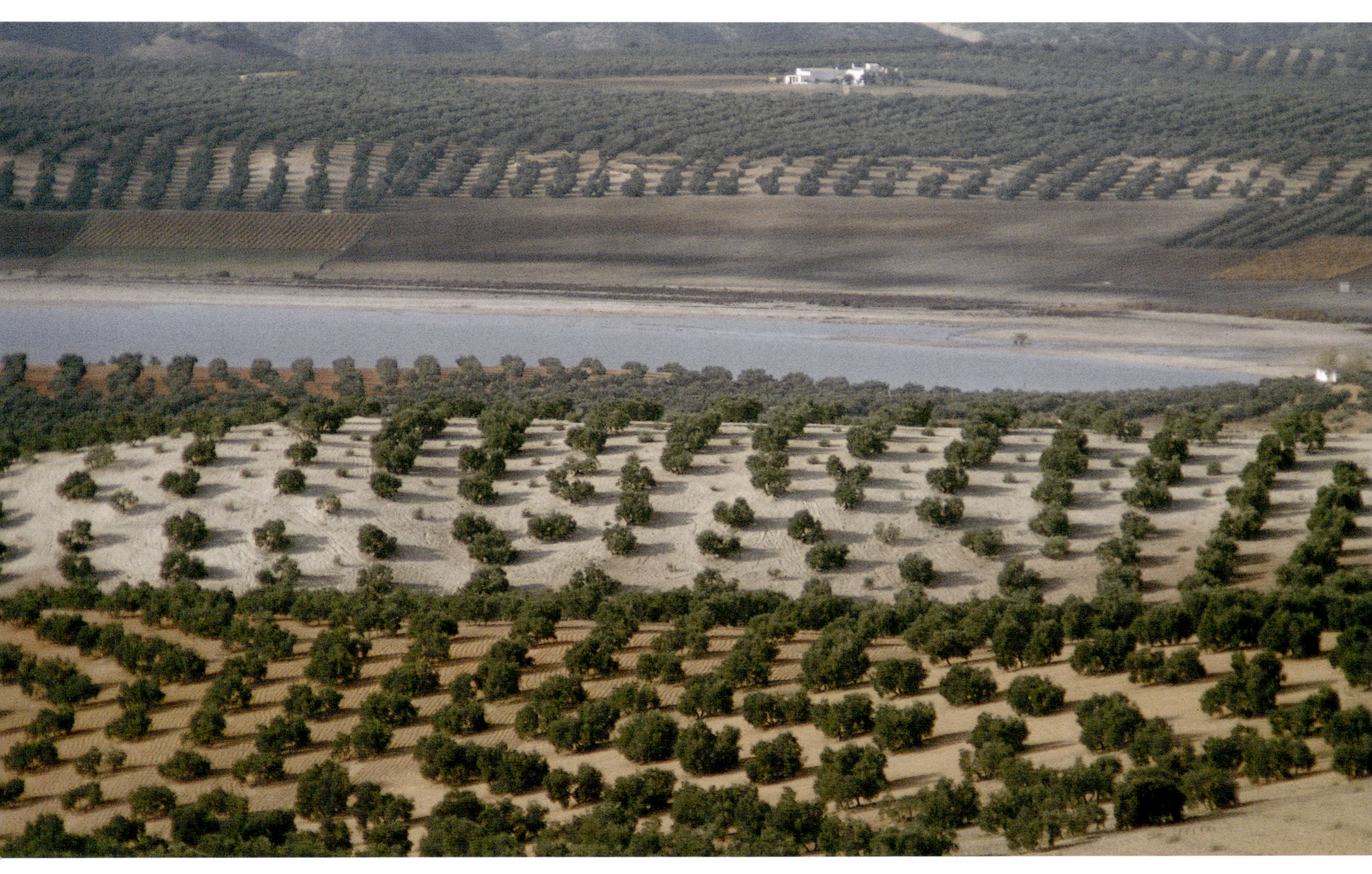

ABOVE
Málaga, Andalucía, in June

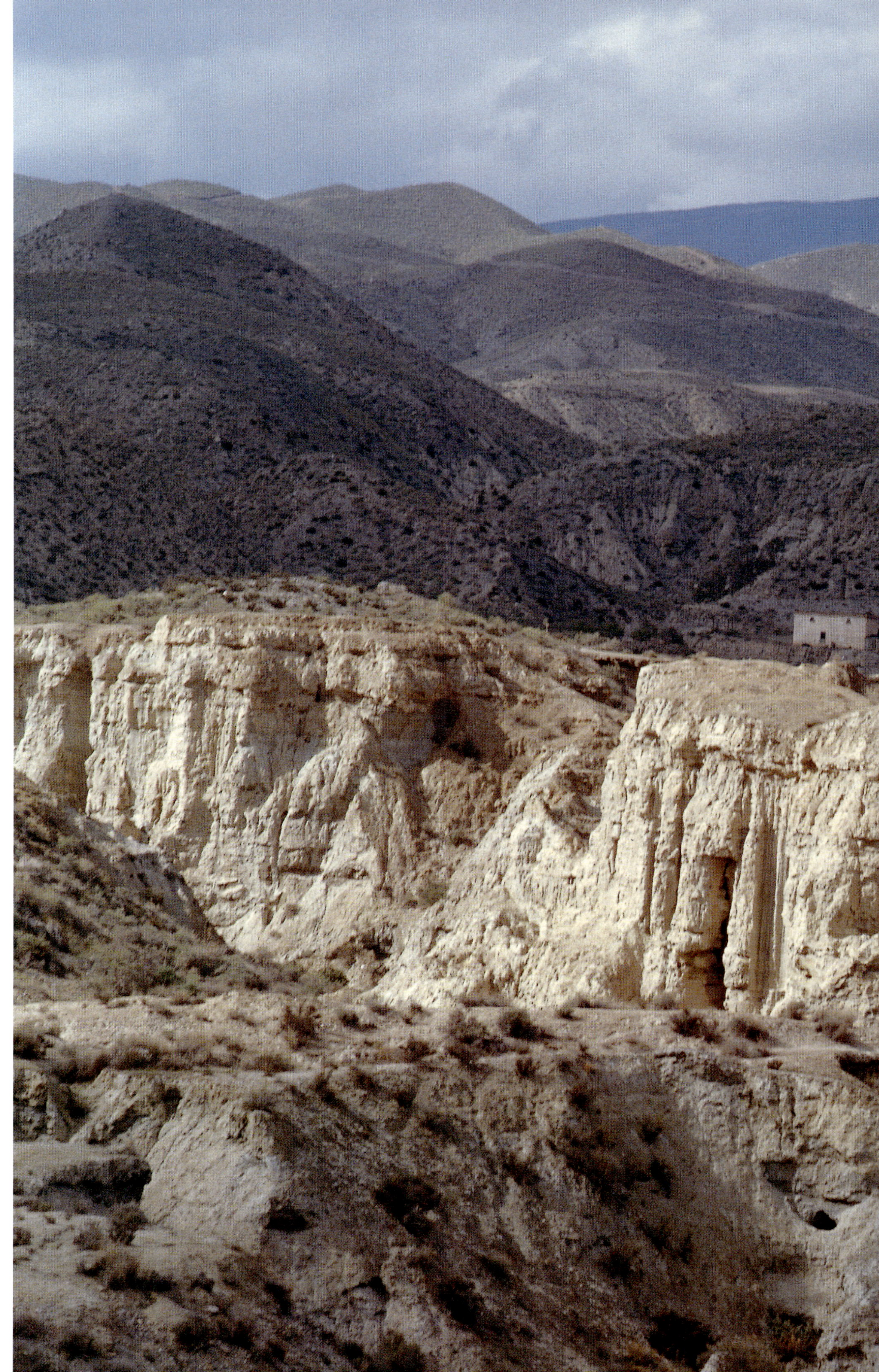

RIGHT
Almería, Andalucía, in March

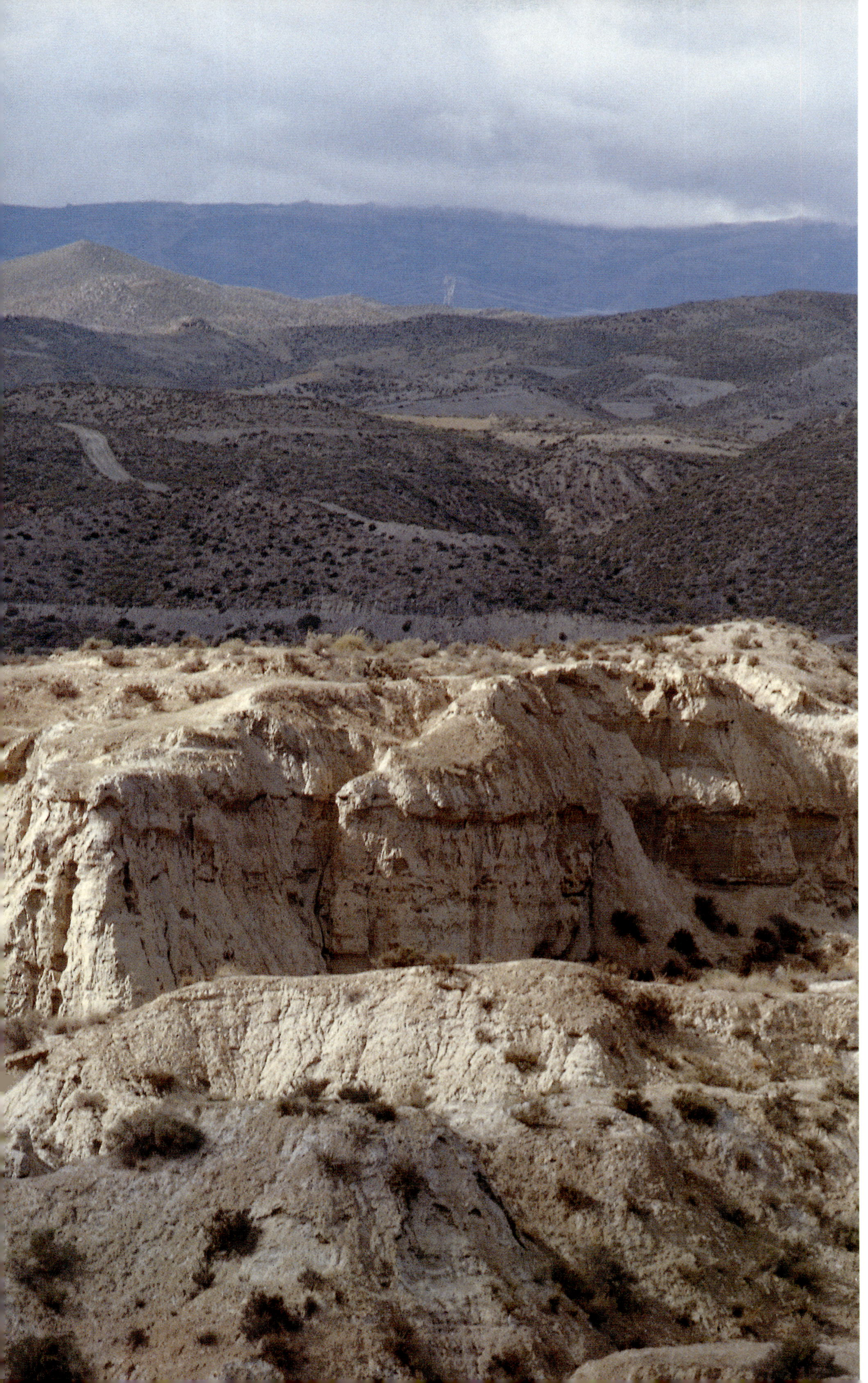

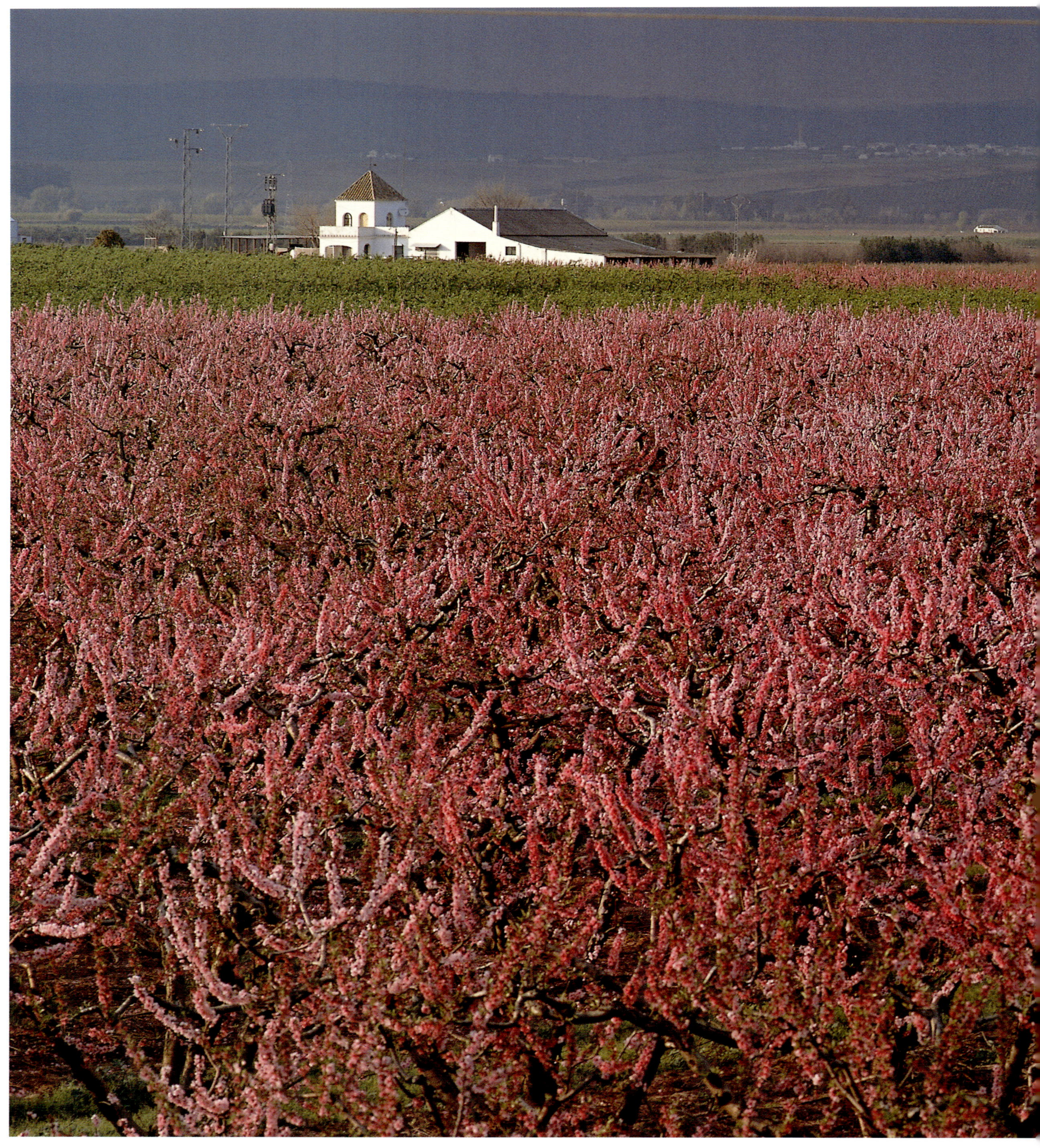

ABOVE
Sevilla, Andalucía, in March

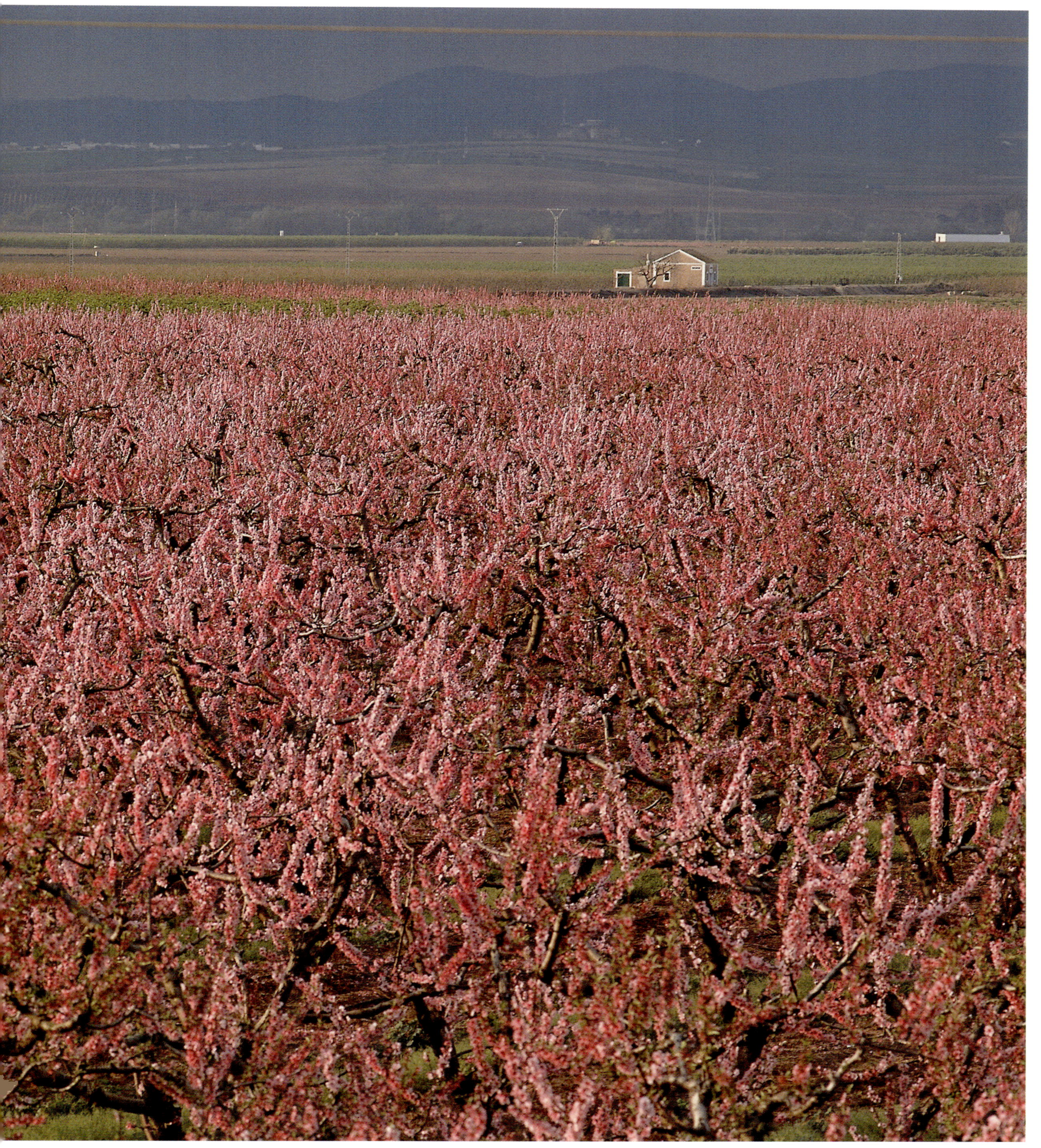

FOLLOWING PAGES LEFT AND RIGHT
Huelva, Andalucía, in September

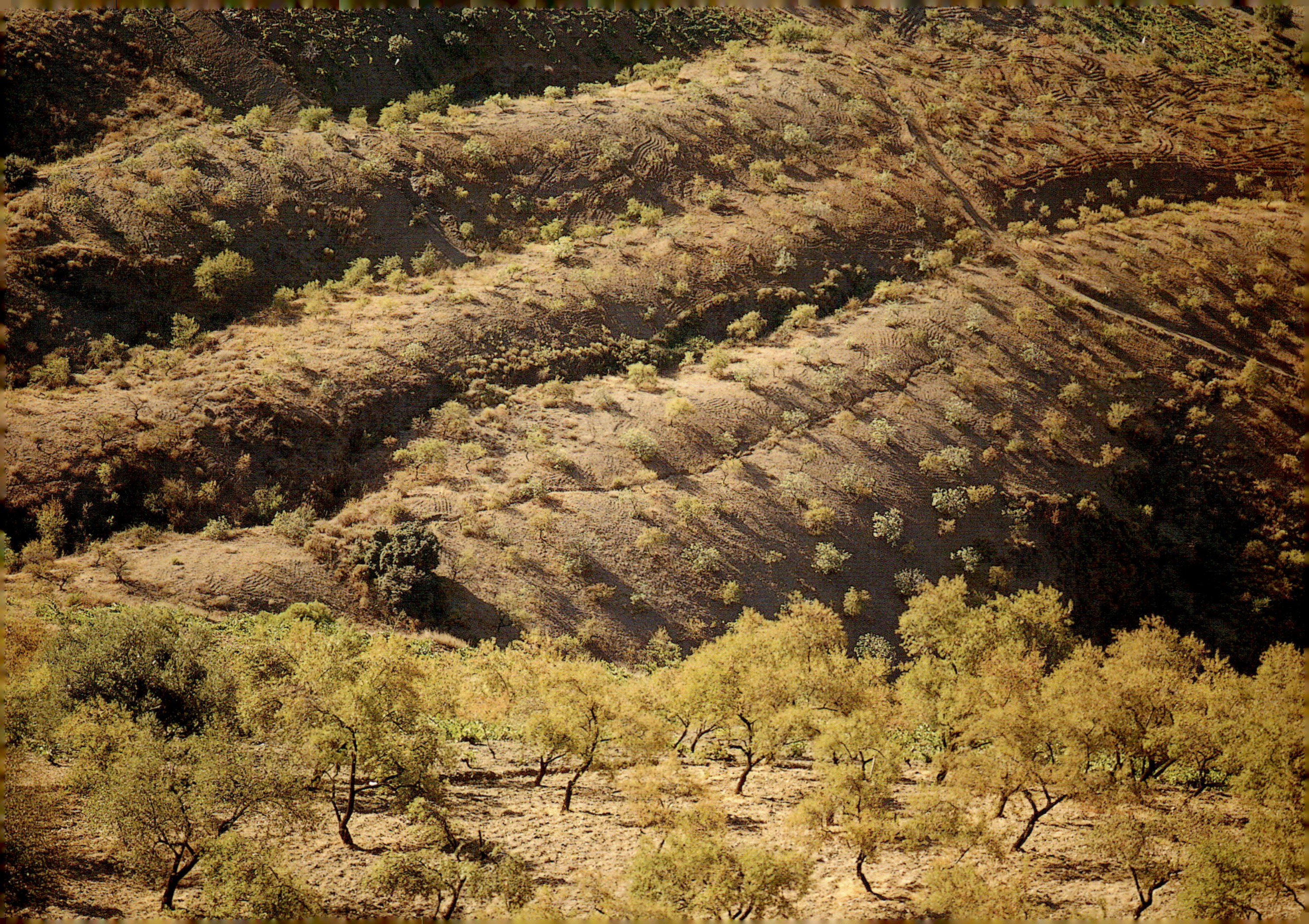

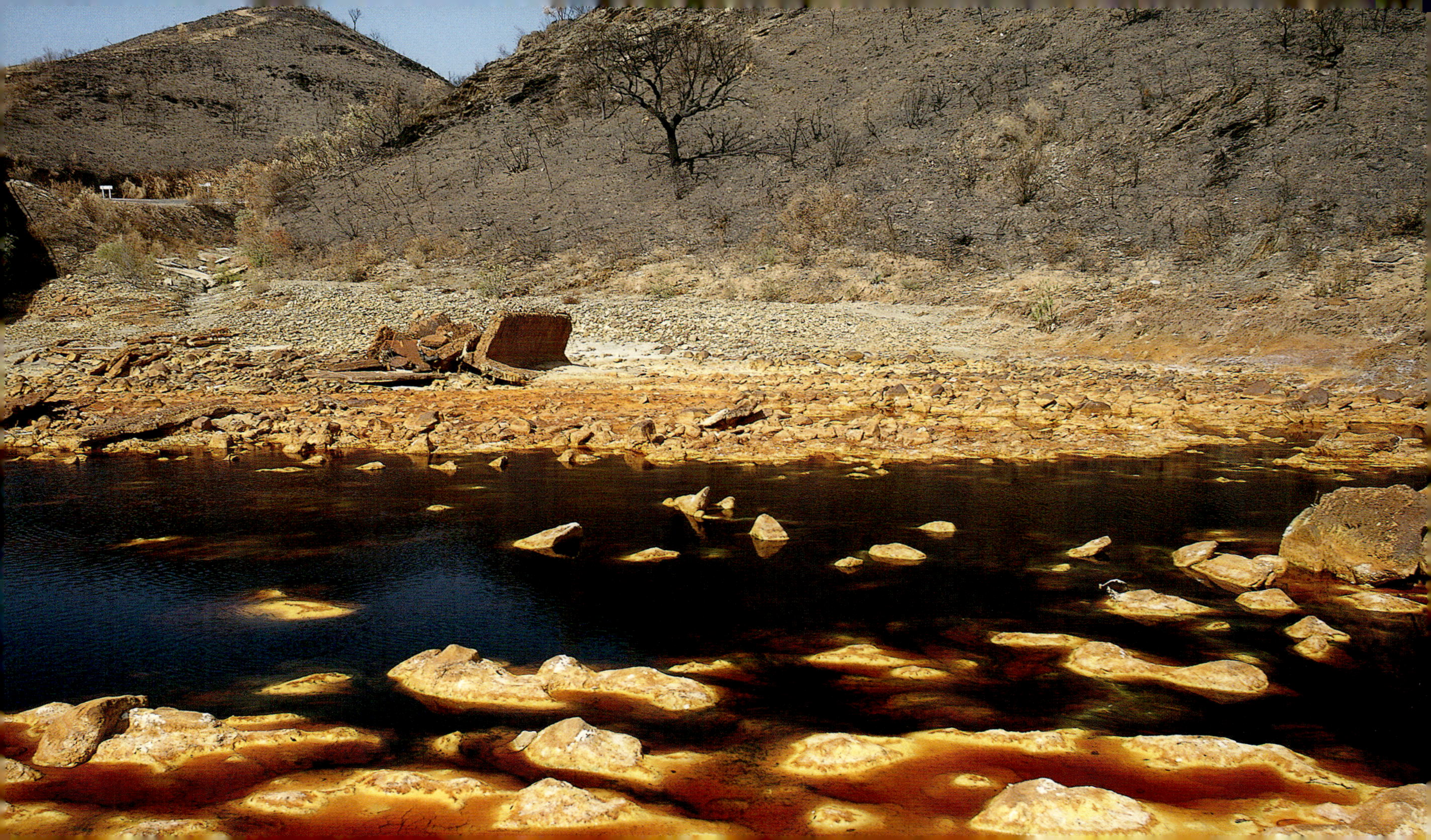

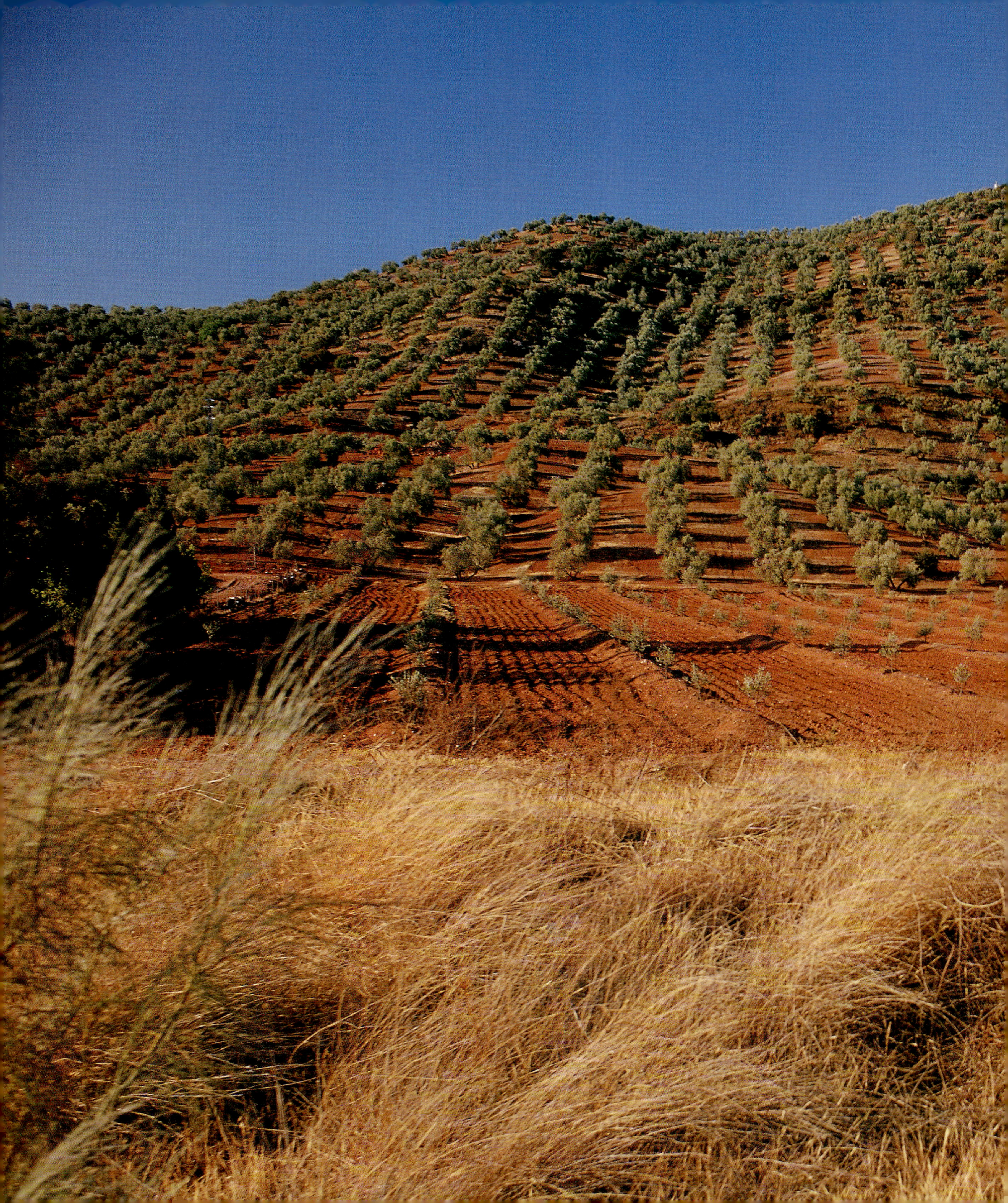

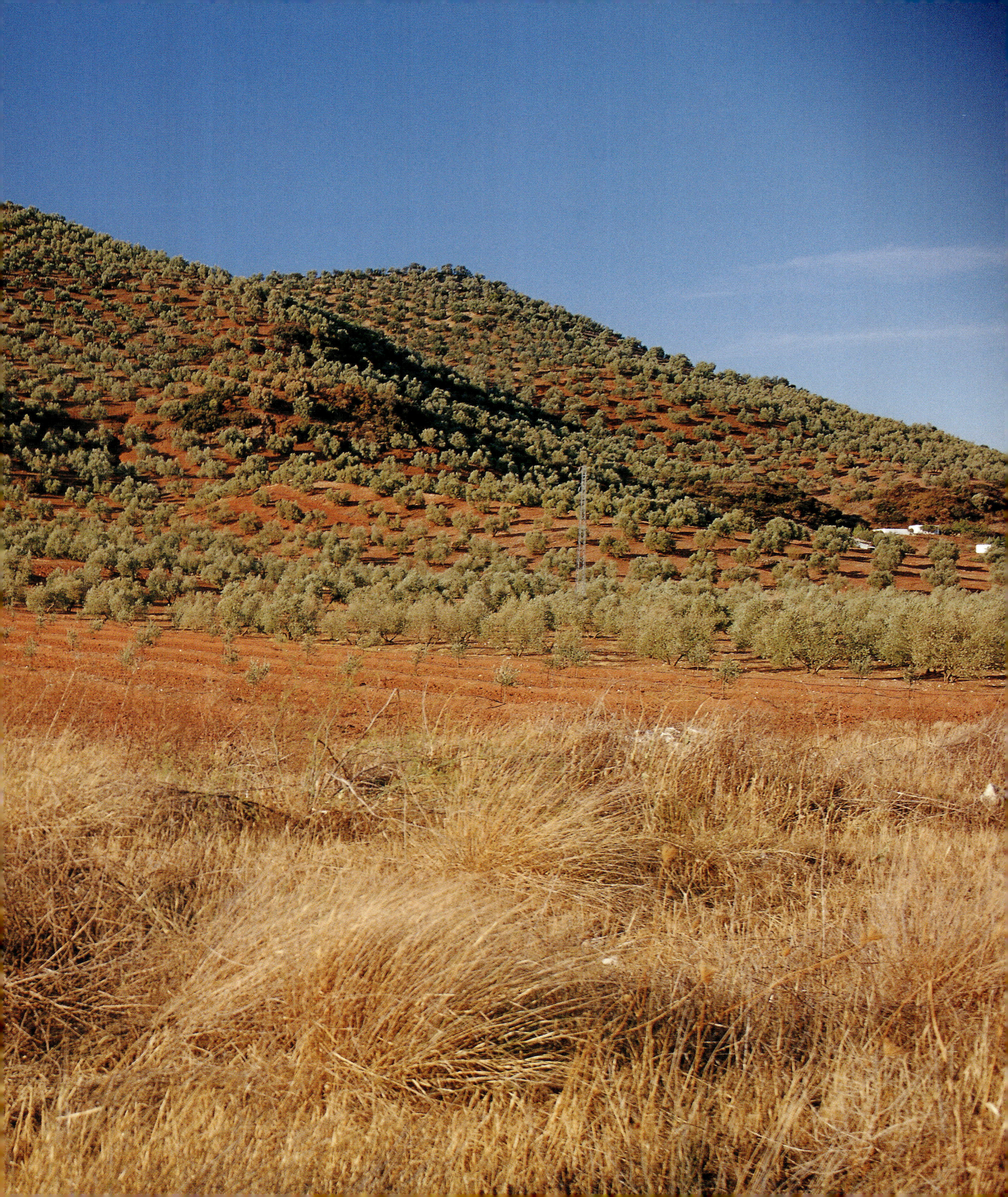

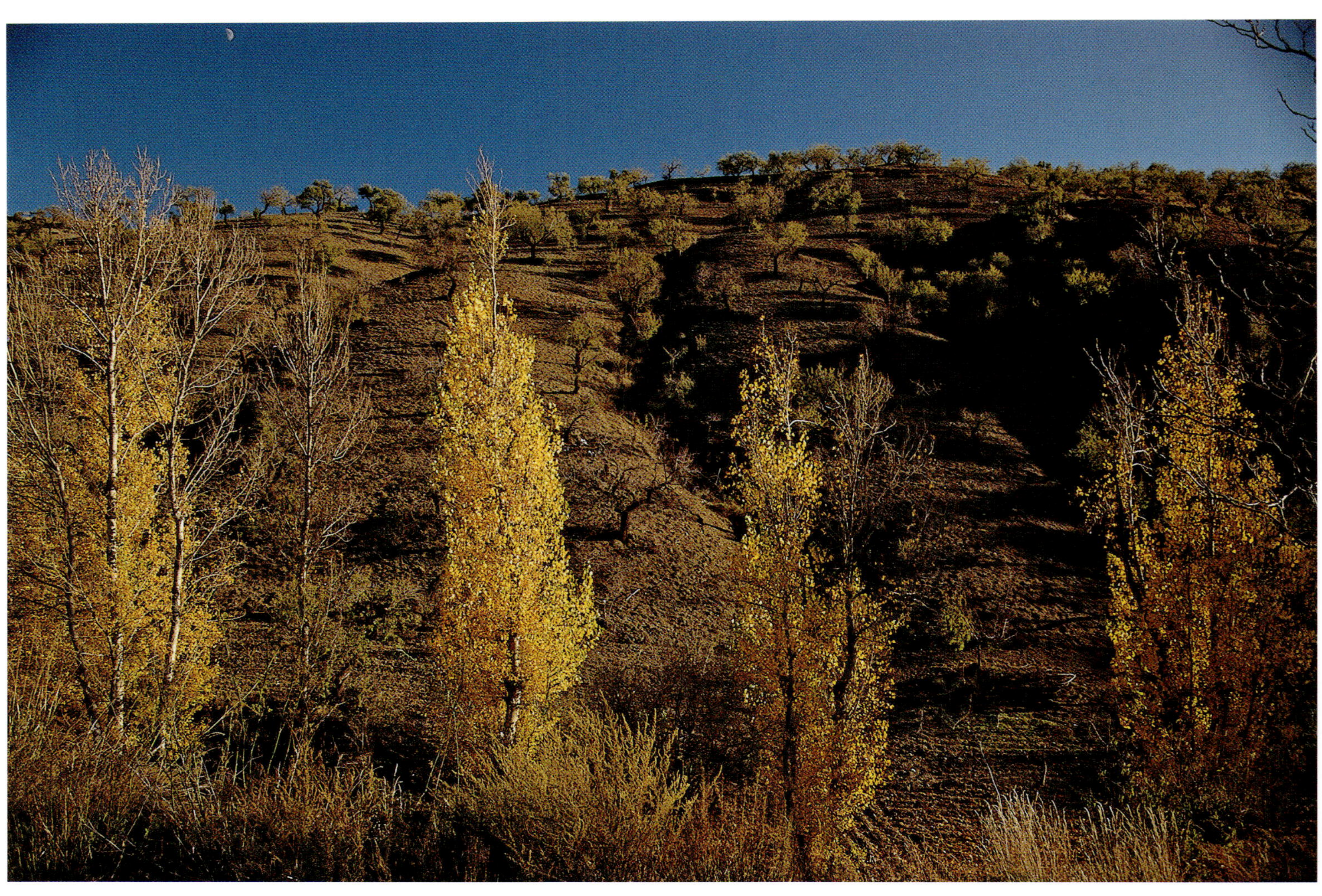

ABOVE
Granada, Andalucía, in November

PREVIOUS PAGES
Jaén, Andalucía, in September

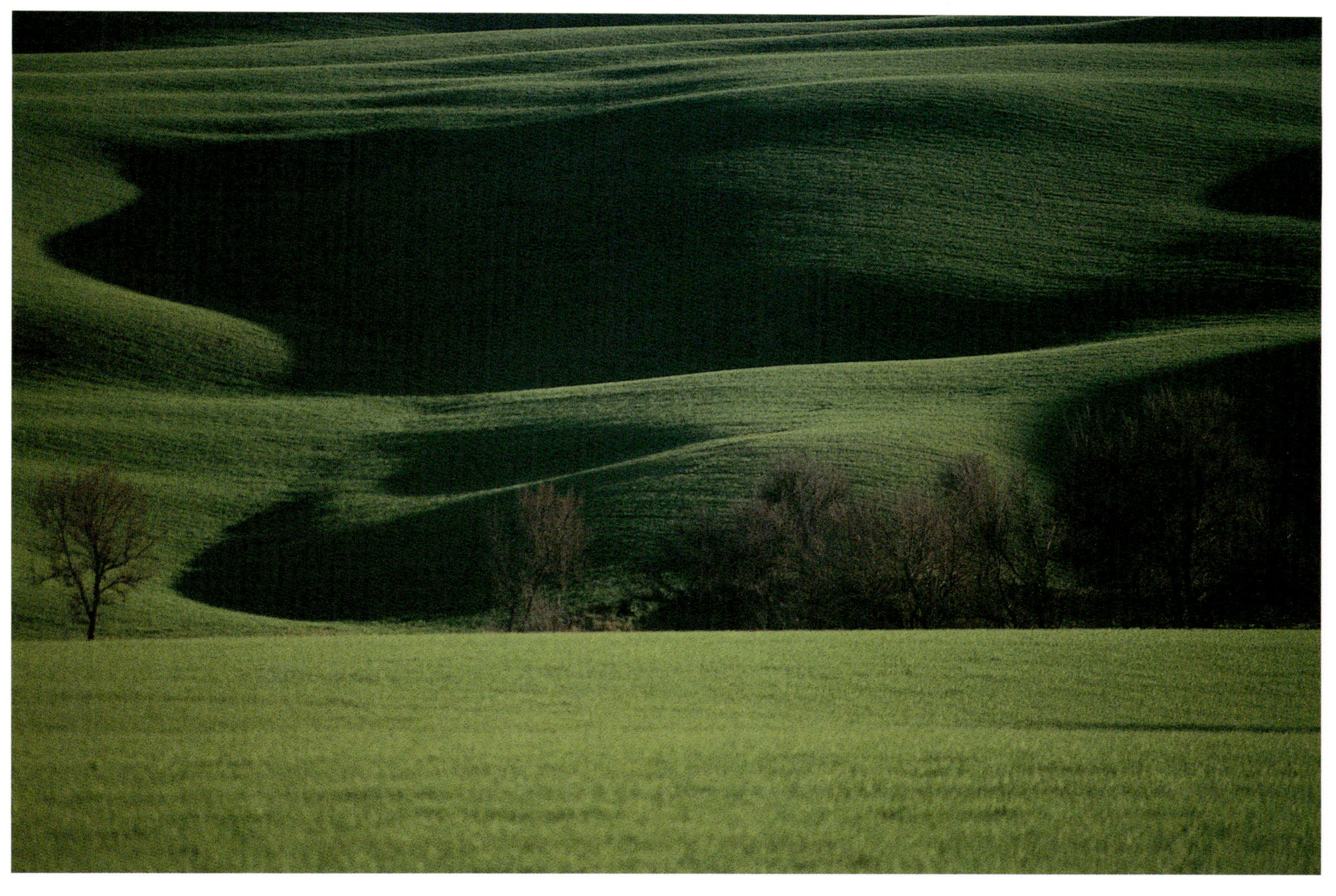

ABOVE
Córdoba, Andalucía, in December

FOLLOWING PAGES LEFT AND RIGHT
Córdoba, Andalucía, in December

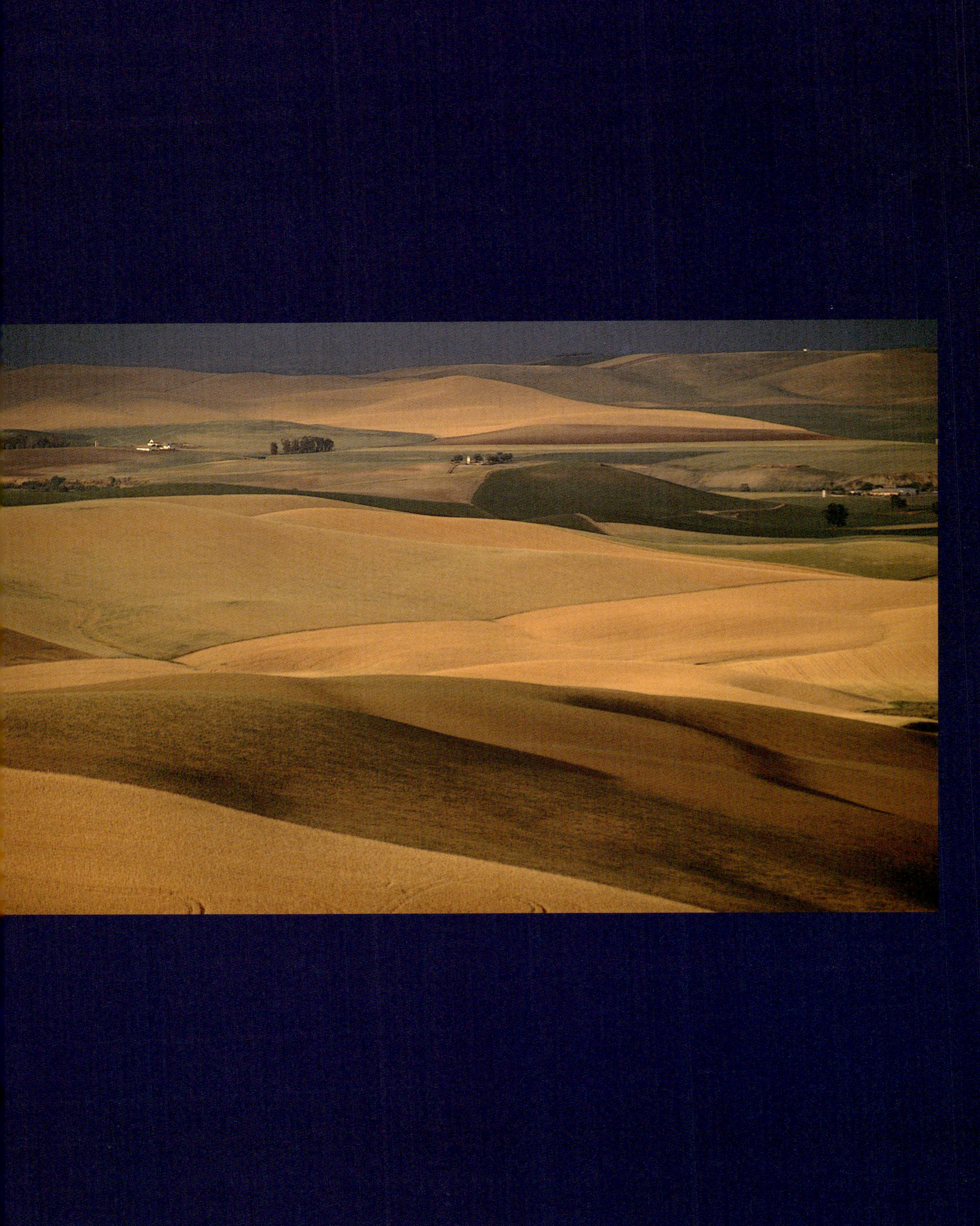

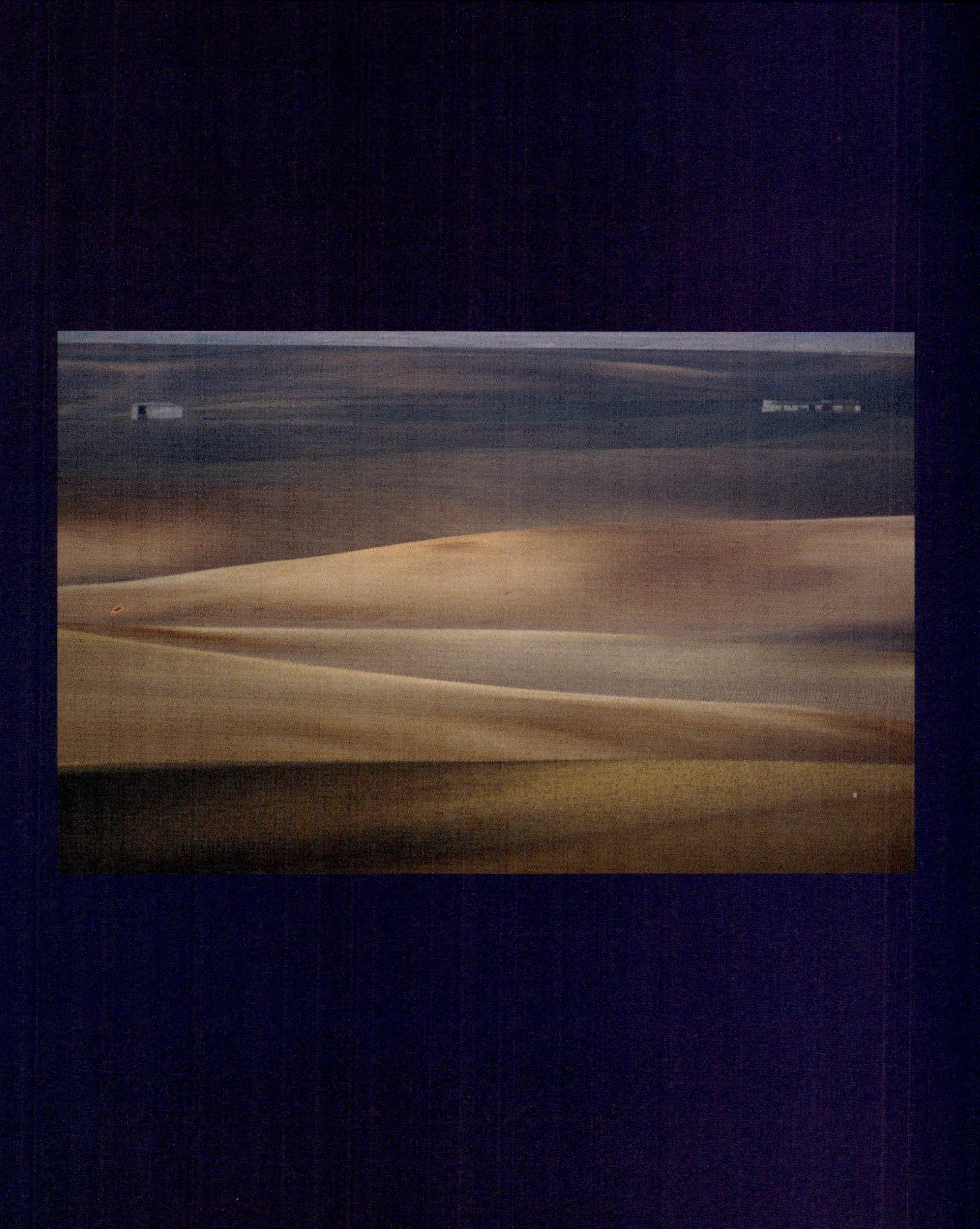

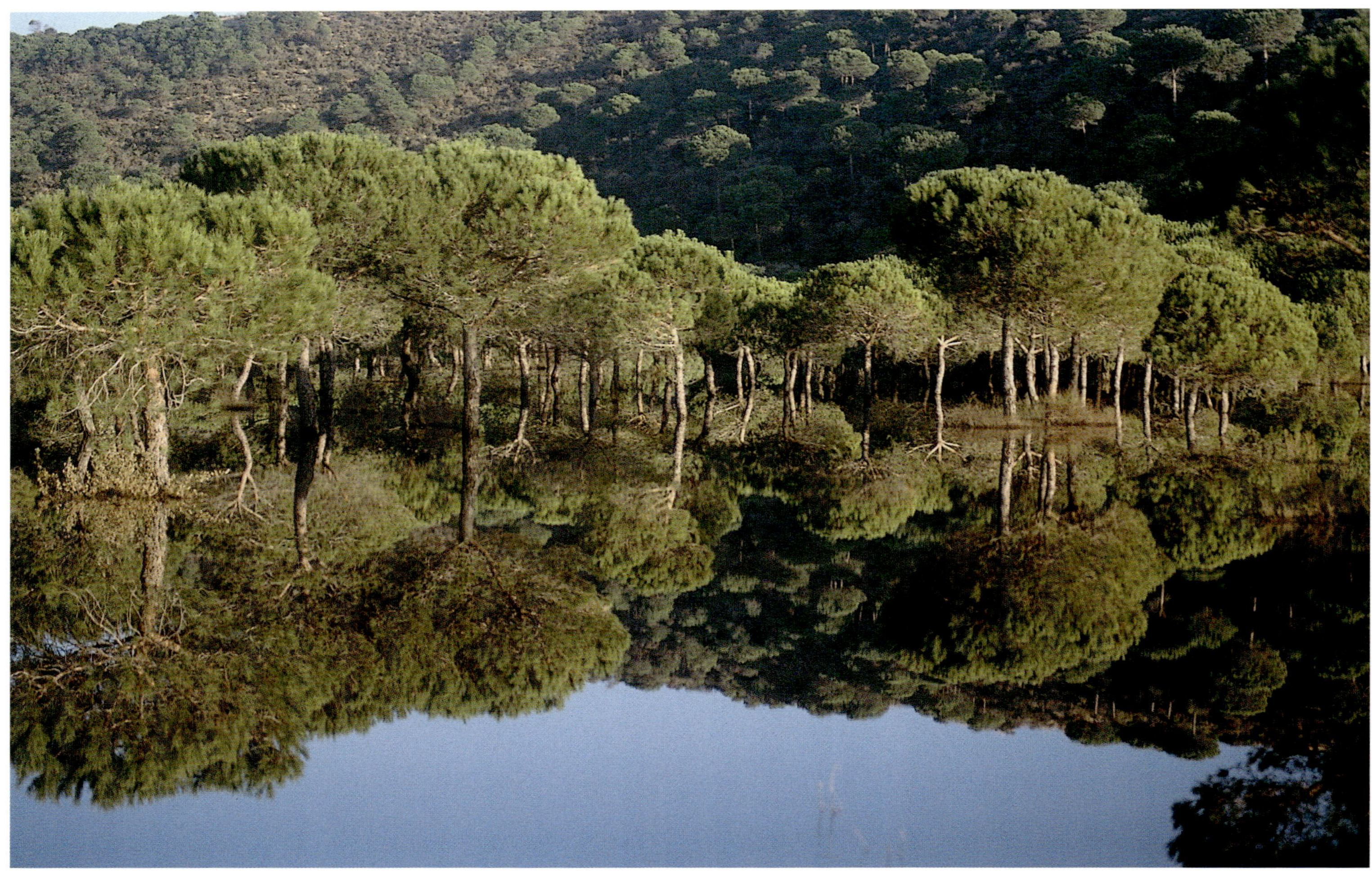

ABOVE LEFT AND RIGHT
Huelva, Andalucía, in December

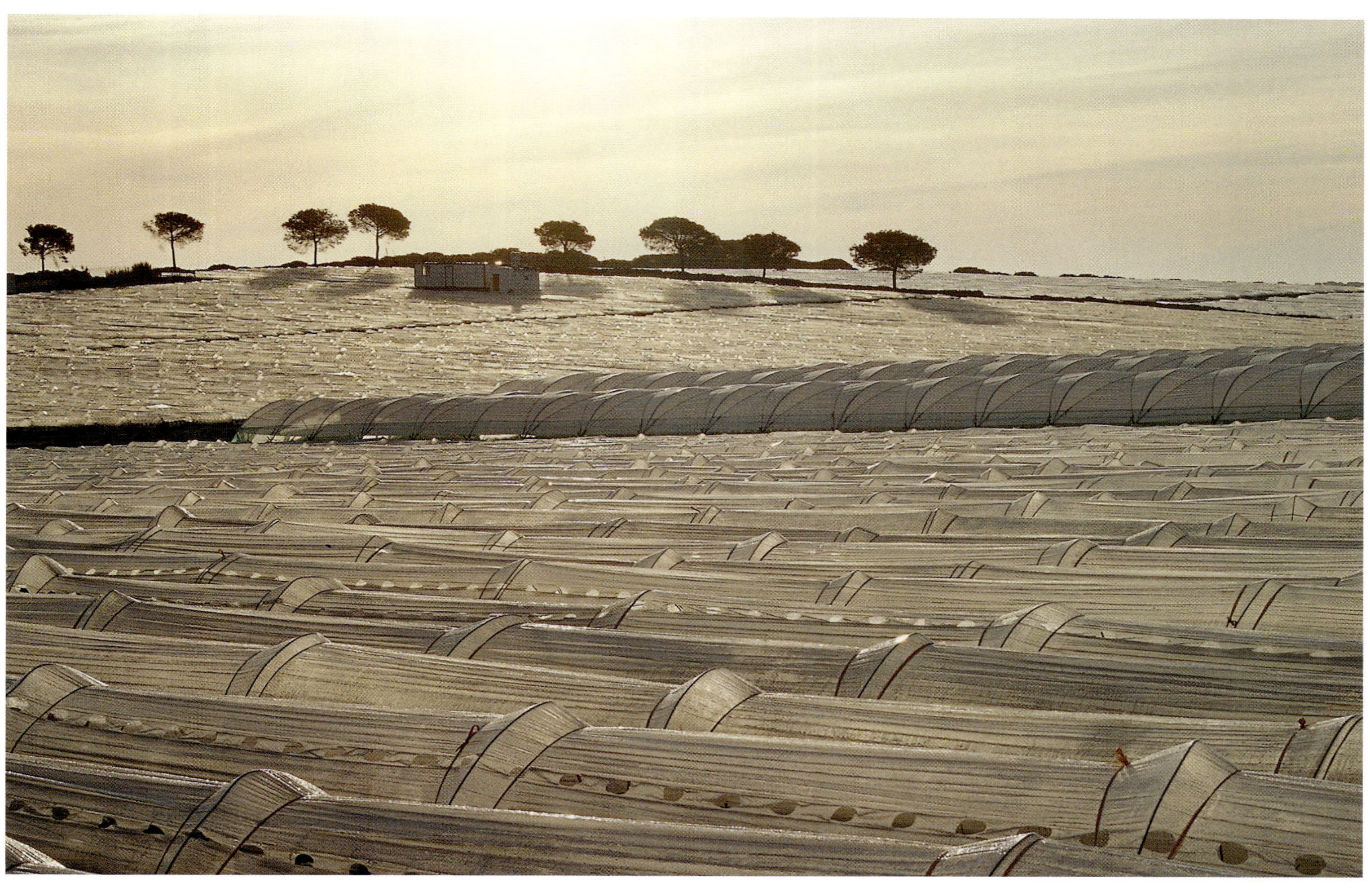

FOLLOWING PAGES
Sevilla, Andalucía, in December

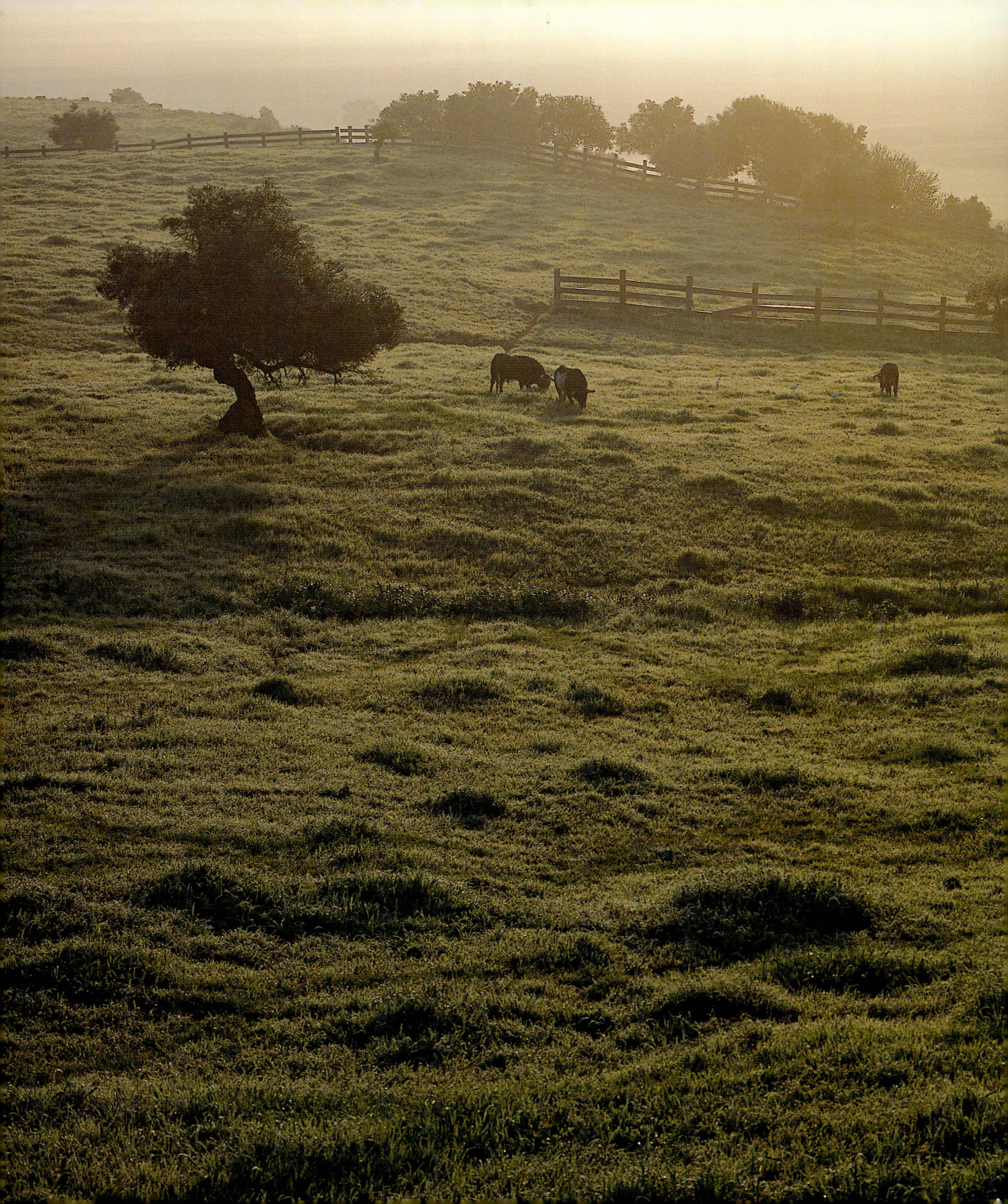

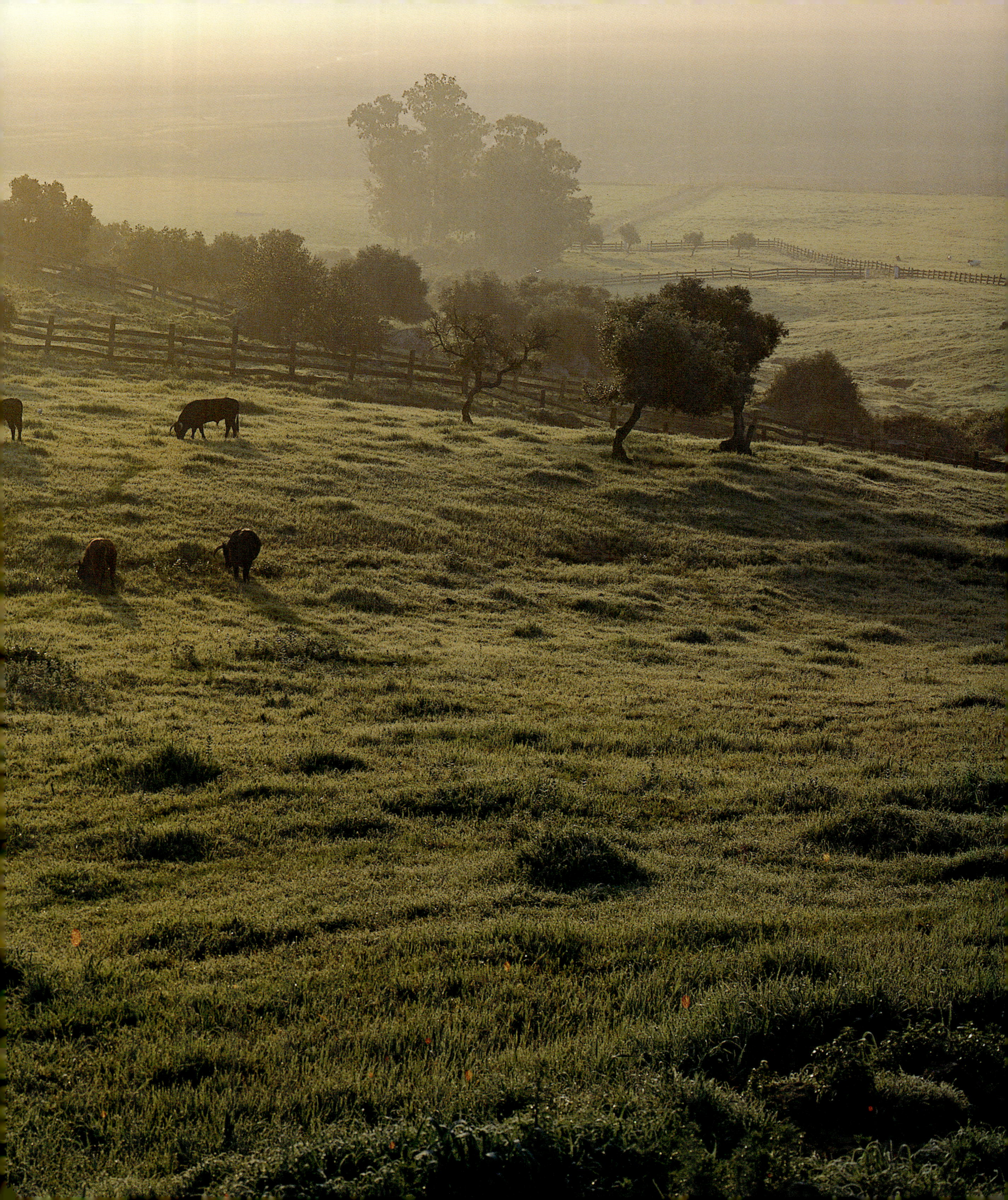

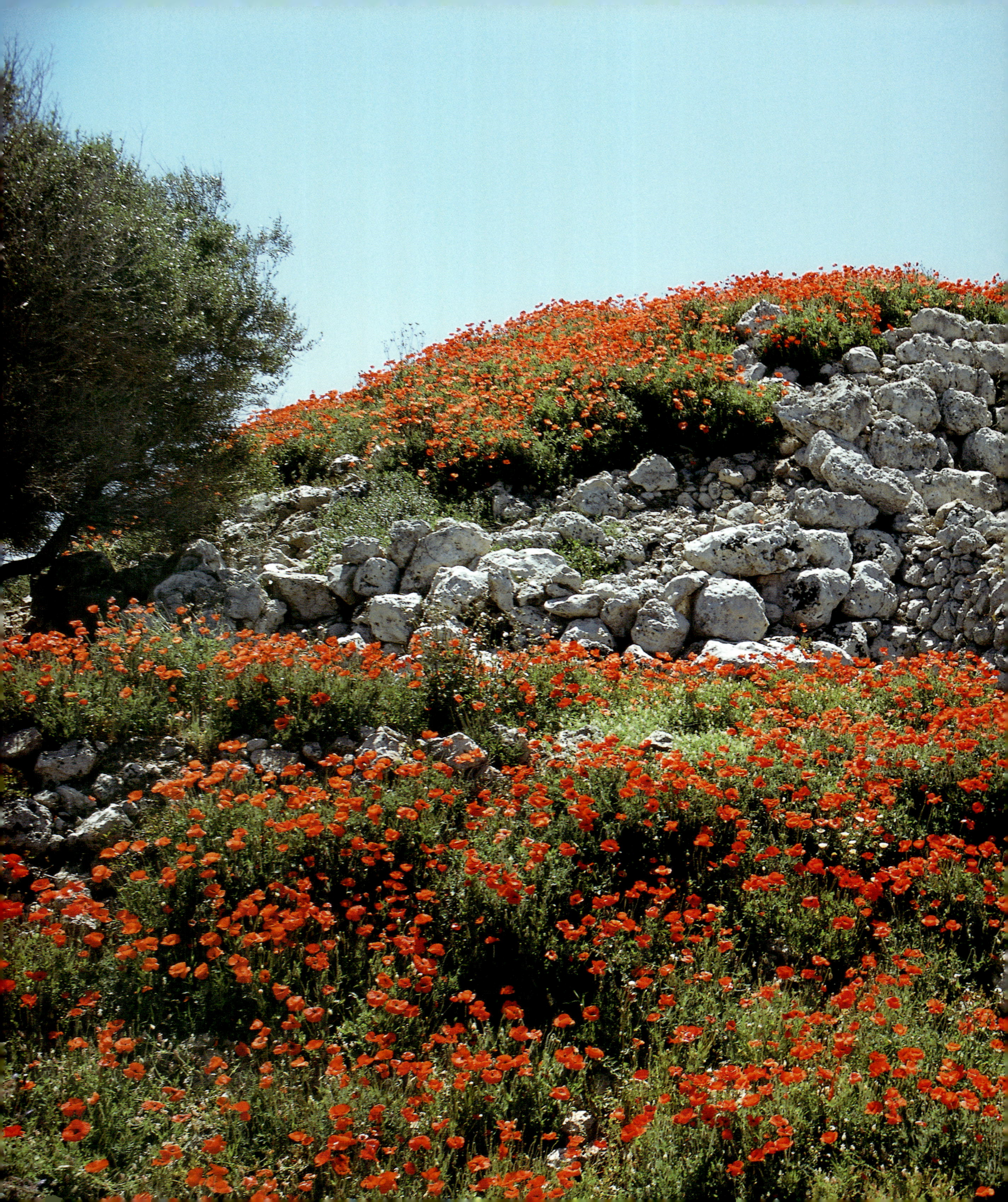

THE MEDITERRANEAN

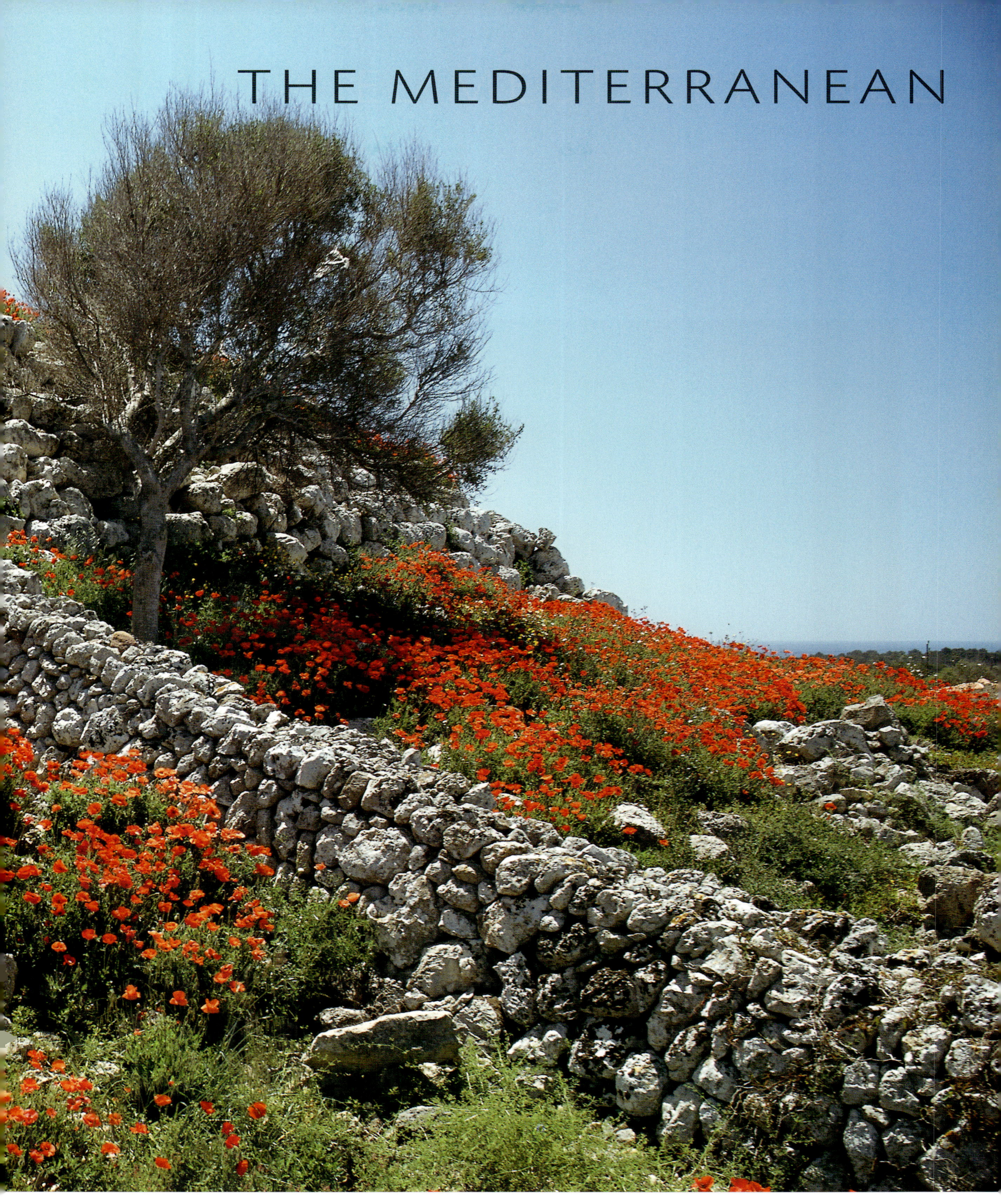

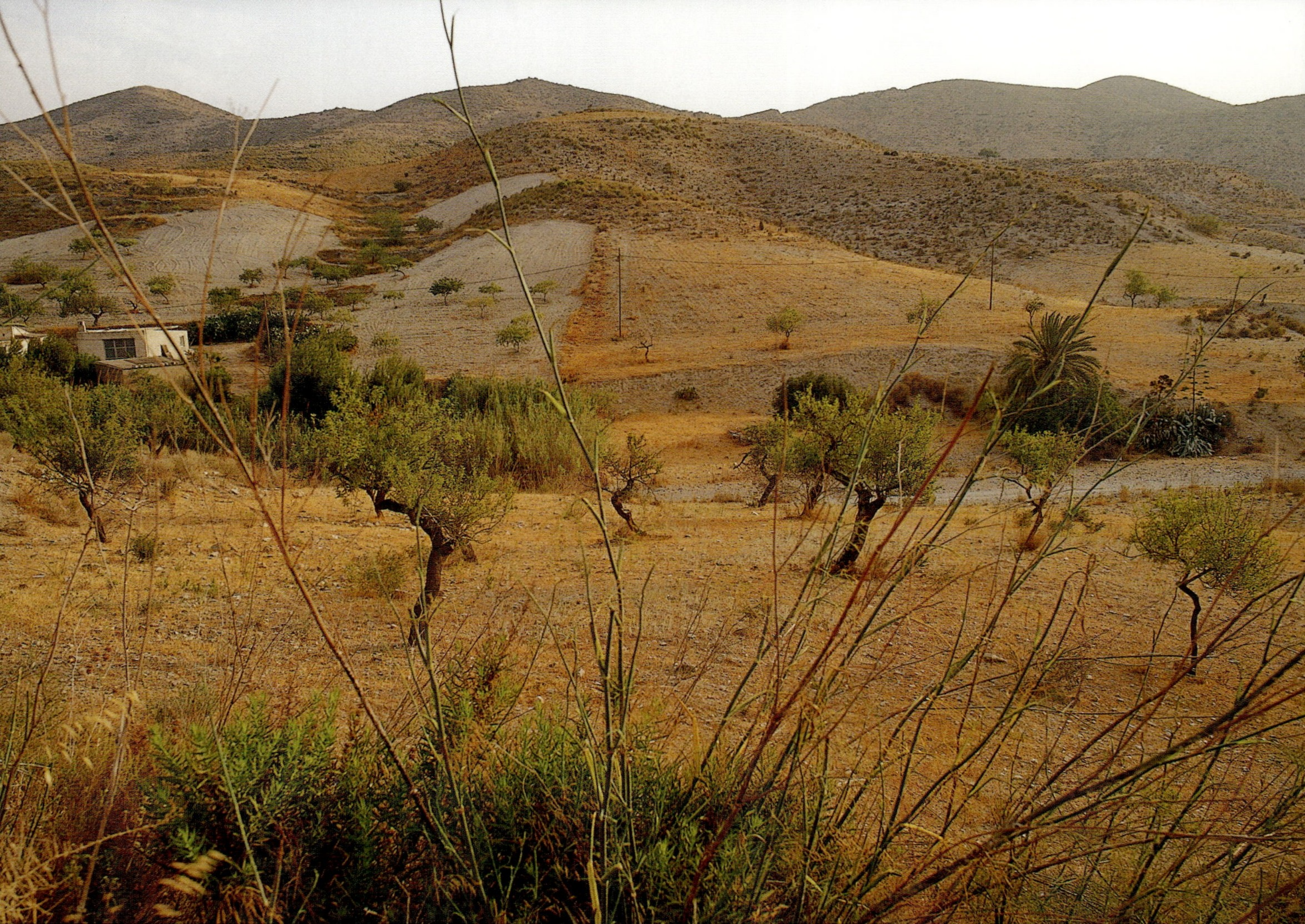

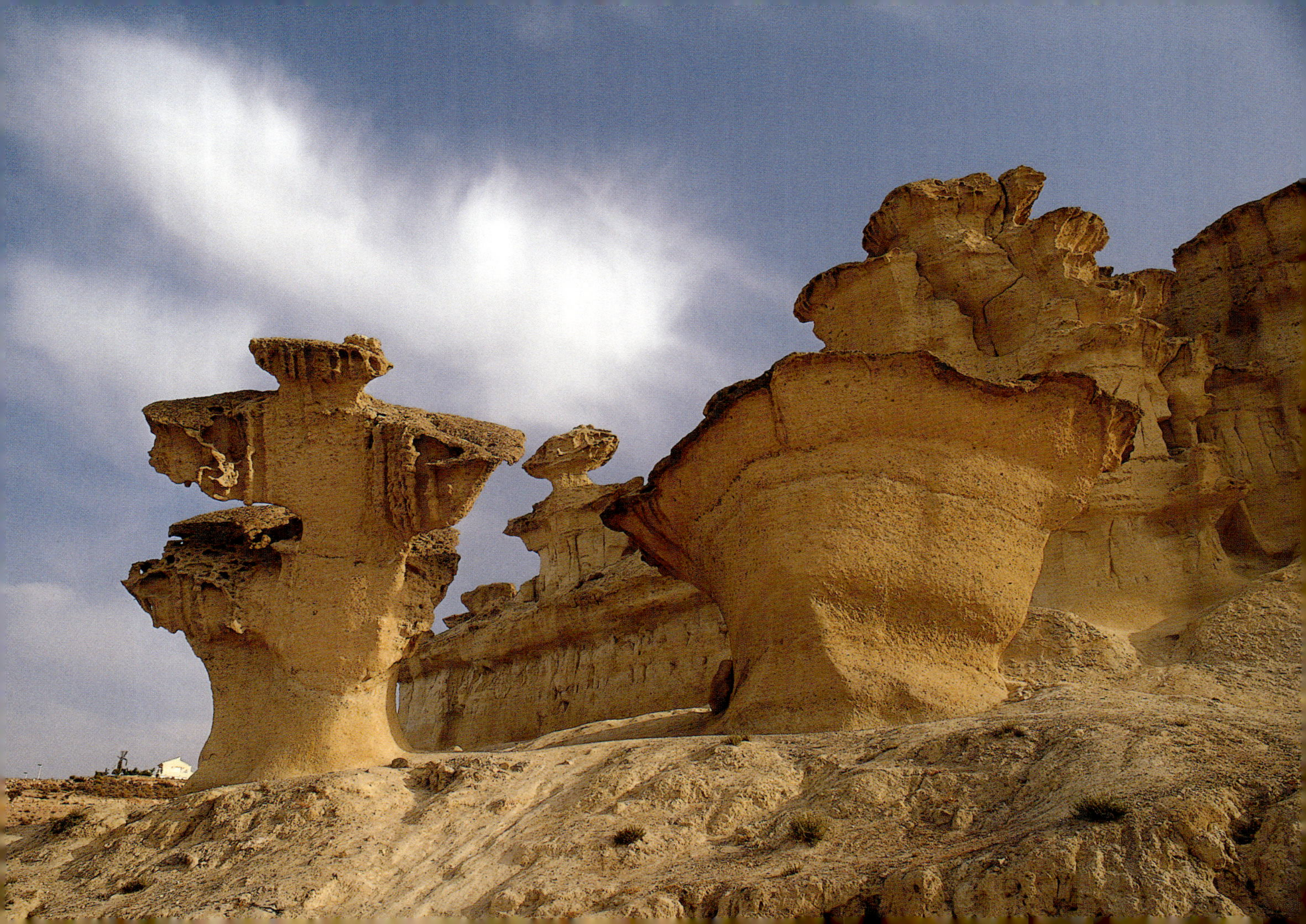

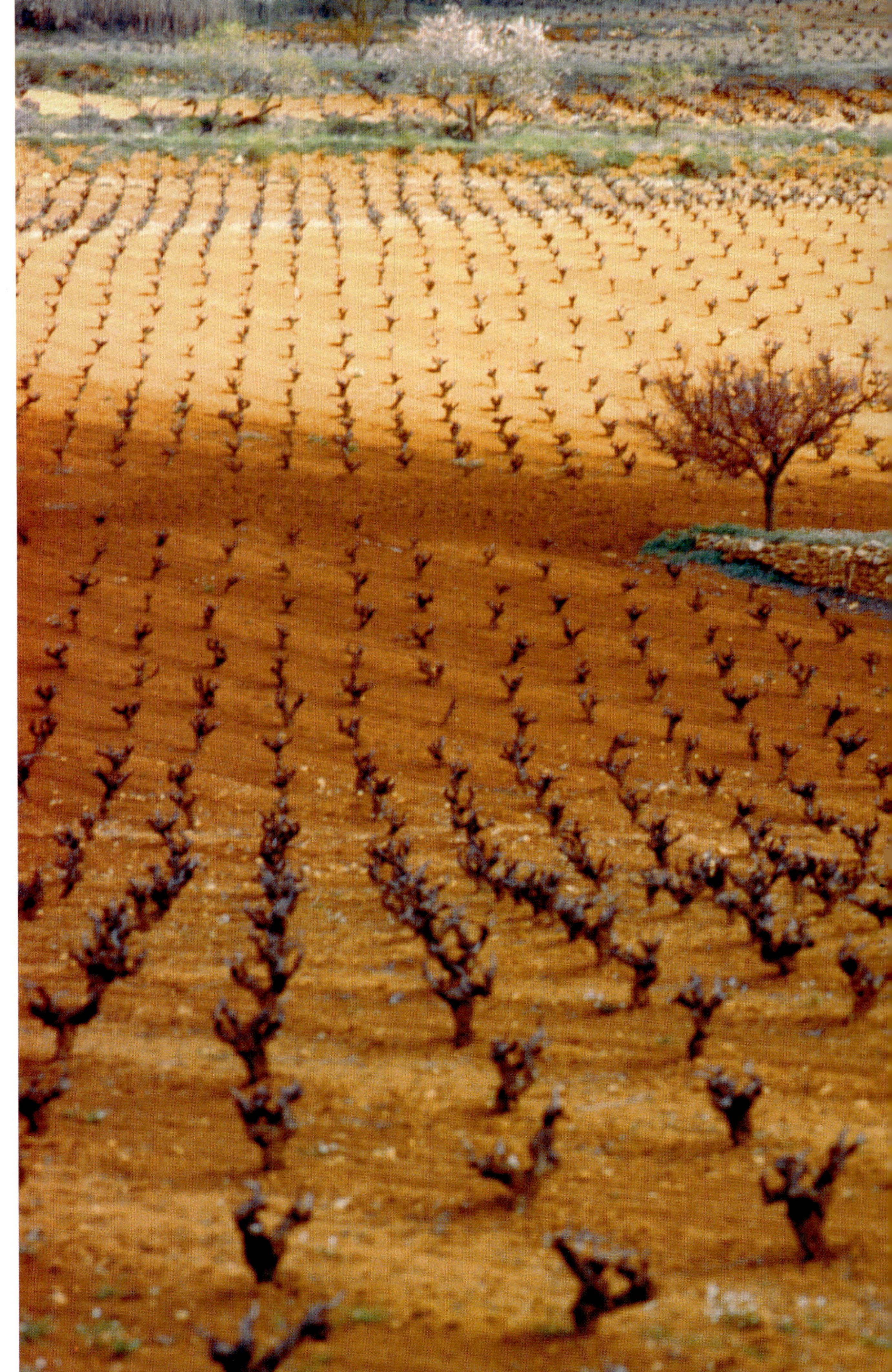

RIGHT
Valencia in May

FOLLOWING PAGES
Ibiza, Balearic Islands, in July

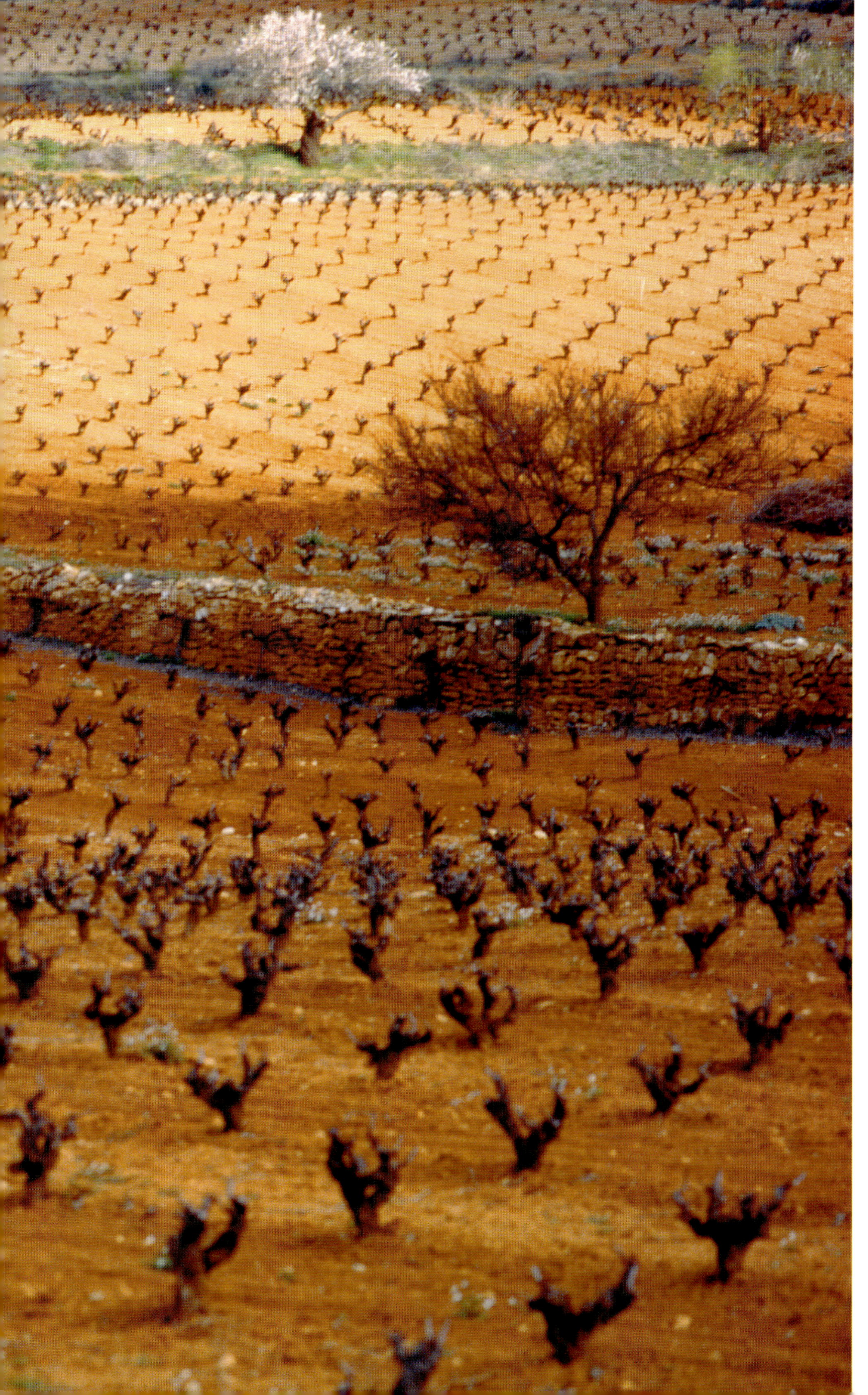

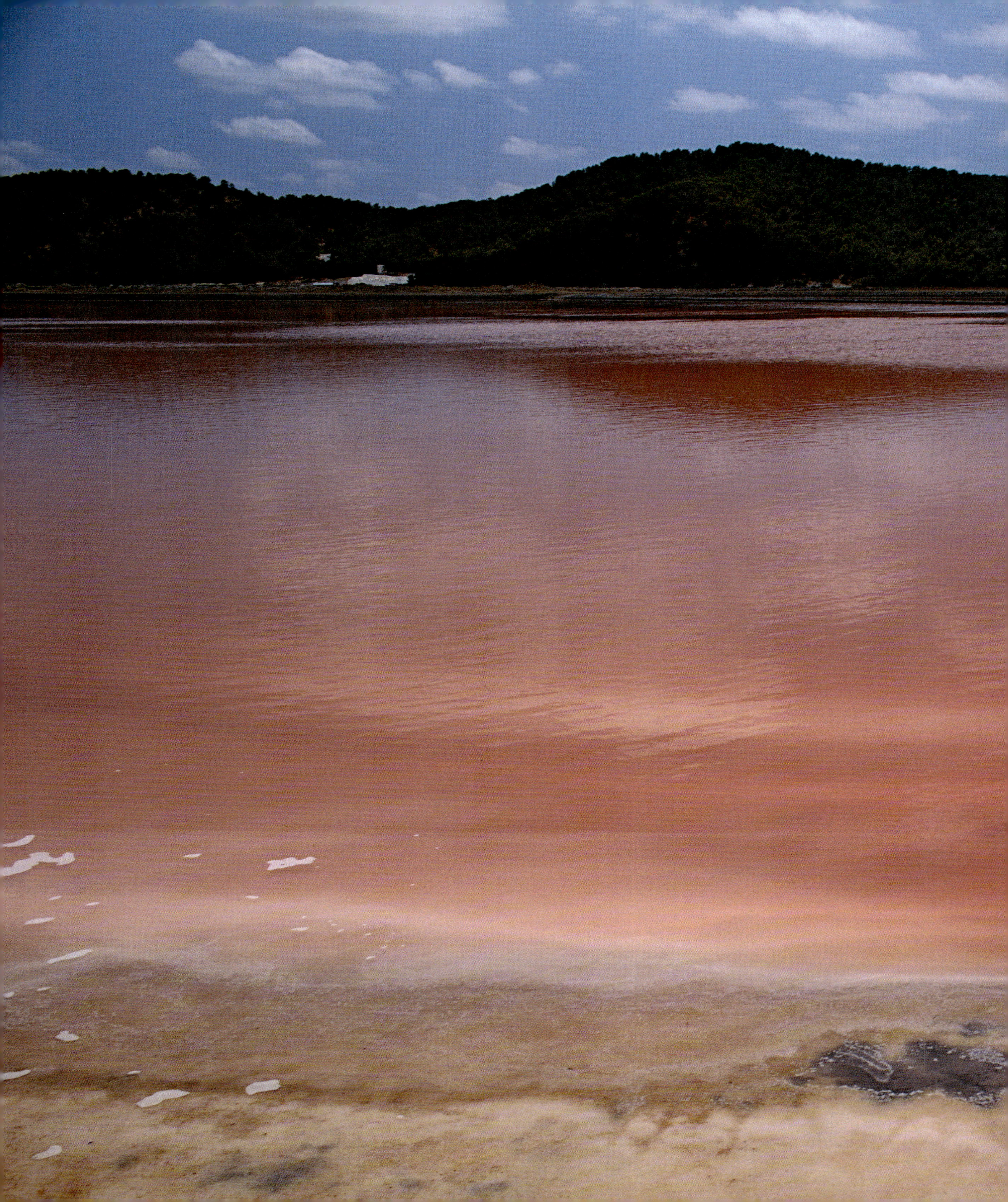

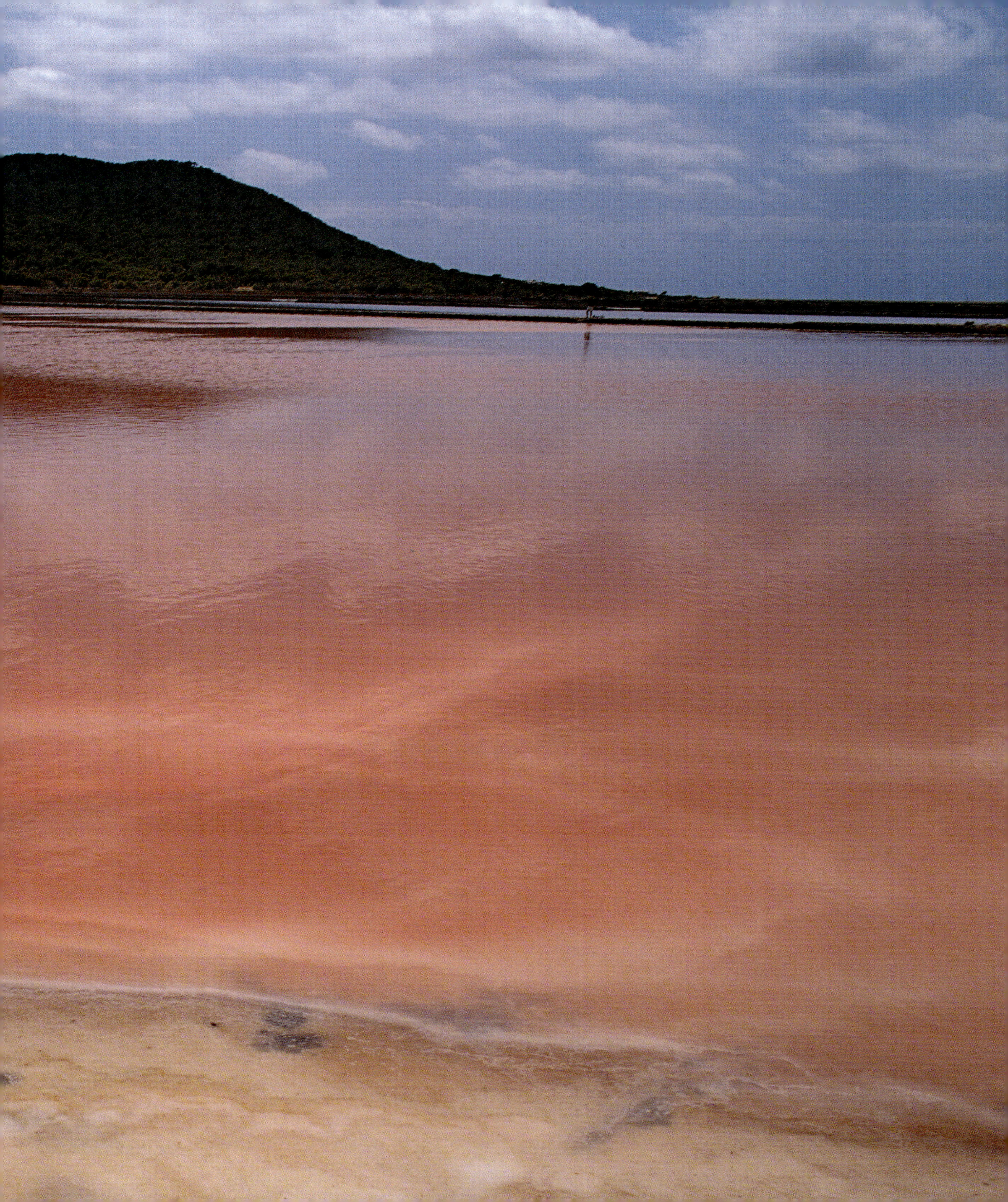

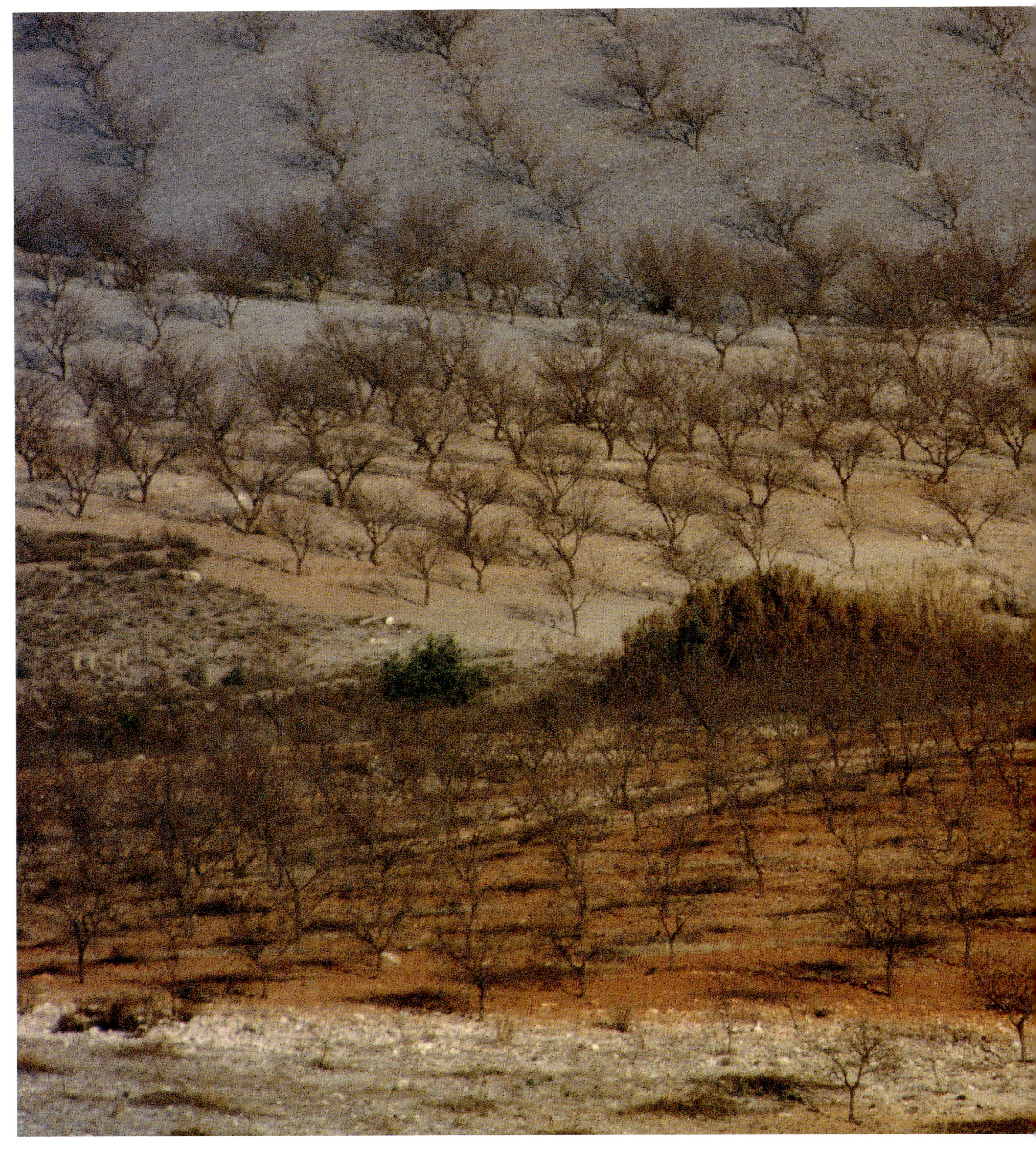

ABOVE
Murcia in December

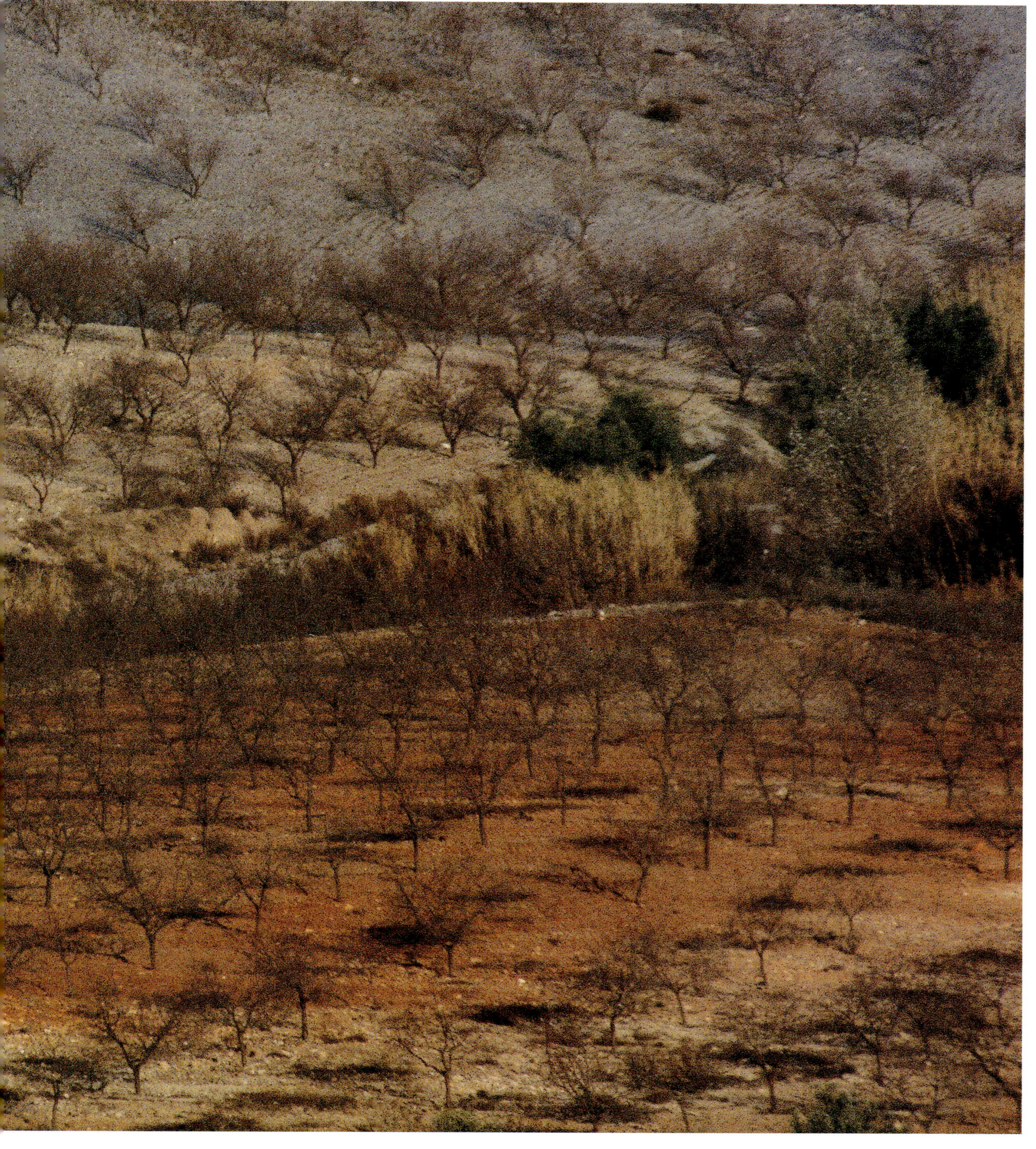

THE CANARY ISLANDS

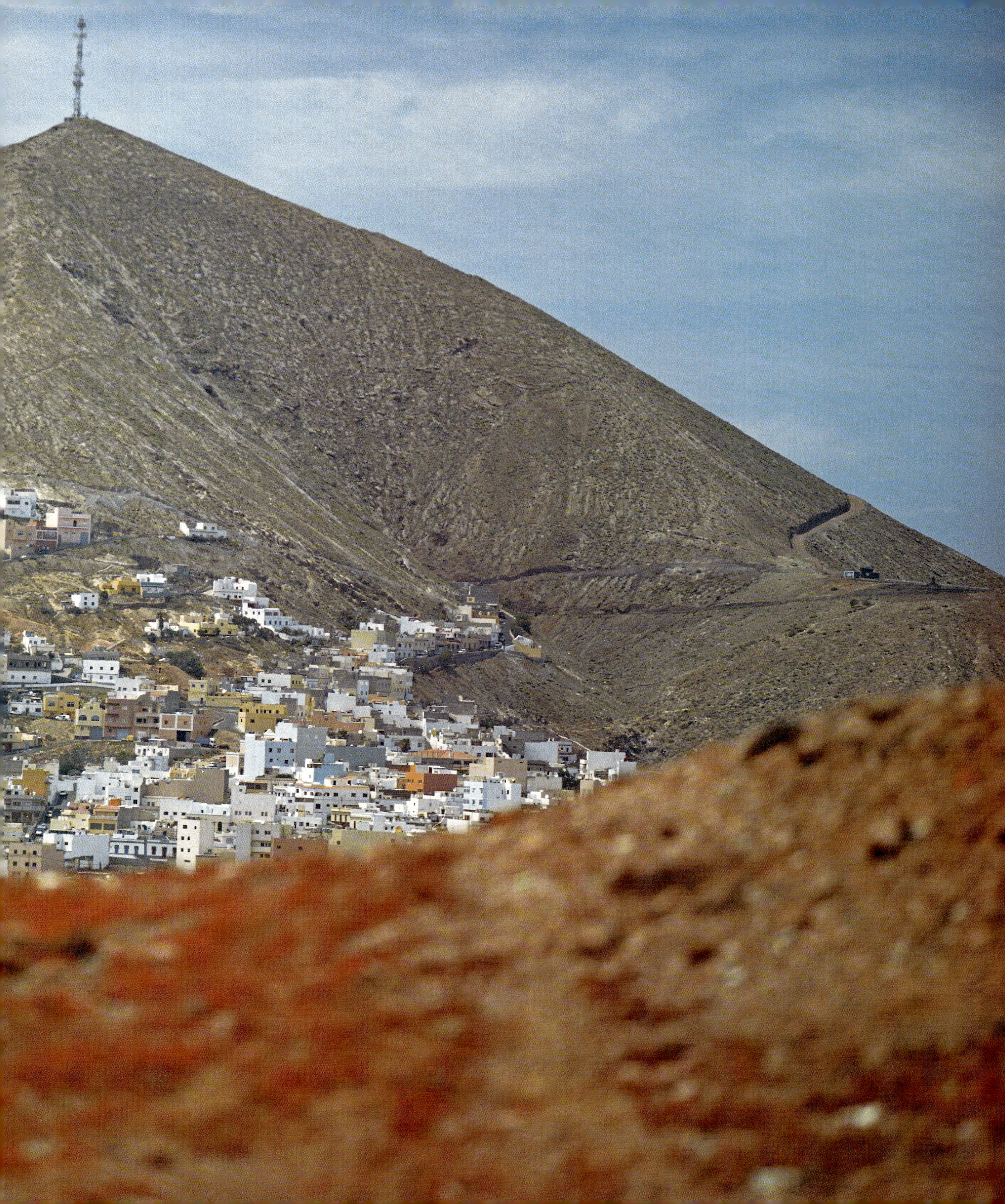

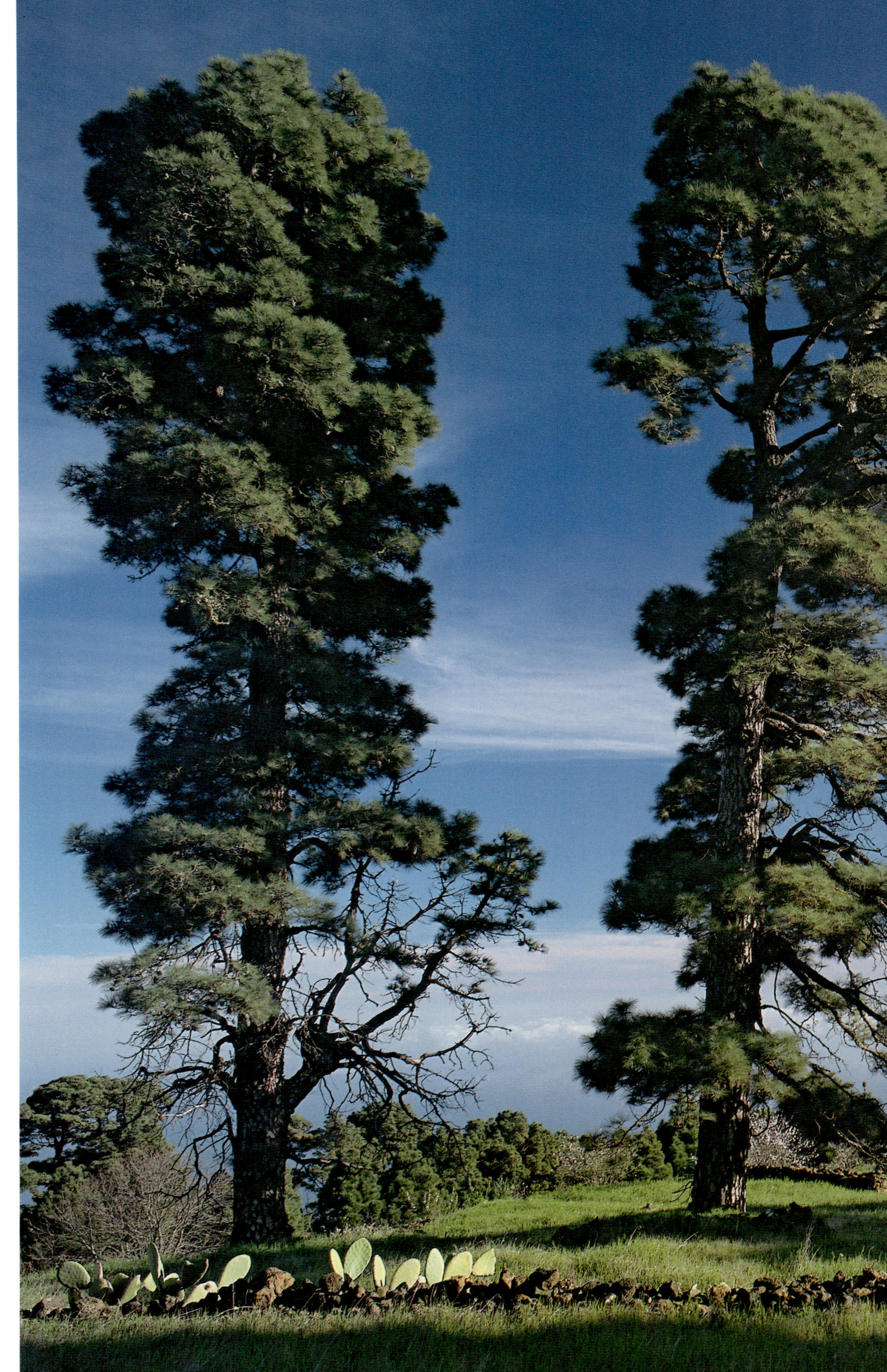

RIGHT
El Hierro in January

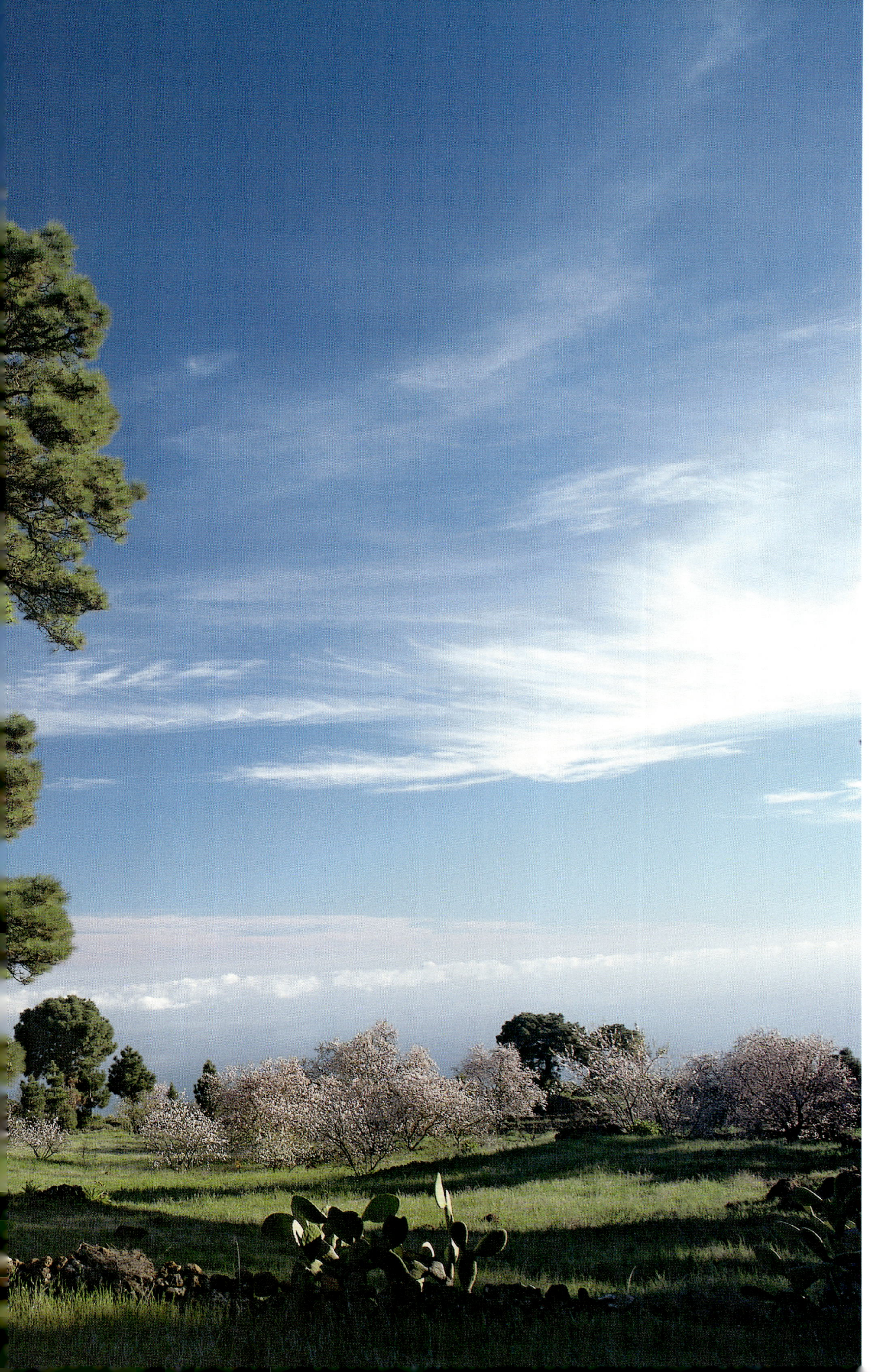

FOLLOWING PAGES
LEFT Gran Canaria in May
RIGHT Tenerife in May

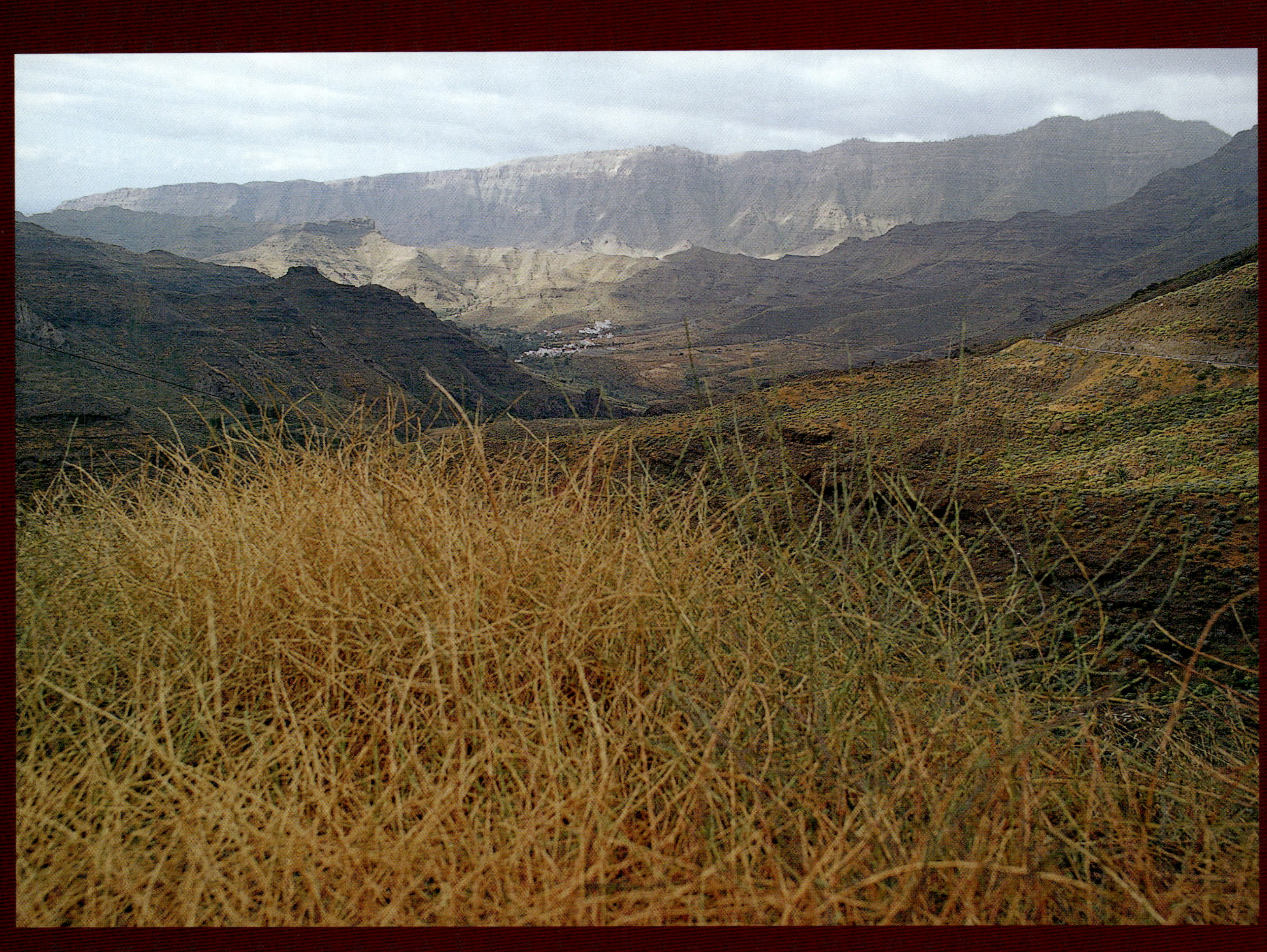

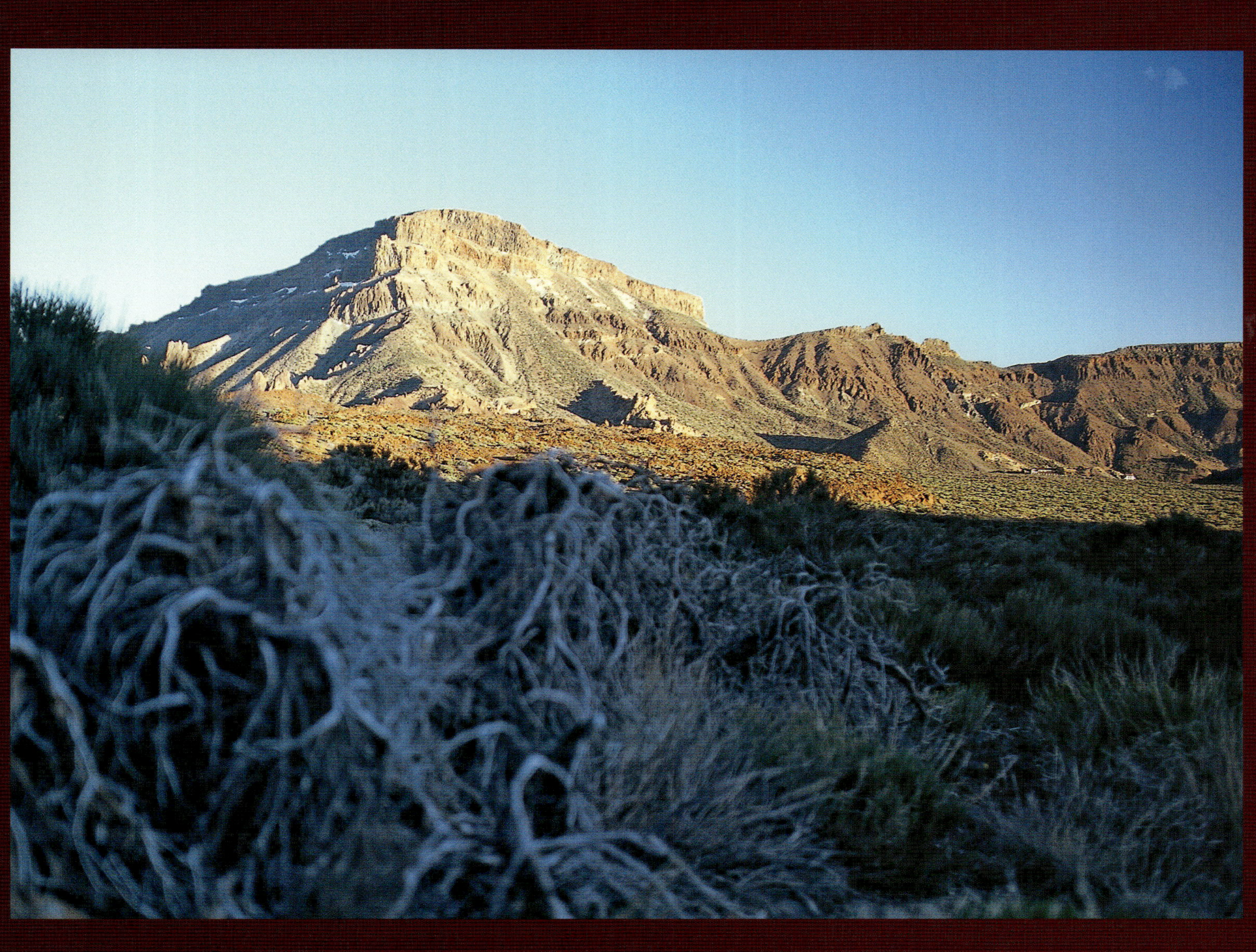

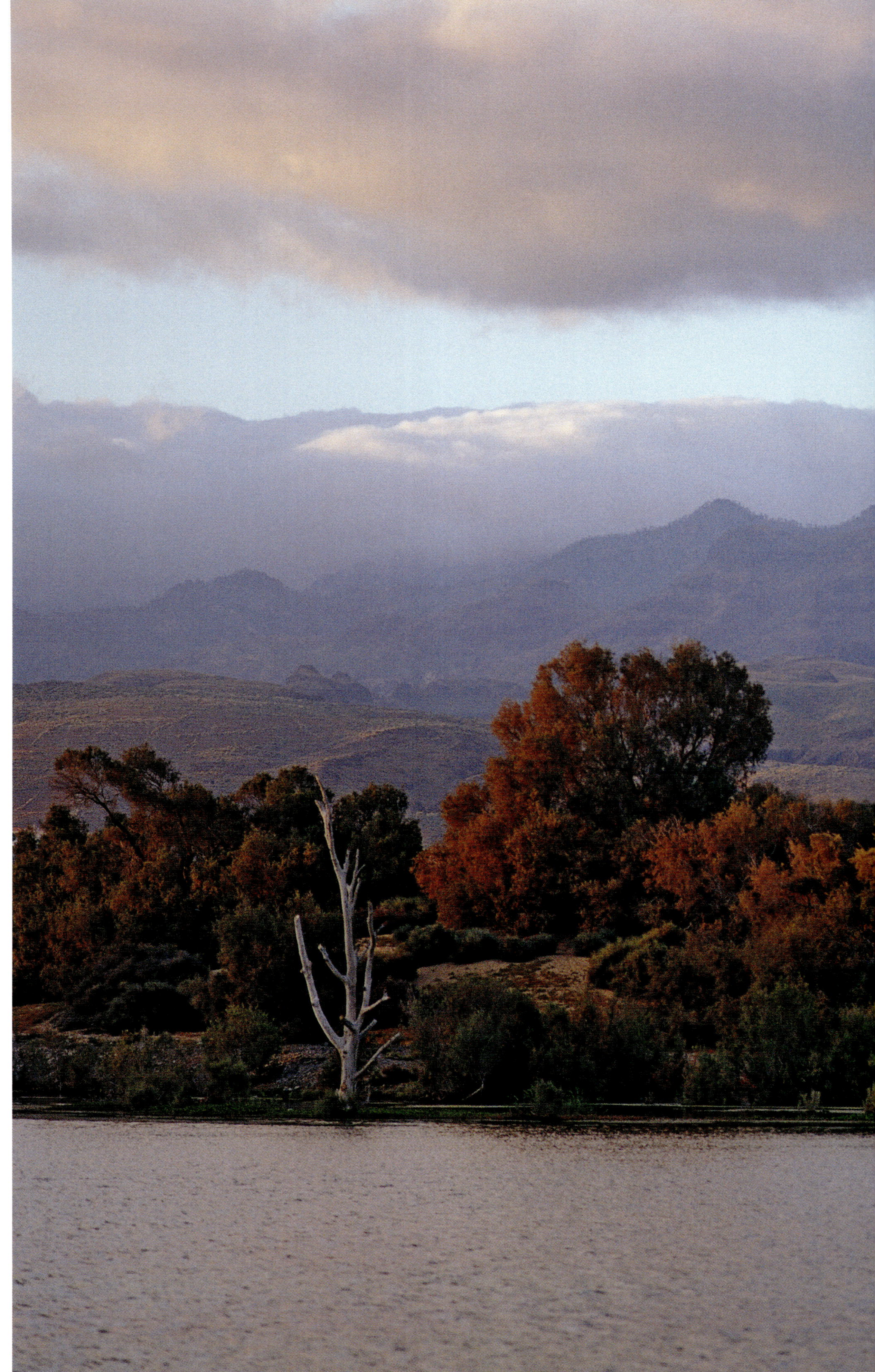

RIGHT
Gran Canaria in May

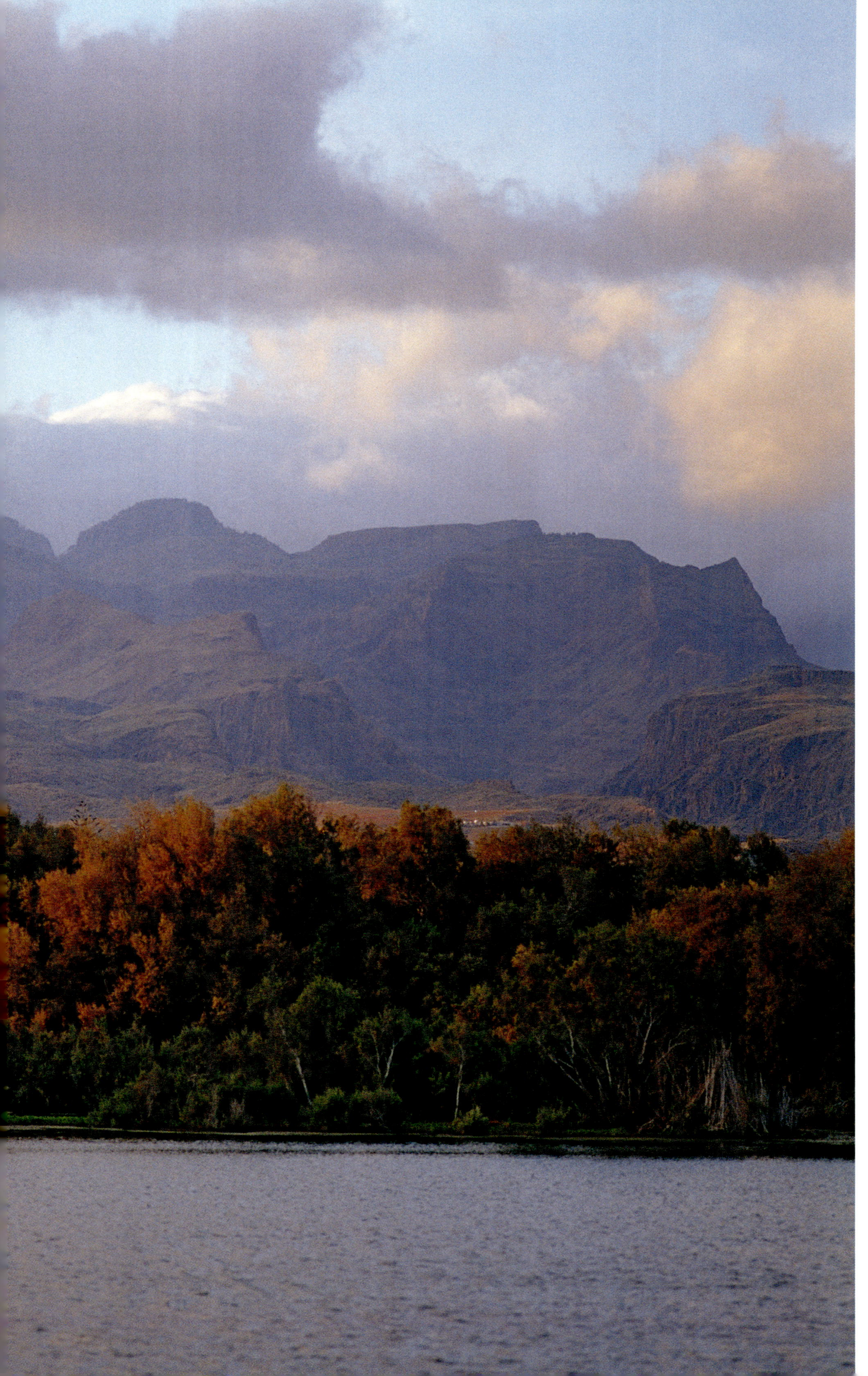

FOLLOWING PAGES
La Gomera in June

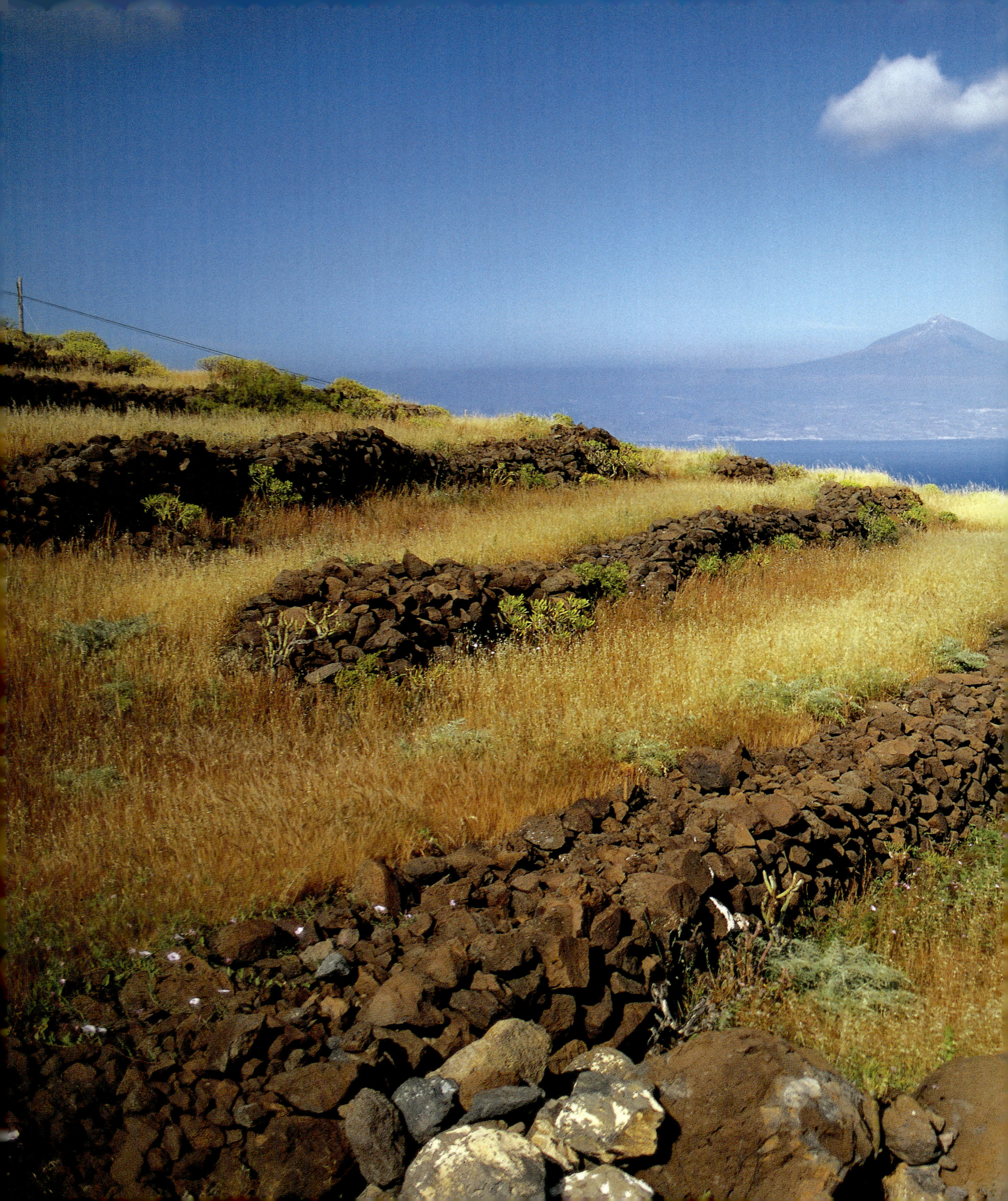

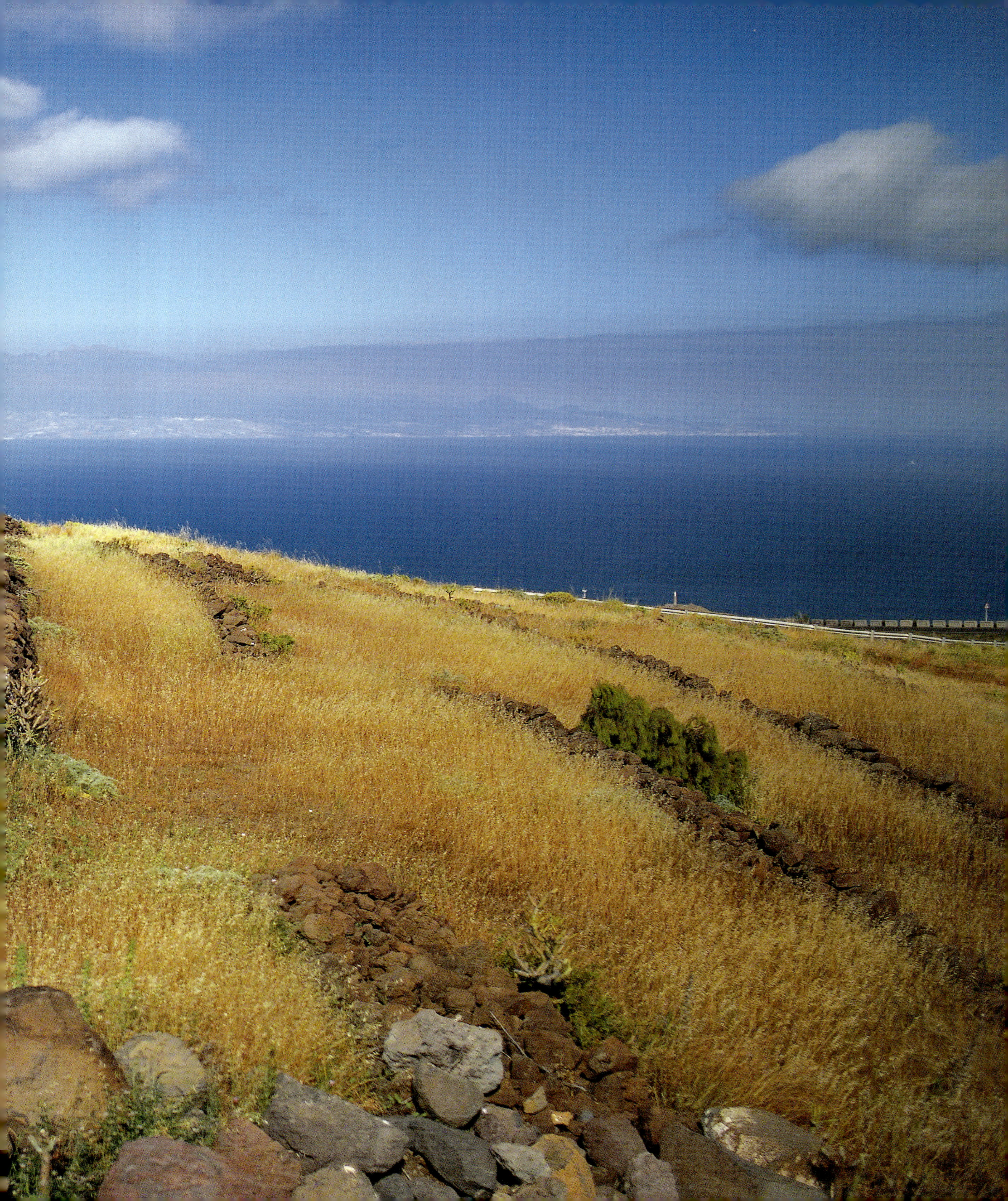

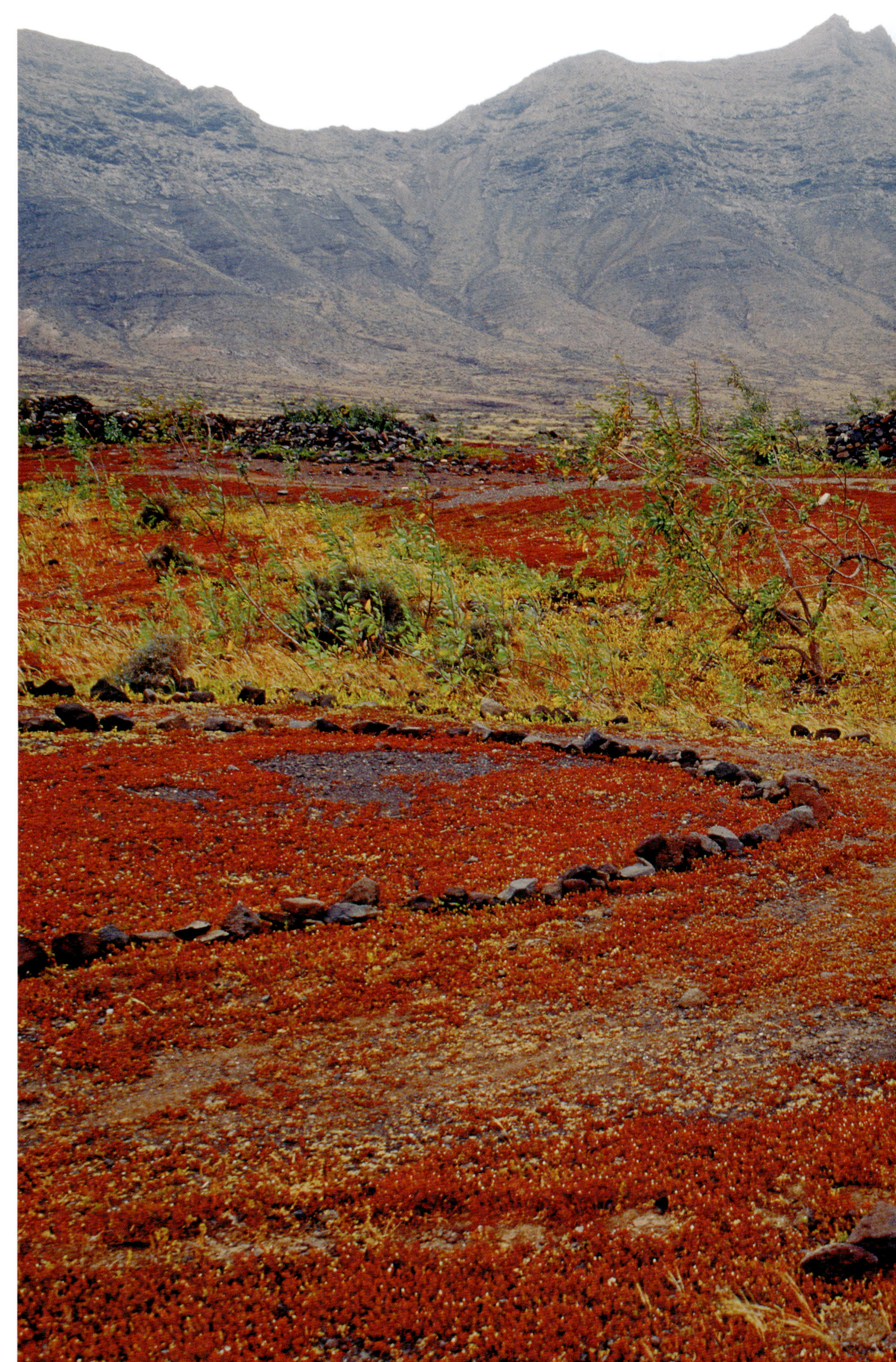

RIGHT
Fuerteventura in May

FOLLOWING PAGES
Lanzarote in October

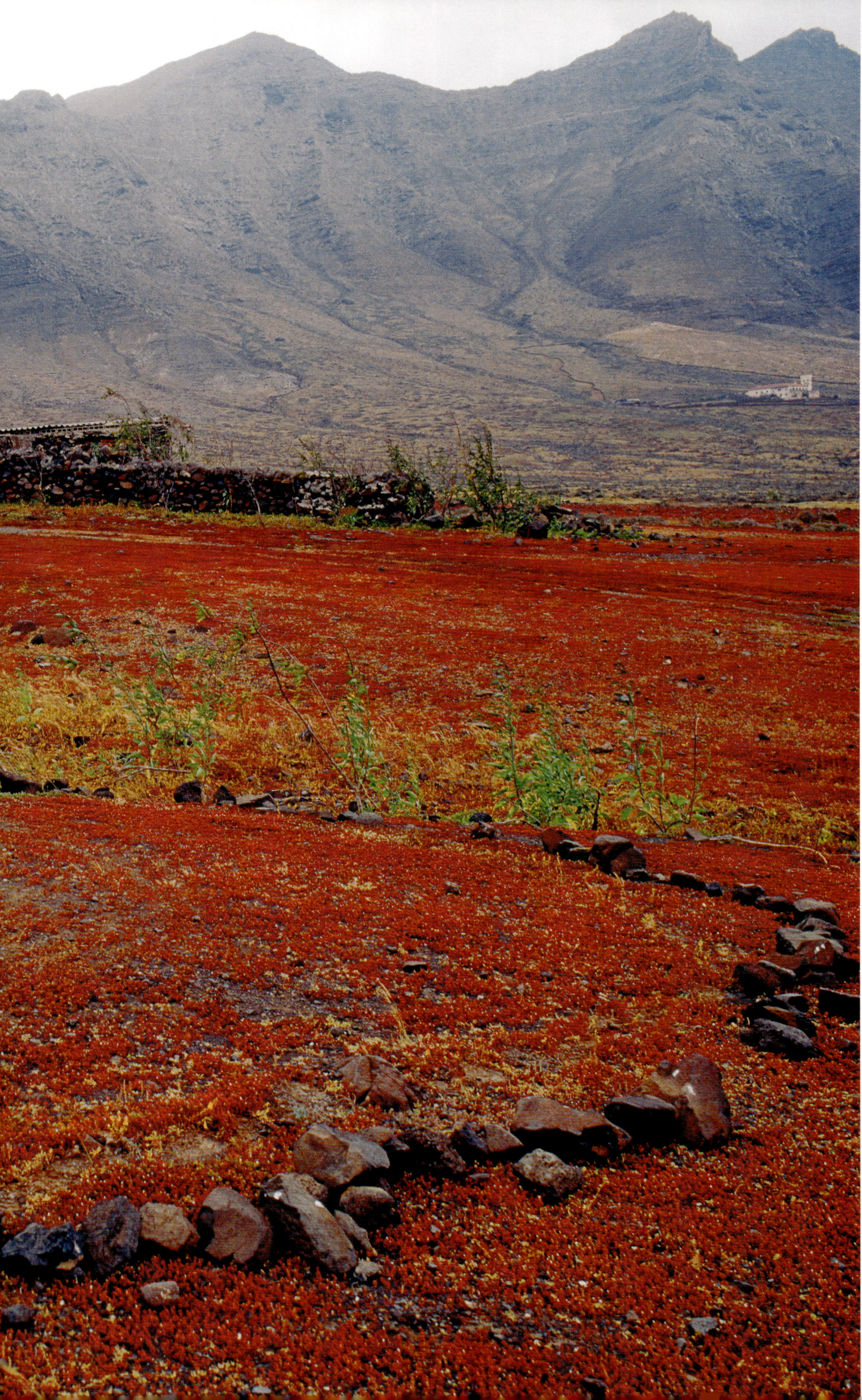

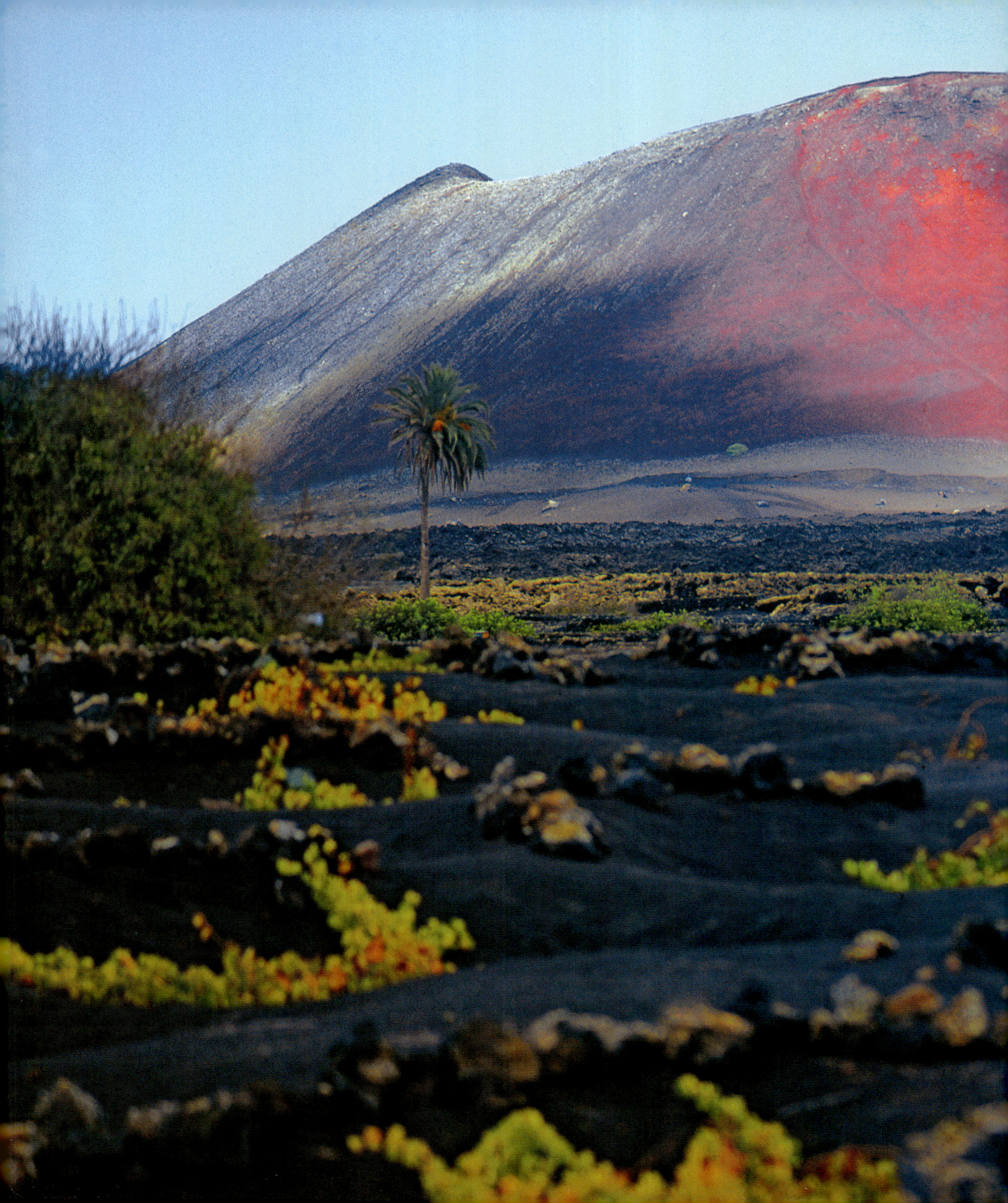

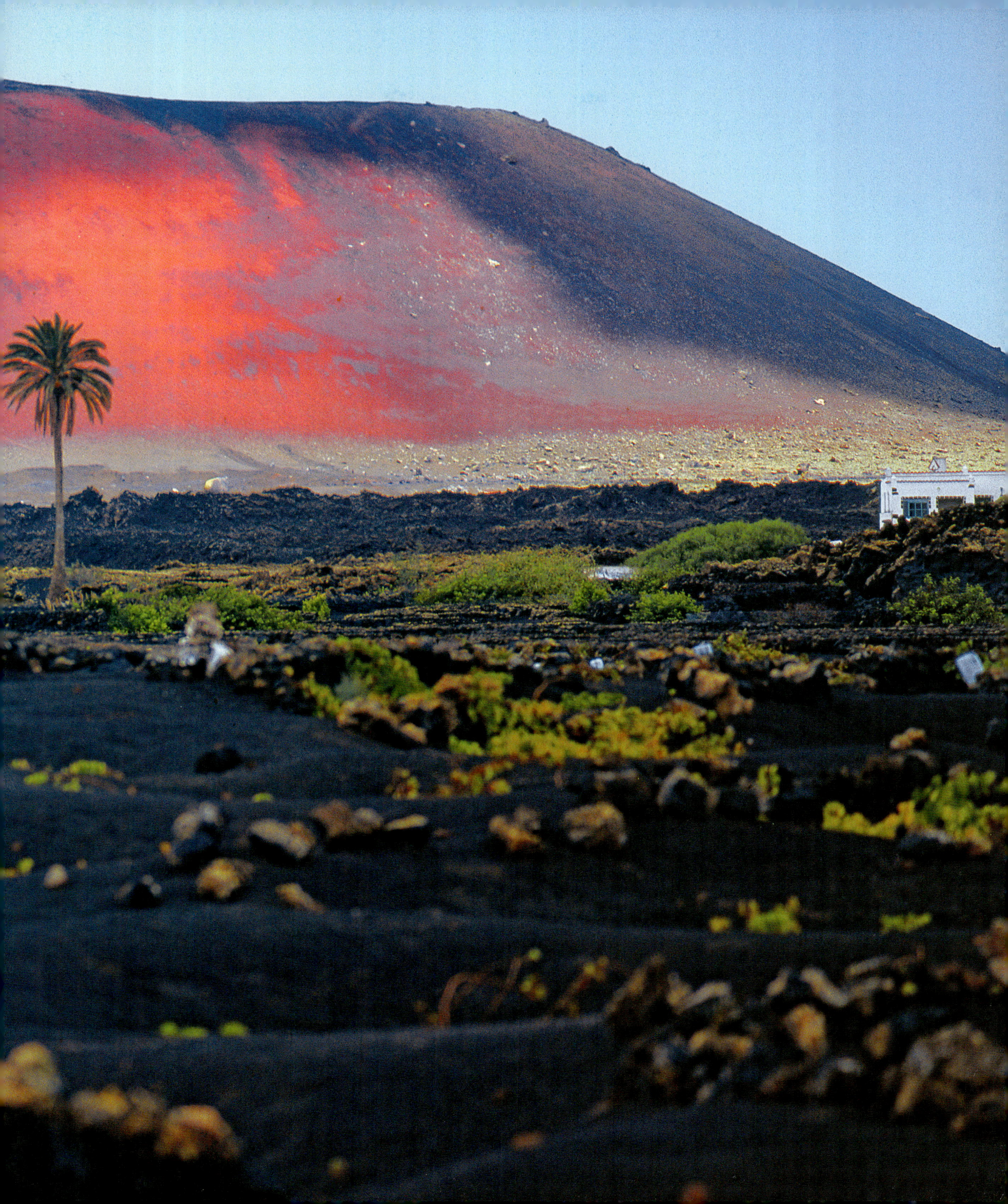

ACKNOWLEDGEMENTS

It would take me another book to recount my interior landscapes: those of the soul, travelled with all who came with me on this journey.

A sketch, then, with my memories of you all: Cesar Canomanuel and Luis Martín Cabiedes, school friends whose friendship I later embraced within the greater school of travel, hunting landscapes, each armed with a camera in pursuit of his distinct prey. Gil Ford, rising from the ashes of a marriage, a brave and liberated companion on our therapeutic trips in search of Spanish handcrafts and fields of light. Natacha Molina, who used to come and visit me to look at photos of 'my' landscapes, with a melancholy look for beauty. Antonio Gómez Rufo, who I first knew as a lawyer, and then as a notable writer, and who for many years has made the case for this book to come to light. Carmen Remírez de Ganuza, with whom I shared a cold day in August watching the winnowing of wheat on an old threshing floor, a Spain now lost for ever – like Carmen, whom I never saw again. Sophie de Puybudet, French woman-child, with the bluest, most hypnotic eyes I've ever seen, and whom I was only able to seduce thanks to the red Castilian moon. Eliana Perinat, ethereal and beautiful as a crystal dream, my companion for many miles in Guadalajara. Consuelo Correcher, shaper of beauty, who organized shows with my Spanish landscape slides through the years, and who has also worked to bring this book to fruition. The permanent smile of Parisian Lucille Hardion, happy in the Castilian sunshine. The hopelessly beautiful face of Ling, like an oriental landscape. Mercedes Temboury, passionate investigator of the paths of thought and disquisition. Coro Egaña, who helped me correct the manuscript and cast her poetic eye over it. The sweet voice of Granada, María Dolores Fernández Figares, who helped me so much with her research into the many visitors to Spain through the years. Cesar Requesens, who found me those travellers' tales in their original languages. Joaquín Fernández de Santaella, an Andalucian gentleman and tortured lover, who gave so generously of his time to refine my words. José María and Michelle Ullrich, ambassadors of beauty, always there to turn dreams into reality. Miguel Cabrera, singsong Canary Islander, iconic gardener, generous as a volcano. Gonzalo Anes, who researched our admired Jovellanos' opinions on landscapes. Maria Cabezuelo who gave me much more than I could give her: a memory of silent empty roads with her beautiful face at my side. Simon Arnold and Victoria Mardon, that beautiful couple from the other side of the world, so close to my heart, with whom I've galloped joyfully through the Balearics, Extremadura and Andalucía. María José, the girl from Valle de Alcudia with the landscape in her face, who watched me watching her in a kiss that nearly got us both arrested among the flowers on the high moor at Alcarria. Chris and Anna Stewart, whose hospitality always delights the body and soul. Alpujarreños by choice, they offered me their landscape and their friendship. The late Victor Carrasco and his widow Libby, joyful creators who shared with such generosity; I only knew Victor had left us when my crying eyes discovered a dreamlike pool covered with white flowers in the countryside of Ávila. Leopoldo Blume, editor of natural wisdom, who believed in this book and brought it to life.

Alberto Sanchez Ibargüen Mencos, that lively breeze of a country man. Pepe Salas' memories of the countryside he loved and endured, conveyed to me since my infancy.

Yolanda Reznak, with whom I shared soulful excursions and melancholy adolescent gazes. Or the painterly eye of Maria Weissenberg, the blonde Viking who added music to so many landscapes and to the times we spent together. Angel Gil, sensitive and faithful friend with whom I have roamed the landscapes both of the earth and of the soul. Javier Mariategui, a gardener and a poet, with whom I experienced the landscapes of Castile and the Cantabrian coast riding our old motorbikes, tasting the soft air of Castile and the sweet, moist air of the North. Paco and Olga Mayans for their generous help in enriching the words of this book. Marta Riopérez and Montse Cuesta, who ran the magazine *Casa & Campo*, promoting the vocation of gardening and the love of beautiful things. Ian Robertson, author of the magnificent book *Los Curiosos Impertinentes* in which I have found so many insights from other travellers, and delighted in recognizing my own feelings in their impressions. Santiago Pozo, a Riojan in Hollywood, with whom I looked for Buñuel's Las Hurdes and shared a passion for cinema.Carlos Cano, the mild-mannered Mexican, always ready to plunge into a road trip. Maria Teresa and Angel Esteban, lovers of rocks and roses. Pio Caro Baroja, in whose beautiful intellectual retreat at Vera, Navarra, I found some of the most lucid landscapes of the soul. Stefan Hall, a warm Viking friend and companion of many years in deciphering the landscapes of the heart. Antonio and Isabel del Real, fellow gardeners who have so admirably created a garden in happy harmony with Tenerife's overwhelming landscape. Clara Villavieja and Juan Carlos Llorente, the fairytale couple of Extremadura, in their fantastical castle. Teresa Mannera, generous and enthusiastic, whom I thank in advance for buying several copies of this book.

Enrique Luis Larroque, lord of the enchanted isle, La Palma, king of the banana trees and kind friend to all things beautiful. John and Marta Veal, our London hosts.

Rene Jamieson, a doting mother who has given me so much support. Your friend and mine, Diana Stobart, who has helped with this book since the very beginning. Karin Silveira, welcoming and benign as Mother Earth, always an inspiration in her pursuit of excellence. Gabriela Bernar, the late Gonzalo Armero, Gonzalo Salas; fond memories of time together talking about landscapes. Miguel Marañon of the Cervantes Institute who promoted the 'Landscapes of Spain' exhibition on the internet.

Isabel Canto, my favourite ER medic, with whom I explored the landscapes of her Segovia and her reckless, generous heart. Merche and Pino del Castillo, offspring of a flying Dutchman, who changed the way I see the Canary Islands for ever, welcoming me with open arms to their world and their circle of friends. Simon Monriker, the English gent living in goat country, who showed me Contraviesa in Granada.

Alberto Mencos and Marisa Llorente, wild bikers on honeymoon and family in the best sense. Patricia Espinosa de los Monteros, who promotes my work. Pablowski Crespi de Valldaura, my favourite poppy-grower, with whom I looked for mind-blowing poppies and mushrooms. Goli Bakhtiar, Persian princess, Amazon of the garden, conqueror of adversity and an open door in the South. Javier and Sita Moro, who introduced me to Dominique Lapierre, who provided the spirited foreword to this book.

And, of course, and above all, my favourite landscapes, my sons, Pelayo and Gaspar, and my wife, Anneli, who has given me so much more than I can express.

Thanks to you all: I have travelled with you all, and with me you all remain.

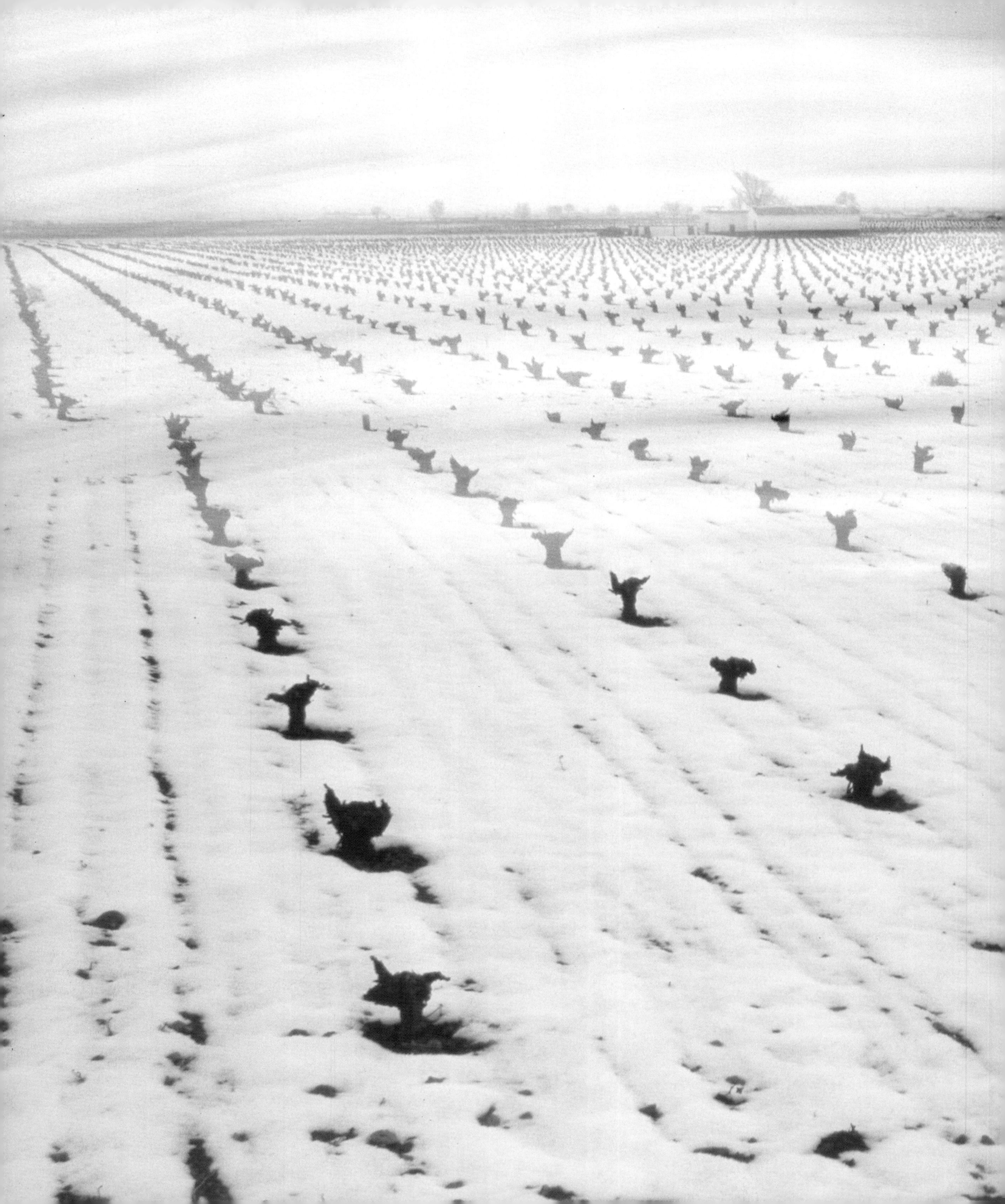